A HISTORY OF ATHEISM IN BRITAIN: FROM HOBBES TO RUSSELL

A HISTORY OF ATHEISM IN BRITAIN:
From Hobbes to Russell

DAVID BERMAN

CROOM HELM
London • New York • Sydney

©1988 David Berman
Croom Helm Ltd, Provident House,
Burrell Row, Beckenham, Kent BR3 1AT

Croom Helm Australia, 44–50 Waterloo Road,
North Ryde, 2113, New South Wales

Published in the USA by
Croom Helm
in association with Methuen, Inc.
29 West 35th Street
New York, NY 1001

British Library Cataloguing in Publication Data

Berman, David
    A history of atheism in Britain: from Hobbes to Russell.
    1. Atheism —— Great Britain —— History
    I. Title
    211′.8   BL2747.3

    ISBN 0-7099-3271-5

Library of Congress Cataloging-in-Publication Data

Berman, David, 1942-
    A history of atheism in Britain.

    Bibliography: p.
    Includes index.
    1. Atheism — Great Britain — History. I. Title.
BL2765.G7B47   1987   211′.8′0941   87-22362
ISBN 0-7099-3271-5

Printed and bound in Great Britain by Mackays of Chatham Ltd, Kent

Contents

Preface   viii

1   *The Repression of Atheism*
I   Doubts and denials of atheism   1
II   Self-fulfilling denials   2
III The crucial clash: Balguy and Curteis   6
IV   Thomas Wise's 'mixt atheism': a key to repression   11
V   Indirect and inadvertent denials: Bentley and Cudworth   16
VI   Freud and the crucial clash   21
VII An atheist doubts his atheism   24
VIII Linguistic analogues and Schopenhauer's explanation   26
IX   Herbert and Fotherby   30
X   The 1697 Act for repressing atheism   35
XI   Repression and suppression   37
XII Conclusion   41

2   *Restoration Atheists: Foundling Followers of Hobbes*
I   Acts against atheism   48
II   Robertson and Bentley   49
III Informers of atheism   51
IV   Lord Rochester, apostate atheist   52
V   Hobbes's denial of atheism and Scargill's confession
     of atheism   57
VI   The atheistic exploitation of the anti-Hobbes literature   61
VII Hobbes's atheism   64

3   *Anthony Collins's Atheology*
I   The deist interpretation   70
II   Collins's atheism: the external evidence   71
III Difficulties in identifying atheism   75
IV   The existence of atheists: opposing tendencies   76
V   The atheistic argument from the eternity of matter   78
VI   Second approach to Collins's atheism: his 'vindication'
     of the divine attributes and Christian prophecies   82

4   *The Suppression of 'Atheism'*
I   Count Radicati   93
II   Charles Gildon   95

III	Blackmore and Berkeley	98
IV	Hume's atheism	101
V	Concluding remarks	105

5	*The Birth of Avowed Atheism: 1782–1797*	
I	The first declaration	110
II	Hammon and Turner	112
III	The *Answer's* atheism	116
IV	*Watson refuted*	120
V	Metaphysical atheism	123
VI	Atheism against deism	126

6	*Shelley's Deicide*	
I	The fourth act	134
II	Denials of Shelley's atheism	136
III	Shelley and the repressive tendency	141
IV	Shelley's system	145

7	*The Struggle of Theoretical Atheism over Practical Atheism*	
I	Atheism and the theoretical/practical distinction	153
II	The orthodox position: Locke and Berkeley	154
III	Prevalence of the orthodox position	156
IV	The anti-orthodox position: Bayle and Shaftesbury	159
V	Variations and transitions in the early eighteenth century	163
VI	Hume's anti-orthodoxy	165
VII	Late eighteenth-century compromises and vacillation	168

8	*The Causes of Atheism*	
I	The triumph of theoretical over practical atheism: the *Answer*	173
II	The birth of Shelley's atheism	178
III	Hogg's role in the birth of atheism	186

9	*The Atheists: 1822–1842*	
I	The *Analysis*	191
II	Grote's atheism	197
III	Richard Carlile	201
IV	Southwell and Holyoake	206

10   *Militant and Academic Atheism*

I   Holyoake and Bradlaugh   212

II   The thorough atheist   218

III G.E. Moore   221

IV McTaggart   225

V   Russell   230

Epilogue: The Ethics of Unbelief   235

Index   248

Preface

God is, for some, an oppressive fiction, while for many others He embodies man's most profound truths. In whichever case, one would imagine that atheism and its history would be of considerable interest. In fact, the history of atheism has been largely ignored; and when not ignored it has been subject to serious distortions. Thus some suppose that atheism has existed from time immemorial; whereas many others claim that there have never been any actual atheists.[1] Both views have confused the history of atheism. They have also helped to enforce an attitude of indifference to the subject. For what is the point of considering the history of something that has either never been born, or was born prematurely aged?

In this study I hope to dispel some of this confusion and indifference by examining the early history of atheism in Britain. There is, I think, considerable wisdom in the maxim that when we are under an emotional spell we should seek to clarify its origins. If this procedure does not bring about illumination, it is likely to be at least a step towards illumination. Few would deny that atheism has been an emotional subject — for atheist and non-atheist alike. More recently a mood of despondent resignation has become noticeable, with some writers doubting whether their efforts are likely to have much effect on those holding the other point of view.

This study is both more and less than a chronicle of British atheism. It is less in that it does not pretend to be exhaustive. There is still much field-work to be done. And one of my aims has been to bring to light vital evidence which has not been noticed by scholars; one example being the first avowedly atheistic book published in Britain (see Chapter 5). The study of early atheism is still at the archaeological or natural history stage. The history of atheism has also been hidden in another way: by covert atheists who have published their atheism in disguised or esoteric forms. Here, too, the textual evidence needs to be excavated and carefully analysed (Chapters 2–4).

While this study aims to reveal covert and overt atheism, it also offers a new perspective which may help to resolve the vexing deadlock between atheists and theists. Since the nineteenth century it has often been said that the speculative atheism of the previous century was shallow because it did not take account of the deep, non-rational forces that have caused mankind to believe in God and religion. Thus Baron d'Holbach's massive attempt to show the falsity of religion and the

non-existence of God has been described as 'frivolous' and 'superficial' by influential historians such as F.A. Lange and Viscount
Morley; for them, what was actually required was an account of the
profound emotional and social needs that belief in God and religion
was (and is) fulfilling.[2] No doubt there is much validity in this anthropological criticism; but it has, unhappily, tended to draw attention away from substantive questions — e.g. Does God exist? — and
towards such genetic questions as: What are the psychological causes
responsible for belief in a heavenly father?

The anthropological approach was pioneered by Feuerbach, Marx,
Nietzsche and Freud. Although these great German writers were
opponents of theism, they were almost entirely uninterested in the
substantive question of God's existence: they largely assumed His
nonexistence, and offered absorbing accounts of the causes which have
brought about, and sustain, belief in God. Perhaps their lack of interest
in the substantive issues was in some measure caused by forces of which
they themselves were only dimly aware, namely, the unwillingness
of their society to tolerate *direct* published avowals and defences of
atheism. German society was prepared to tolerate (reluctantly, of
course) *indirect* expressions of atheism, but not open professions; and
the genetic approach lent itself, more than the substantive, to indirect
expression. Thus one finds almost no direct published denials of God's
existence, or open avowals of atheism, even in such allegedly strong-
minded German atheists as Schopenhauer and Marx.

These observations point to what I have called 'a new perspective'.
This new perspective does not deny the utility of the genetic approach,
but it broadens and redirects it. Instead of asking why nearly all people
at nearly all times have believed in God, I try to answer these
questions: What are the psychological and social forces that have
prevented the emergence of atheism in nearly all people at nearly all
times? Why has atheism arisen so late, so erratically, and so feebly?
What are the pressures that have made the public avowal of atheism
so difficult? The pathological study of atheism goes back at least to
Plato's *Laws*. What is now required is a wider examination: one which
impartially takes account of atheism as an object of normal as well
as abnormal psychology and which is prepared to treat the pathological
study of atheism as itself a form of pathology.

Thus in Chapter 1 I examine more than 25 instances in which the
existence of atheists were doubted or denied. I argue that most of these
doubts and denials were part of a widespread and potent (but not conscious) tendency to repress speculative atheism, and that they help to
explain the surprisingly late emergence of avowed atheism towards the

end of the eighteenth century. The denial of atheism is a theme which runs through this book: from Lord Herbert of Cherbury to Lord Rochester, to Hume and Shelley, Holyoake and Bradlaugh, and finally to T.S. Eliot's reaction to Bertrand Russell.

This study has, then, two general aims: to exhibit the actual history of atheism and to determine the causes which have prevented or encouraged atheism. Those readers primarily interested in the first may wish to begin with Chapter 2, moving then to Chapters 3, 4, 5, 6, 9 and 10.

Portions of this book originally appeared in the *Journal of the History of Philosophy,* vol. XXI, no. 3 (1983); *Proceedings of the Royal Irish Academy,* vol. 75, no. 5 (1975) and vol. 82, no. 9 (1982); *The Freethinker,* vol. 102, no. 10; *Topoi,* vol. 5 (1986); *Question* 11, (1978); and *Trivium,* 12 (1978). I am grateful for permission (where necessary) to use this material. I am also grateful to Anne Burke for her skilful typing of the final version of the manuscript.

Notes

1. See below, especially Chapters 1, 4 and 9.
2. See Lange's classic *History of materialism,* trans. E.C. Thomas (London, 1925), with an introduction by Bertrand Russell, especially vol. 2, pp. 96, 116–17 and 121–2, and Morley's *Diderot and the Encyclopedists* (London, 1923), especially vol. 2, pp. 166–7 and 187.

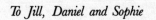

To Jill, Daniel and Sophie

1

The Repression of Atheism

I. Doubts and denials of atheism

A typical doubt concerning the existence of atheists is expressed in Thomas Broughton's *Bibliotheca historico-sacra* (London, 1737). According to Broughton: 'there is room to doubt, whether there ever have been thinking men, who have actually reasoned themselves into a disbelief of a Deity'.[1] We find a more emphatic statement in a later and more famous reference work, the *Encyclopedia Britannica* (Edinburgh, 1771), in its article on 'Atheism':

> Many people, both ancient and modern, have pretended to atheism, or have been reckoned atheists by the world; but it is justly questioned whether any man seriously adopted such a principle. These pretensions, therefore, must be founded on pride or affectation.[2]

Another piece of evidence also drawn from the popular literature of the eighteenth century is from an essay in the *London Magazine* of 1734:

> A contemplative *Atheist* is what I think impossible; most who would be thought *Atheists*, are so out of Indolence, because they will not give themselves Time to reason, to find if they are so or not: It is rather from Wantonness of their Heart than the result of their Thoughts.[3]

In this passage the anonymous essayist does not merely doubt whether there are or have been any atheists: he denies the possibility. However, in all three statements a qualification is made: it is not

1

atheism as such that is doubted or denied, but a certain sort of atheism, atheism that is 'reasoned' (Broughton), 'serious' (*Encyclopedia*), or the 'result of ...thought' (Essayist). Those who adhered to such atheism would be 'thinking men'(Broughton), or 'contemplative atheists' (Essayist). The standard name given to these men or their doctrine was 'speculative atheists' or 'speculative atheism'.

Writers who deny the existence of speculative atheists do not generally deny that there may be other, non-speculative, types of atheism, 'founded on pride or affectation' (*Encyclopedia*) or on 'indolence' or 'wantonness of heart' (Essayist). As far as I am aware, there is no generally accepted name for this type of atheism. I shall call it 'unthinking atheism'. The term 'practical atheist' was commonly used to describe someone who, although he professed a belief in the existence of God, acted as though God did not exist. The immoral behaviour of the practical atheist was supposed to show that he did not really believe in God. So immorality might be either a *cause* of unthinking atheism or an *expression* of practical atheism; and practical atheism itself would be regarded as the very probable *effect* of speculative atheism.

Unthinking atheism was recognised even by those writers who did not deny the existence of speculative atheism. Samuel Clarke, for instance, allows that there are speculative or reasonable atheists, and in his 1704 Boyle lectures he undertakes to deal with them by reason alone. But he is also aware that there is a different sort of atheism to which he is *not* addressing his lectures. This sort is caused by stupidity, ignorance and immorality.[4] Some writers showed considerable interest in identifying and describing the various causes of unthinking atheism. Thus in his *Thoughts concerning atheism* (London, 1695) John Edwards identifies at least ten distinct causes or occasions of unthinking atheism.[5]

II. Self-fulfilling denials

Having presented evidence of three eighteenth-century writers who doubt the existence of speculative atheism, I shall now consider the meaning of their doubts. The most straightforward explanation is that they are simply stating a fact: there are no speculative atheists. In the same way, one might deny the existence of ghosts, fairies or the music of the heavenly spheres. It is possible that the disbelief expressed in Broughton, the *Encyclopedia* and the Essay is as straightforward as the denial of ghosts. Indeed such disbelief would not have been altogether unreasonable, especially in the case of Broughton and the Essayist, for the first published avowal of speculative atheism appeared in 1770 on the Continent and in 1782 in Britain.[6]

But there is a difficulty with this straightforward interpretation: most of those who deny the existence of speculative atheism also, although indirectly, assume its existence. Often in the very same passages in which they deny the existence of speculative atheism, they oppose and try to refute it. But if they do not believe, in some way, in the existence of speculative atheism why should they try to confute atheism? So, for example, the passage from the Essay is taken from the concluding paragraph of a work entitled 'The folly and absurdity of atheism'. In most of this work the anonymous writer argues for the existence of God and the falsity of atheism. He tries to impress us with the astounding complexity of the natural world, and hence the great unlikeliness of its being the result of chance. He asks, for example: 'Can you think that the *Crystalline Humour*, the *Retina*, the *Optic Nerve*, all which are assistant to convey Sight to this little Product of *Nature* [a mite], are the Product of *Chance?*[7]

The Essayist goes on at some length in this vein; his aim is to show the absurdity of supposing that chance, rather than God, explains the complexity and orderliness of this world. But if atheism cannot be seriously held, then against what and whom is he arguing? And why is he taking his unnamed and impossible opponents so seriously? Why, in short, is he bothering to argue at all? If it were *really* impossible for anyone to be a speculative atheist, then there would hardly be much point in his warmly dissuading people from that disbelief. But since he is trying to dissuade and convince, it seems likely that (in some way) he does believe that speculative atheists exist or are at least possible. If it were impossible not to believe in God, then the Essayist's persuasive efforts would be as senseless as it would be to persuade someone to sit down when that person was already seated.

Of course it might be suggested that since the Essayist allows that unthinking atheists exist — those whose atheism is caused by indolence, affectation, etc. — his arguments may be directed against them. If this were so, his denial of speculative atheism might be rescued from absurdity. Although this interpretation is possible — and it resembles the construction one denier put on his denial (see below, Section IX) — it is not very satisfying. For one thing, if the unthinking atheist, being opposed, became an atheist as a result of

3

causes and not reasons, why should the Essayist expect to reason him out of his unthinking atheism? Samuel Clarke, as we have seen, is quite clear that there is no point in reasoning with unthinking atheists. Having distinguished unthinking and practical atheists from speculative atheists, he says that the latter 'are the only atheistical persons, to whom my present Discourse can be supposed to be directed, or indeed who are capable of being reasoned with at all'.[8] Of course we should expect the learned Dr Clarke to be clearer about this subject than an anonymous essayist in a monthly magazine. Nor would I claim that the suggested interpretation is impossible either on psychological or linguistic grounds. However, it seems to me more probable that because the Essayist feels that his argument from complexity is not vain, he does believe — although not very clearly or consciously or constantly — in the possibility of speculative atheists. But why, we then want to know, did he bother denying their existence?

There are many ways in which one can defend oneself and attack an enemy. For our purposes these ways can be reduced to two, and these two can be illuminated by an analogy developed by Freud. There are, says Freud, two main techniques for preventing an unwelcome guest from visiting one's house. First there is the straightforward and rather crude technique: when he comes into my house I can tell him or force him to leave. But there is a more subtle way: I can post a guard at my door to stop the interloper from entering.[9] The application of this analogy, or model, to the Essay should be clear. The writer starts off with the first technique: he tries to show the falseness of speculative atheism. But then — perhaps sensing the weakness of this direct technique — he uses the more subtle tactic. Having taken up cudgels against the speculative atheist, he decides (or wishes) that there were really no such opponents. His denial of speculative atheists is designed, I suggest, to be self-fulfilling: it places a guard at the door.

The Essayist may have dimly thought: 'If my argument from complexity fails, I need not worry, for there are no atheists anyway; and if there are atheists, I need not worry, for I have my argument from complexity'. But what the Essayist fails to see is that there is a conflict in his twofold consolation. In making preparations for ejecting the unwanted guest the Essayist is showing his lack of confidence in the guard posted at his door: he does not really believe that there are no speculative atheists. The two tactics do not go consistently together: there is a crucial clash or conflict which reveals — rather like a perceptual illusion — that what we are hearing or looking at is not what it appears to be. The clash compels us to look deeper than a straightforward interpretation.

The deeper explanation which I have suggested is that the denial, at least in the Essay, is a technique for inhibiting or combating atheism. Yet I am not claiming that the Essayist was trying to suppress atheism. His denial is a case of repression of atheism. Repression is generally defined as the expulsion from consciousness of ideas or experiences that are unpleasant or threatening to the ego. Suppression differs from repression in its being conscious; and both differ from ordinary unconscious forgetting in their being motivated or purposeful. By the repression of atheism I mean the conscious disbelief in the existence of atheism, and the unconscious wish or tendency to inhibit atheism by means of the conscious disbelief and its verbal expression. By the suppression of atheism I understand the conscious wish to inhibit or eliminate atheism by denying its existence.

Before considering possible objections to my repressive interpretation of the Essay, I should clarify certain points. Firstly, it will be noticed that I am more concerned with the *action* of repression than with the *state* of being repressed. I also tend to conflate 'expulsion from consciousness' with the inhibiting or eliminating of atheism. What I have in mind here is that the repressive denial is unconsciously directed at expelling an idea or belief from the public mind (which includes the mind of the denier), or from the stock of ideas or beliefs that are taken seriously by the public mind. I call the process 'repression' and not 'suppression', because the public mind is unaware of the design to inhibit or expel the idea or belief by means of a certain mechanism — in our case disbelief or verbal denial.

Clearly there are difficulties in my interpretation of the Essay as repressive. Consider the following objection: how do we know that the Essayist is hostile to atheism? Surely we gather it from his abusive remarks and condemnation of atheism. But then why not simply conclude that he consciously aimed to inhibit atheism by means of his denial? The more we become convinced that his denial was *aimed* against atheism the more we shall be inclined to see it as a suppressive device. For if we assume that the Essayist did not wish to state a fact, should we not then accept the next plausible explanation, namely that he was using his denial in much the same way as someone who says: 'Surely you don't believe that! Not even *you* could believe that!'

This is a natural objection; but consider the implications of our endorsing it. We should have to assume that the Essayist was writing in bad faith, and that he possessed a considerable degree of mental sophistication. We should have to imagine his saying something like this to himself: 'I shall deny the existence of speculative atheists — who do or may actually exist — in order to discourage such atheists.' I find this difficult to believe, especially of an Essayist writing some 35 years before the first avowal of speculative atheism. Moreover, if the Essayist were really so sophisticated, one might expect him to keep the denial separate from any arguing against atheists — for fear that the latter might engender suspicions about the former. Hence I conclude that the Essayist's denial was not consciously but unconsciously aimed at inhibiting atheism. The unconscious design of the denial was to be self-fulfilling: to make, or keep, the non-existence of atheism a fact. At the same time, I do not want to say that the unconscious purpose was deeply unconscious. The fact that the crucial clash is on the surface indicates, I think, that the purpose was not deeply unconscious. However, this is a problem to which I shall have to return.

III. The crucial clash: Balguy and Curteis

My primary reason for inferring a repression of atheism in the Essay was the discovery of a clash between the Essayist's denial of speculative atheists and his attempt to defend theism and attack atheism. Now this crucial clash — as I shall continue to call it — can be observed to a greater or lesser extent in many of the denials of atheism. Consider the following statement from the moral philosopher, John Balguy:

> Of all the false Doctrines, and foolish Opinions, which ever infested the Mind of Men, nothing can possibly equal that of Atheism; which is such a monstrous Contradiction to all Evidence, to all Powers of Understanding, and the Dictates of common Sense, that it may be well questioned whether any Man can really fall into it by a deliberate Use of his Judgement.[10]

Balguy's statement has more in common with the Essay than with Broughton or the *Encyclopedia*: although he is less emphatic than the Essayist, he agrees with him in doubting whether 'can really' be speculative atheists. After issuing the doubt, Balguy goes on to argue, with great rhetorical flourish, that nature clearly reveals itself to be the production of God. For example: 'The meanest Insect we can see, the minutest and most contemptible Weed we can tread upon, is really sufficient to confound Atheism, and baffle all its Pretensions' (p. 2). His approach, even down to his example, is very close to the argument from complexity in the Essay. The example in the Essay was a mite; Balguy is less specific, with 'the meanest Insect'.[11] The final clause recalls the *Encyclopedia*: the pretensions of atheism are chastised. But again as in the Essay the reader is presented with the alternative of explaining the complexity of nature by recourse either to God or to blind chance:

> Let any Man survey the Face of the Earth, or lift up his Eyes
> to the Firmament; let him consider the Nature and Instincts
> of brute Animals. ... Will he presume to say or suppose that
> all the Objects he meets with are nothing more than the Result
> of unaccountable Accidents and blind Chance.[12]

Balguy then concludes with another doubt concerning atheism similar to the one with which he began: 'In short, [atheism] offers such Violence to all our Faculties, that it seems scarce credible it should ever really find any Footing in human Understanding'. Balguy suggests that atheists 'may well be thought wilfully deaf and obstinately blind' to the existence of God. But if this is so, why should he bother trying to persuade these unthinking atheists that God exists? If they are obstinately refusing to believe, why should they be affected by his appeals to plain matters of fact and reason? Surely what is needed is to affect the will and not the understanding of these unthinking atheists. It would be more appropriate to threaten than to argue with them. But since Balguy — like the Essayist — does argue, I think we must suppose that at some level he believes there are atheists. The authenticity of the denial is called into question by the argumentation, which shows that the denial is something more than it appears to be.

This crucial point is dimly perceived by Thomas Curteis in his *Dissertation on the extreme folly and danger of infidelity* (London, 1725); but that does not prevent some of his statements from clashing with each other. Curteis believes that the idea of God is both innate and universal. No traveller, he writes, 'could ever yet out-travel the Notion of a DEITY; nor the Exercize of some Kind of religious Worship, as the result thereof' (p. 22). Having said this Curteis quite properly remarks that it 'might seem altogether needless' to insist on God's existence (p. 24). Why insist on something which everyone knows? But Curteis none the less does go on for a dozen pages to insist and argue. He makes extended use of the complexity argument, showing the 'wonderful Frame of the Terrestrial World' (pp. 25–8). He also uses the innateness of the idea of God as a premise for an argument for God's existence. Because the soul has an 'innate impression of DEITY', there must be such a being. The 'natural disposition, or at least irresistible impulse, even in the worst of Men, to acknowledge a DEITY, whensoever they give way to serious Thought' shows that there is a real object answering to that innate propensity (p. 36). But after having argued for the existence of God, Curteis returns to his initial position — he doubts whether there are atheists, and hence whether it is necessary to argue at all. On page 34 he writes:

> And yet, after all, 'tis very questionable, Whether there ever was any such Monster in Nature, as a serious, close-thinking, or speculative *Atheist*: who liv'd and died so, in the clear Exercize of his Reason and Senses. The most of those Few among the Ancients who were reputed such, did much more contemn and dishonour a Deity in their Practice, than they were willing or forward to declare it in Opinion. Nothing in the world could be so difficult as to say or write any Thing plausible in Defence of the latter; when the Voice of Nature and the general sense of Mankind, was against them.

As with other doubters of atheism, Curteis reclassifies alleged speculative atheists: they become practical atheists. But there is a note of uncertainty in his doubt; this appears in his watered-down formulations of the arguments from innateness and consensus, and also from his qualifications: not only must the putative speculative atheist be serious and close-thinking, but he must also live and die in his unbelief. Curteis places considerable weight on this last condition:

> in the Time of Health and Ease ... they were averse to the Acknowledgement of a Supreme *Being*; yet, in Extremity of Distress or Danger, and especially under the shocking apprehensions of Death, they were usually as forward as other persons, in Acknowledging His Power and Sovereignty.[13]

In short, Curteis moves variously from taking atheism very seriously to dismissing it as virtually impossible. Indeed, in some places, rather than dismissing the danger and extent of atheism, he exaggerates it. In the Introduction, for example, he asks: 'What shall we say then to the pernicious and growing sect of our modern *Deists* or rather *Atheists* in masquerade (tho sheltring themselves under the general name of *Christians*);' (p. 12). Here, instead of reclassifying speculative atheists as practical atheists, he reclassifies some deists and Christians as atheists; rather than diminishing the class he enlarges it. But the more important conflict is between his doubts concerning speculative atheists and his arguings for the existence of God. If the generality of people believe in God, if most alleged speculative atheists are really practical atheists, and if those few inconstant speculative atheists abandon their atheism when confronted with distress, danger or death — what is the point of arguing for God? Whom can it affect? Not the believers, nor the practical atheists, nor even the inconstant speculative atheists — for they are affected by practical and non-intellectual factors. There is, in short, a crucial clash, which, I have maintained, points to repression.

A parallel example may help to illustrate my claim. Suppose we have rented a flat, and an agent of our landlord arrives and says: 'There are no mice here, but I shall now set to work exterminating them.' Would we not assume that there were indeed mice in our flat, especially if the agent started to do as he said he would? We might still be puzzled by the first part of his utterance, but on reflection we might suppose that it was designed to reassure us. This is not to say that we could not invent a story in which the agent really believed that there were no mice, even though he went ahead laying poison and setting traps. He might, for instance, tell us as he was leaving that he went through the motions of exterminating mice (even though he did not believe there were any) because he had been paid to do so, and it is a rule with him to do what he is paid to do. But this, although possible, is surely less plausible. Yet, in whichever case, it is clear that there is a conflict between his words and his deeds which calls for the reinterpretation of one or other. Take another slightly different example. Imagine a discussion between father and son in which the son tells his father that he has become a pessimist. To this the father replies: 'Do not be silly; it is quite impossible for someone of your age to be a pessimist.' But some time later in the conversation we hear the father shouting angrily: 'If I hear that you are still a pessimist, I shall make you wish that you were not.' Here again we seem to have a conflict: one utterance cries out to be reinterpreted and thereby reconciled with the other.

9

I think we should say much the same about the statements of the Essayist, Balguy and Curteis. There is a conflict — though perhaps not so immediately evident — between their denials or doubts and their argumentation. One should be reconciled with the other; and as the argumentation is more extensive, more laborious and more compelling, I have reconciled the denials with it. Of course there is an important difference between my two hypothetical examples and the Essayist, Balguy and Curteis. In the former, and especially in the mice example, we are inclined to construe the denials as consciously designed: the agent intended to make us believe there were no mice. Whereas in the cases of the Essayist, Balguy and Curteis I have argued that their conscious or verbal doubts and denials of atheism were unconsciously designed to combat atheism and defend theism.

At the same time, I would not wish to maintain that the denials of atheism are quite as simple as my two-tier interpretation may seem to imply. There is more to such denials than a clear-cut conscious negation on one level and an unconscious plot to inhibit on the other. For example, we can detect in at least some of the denials an expressive element. That is, when they deny the existence of speculative atheism they may also be expressing their disapproval of atheism. The abusive language in the denials of Balguy and Curteis indicates that they have an expressive dimension. Balguy speaks of atheism as a 'monstrous' and 'foolish' opinion that has 'infested' men's minds; and Curteis refers to the putative atheist as a 'monster'. This expressive element may be seen as mediating between the unconscious desire to discourage atheism and the conscious intention to deny it. After all, a man who expresses his disapproval of someone in that person's company often wishes to hurt the person. When someone says 'I hate you!' he may well intend to *express* his displeasure and also to evoke an unpleasant sensation in his listener. An expressive utterance may be the vehicle for bringing something about. Hence I would argue that the abusive language of Balguy and Curteis reveals the deeper intention behind their denials. We see that the denier is not making a dispassionate negative judgement: he is expressing his annoyance at atheism. The disapproving and abusive utterances of Balguy and Curteis also support our reinterpreting their denials to conform with the destructive aim of their argumentation, rather than vice versa. The abusive nature of their denials suggests that they have an inhibitive role, and not merely a factual one. But how can we be sure that their denials were aimed at inhibiting atheism? It is this part of my thesis that still needs further defence, which I hope to provide in my commentary on the next denial.

IV. Thomas Wise's 'mixt atheism': a key to repression

In his introduction to *A confutation of the reason and philosophy of atheism* (London, 1706) Thomas Wise offers some justification for the publication of his book: he would not have bothered writing a book against atheism, he says, if various 'Atheistic Doctrines' had not been 'boldly vented and publicly asserted in this ... Age of ours.' This apology is then followed (p. 2) by this qualification:

> Not, after all [Wise asserts], that I suppose there are or ever have been any *absolute speculative Atheists*, or such as fully answer that Character, being thorowly grounded and convinced in their Minds, *that there is no God*; and so not only hardily, rashly and by fits, but deliberately, intelligently and constantly, as well in old Age and in Youth, as well as in view of Death as well as the jollity of Life, stand firm to that Principle, and withal can produce such reasons for it, as are sufficient for their Minds to acquiesce in, and with themselves to weigh down the Scale, against all the other Reasons they know to the contrary. And therefore I could wish that the term *Atheist*, as Men are apt to understand it in this sense, were not so generally us'd; because from hence it is observable, that the Ignorant, but *wickedly inclined*, do think to justify themselves by Example. Telling us that ... *Diagoras, Theodorus, Epicurus, Lucian* &c have been *Atheists,* and therefore they also may safely be such. Whereas it is certain, that those and some others who have heretofore come under that character, yet were not *Atheists* in the sense before-mentioned.

Wise's long and contorted qualification throws a new and stronger light on our subject. Not only do we find here a denial of speculative atheism, but we can also observe the deeper motivation behind that denial. It is dangerous to give the impression that there have been speculative atheists, Wise feels, because some potential atheists might support their tendency to atheism with that knowledge. Precedents may encourage others. There is a converse conclusion to this, which Wise does not draw: that the general disbelief in speculative atheists will of itself prevent or discourage atheism. Wise does not draw this conclusion but he acts in accordance with it. He proposes that the term 'atheist' should not be generally used (or understood) in the sense he stipulates: as meaning absolute speculative atheist. He affirms that the use of the term (with its particular meaning) will

11

encourage atheism. But he must also have felt that if the term is not used, and if the thing it refers to is regarded as impossible, then this would be likely to discourage atheism. Consequently we find in Wise's statement not only (1) a denial of speculative atheism, but also (2) a proposal for discouraging atheism which is associated with the denial of atheism.

Now it might seem that there is a direct conflict between (1) and (2); for if speculative atheism is and must be non-existent, then there is no point in proposing techniques for discouraging it. But, in fact, the conflict is not quite so straightforward. Firstly, Wise does not explicitly deny the existence of speculative atheists, but only *absolute* speculative atheists. Secondly, the sort of atheism which his linguistic reform is avowedly aimed against is not pure speculative atheism, but the atheism of the 'ignorant, but wickedly inclined'. However, it is hard to take Wise's avowals altogether seriously. There are good grounds for holding that what he was primarily afraid of, and what he hoped to discourage by means of his denial, was speculative, and not unthinking or practical atheism. I shall argue that Wise's statements do exhibit the crucial clash, although by no means perfectly. The clash is imperfect, not because Wise denies only absolute speculative atheism, but also because he shows signs of being aware that his denial may help to discourage atheism. But if he is even partly aware that his denial and linguistic reform are likely to discourage atheism, then we have something approaching suppression rather than pure repression of atheism. However, the imperfection of the clash in this case allows us to observe more easily the purpose of the denial. Thus we may use Wise's denial as a key for the understanding of other denials. (We may now be tempted to see Curteis's qualifications as having an eliminative function: to define speculative atheism out of existence.) One must, after all, reach that which is deeply unconscious by means of that which lies less deep. Hence if we find denials of atheism which resemble Wise's, without showing the same partial self-awareness of their inhibitive role, we may justifiably suspect them of being repressive. We would then be interpreting a denial as repressive by the help of a more transparent repressive/supressive denial. I think this is a useful and perhaps necessary procedure when trying to identify types of repression. It is, however, based on the perhaps questionable assumption that the difference between repression and suppression is largely a matter of degree rather than of kind. Yet this (as we shall see in Section IX) was the opinion of Freud.

I must now support the claim made above — that the sort of

atheism Wise was aiming to inhibit by the linguistic reform associated with his denial of speculative atheism, was not merely practical or unthinking atheism but speculative atheism. We may first note that Wise himself allows that the variety of atheism that he will attack in the body of his work is more than practical and/or unthinking atheism. This is not merely an inference I have drawn — as in the case of the Essayist — from his arguing against atheism. In the present instance Wise himself says that the atheism he will be opposing is a mixture of practical and speculative, for which he coins the term 'mixt atheism'. There are some men, he writes, who are not able 'to convince themselves fully that there is no God, yet venture to live as if there were none'. 'And these in reference at once to Speculation and Practice may be termed *mixt Atheist*' (p. 3). So there is in mixt atheism a rational element tending towards rationalising, and this is the sort of atheism that Wise intends to do battle with in the body of his work. By means of this new, partly speculative, class of atheists Wise is able to escape (to a considerable extent) the crucial clash I have identified in the Essay, Balguy and Curteis. Wise is not denying the existence of speculative atheists and then trying to argue them out of their atheism.

But what is Wise's opinion of just plain speculative atheism? He allows mixt atheism and denies absolute speculative atheism, but as to his opinion of the middle area — of plain speculative atheism — he leaves us in doubt. However, I think we can see in his account of absolute speculative atheism a tendency to identify it with plain, unqualified speculative atheism, and also a wish to show that both are impossible. It will be noticed that his conception of absolute speculative atheism is quite unrealistically attenuated. Wise has hedged it around with so many qualifications and necessary conditions as to make the thing almost impossible. On these conditions it would be difficult for anyone to be an absolute believer in anything. What theist, for example, has 'deliberately, intelligently and constantly ... in old age and in youth ... [stood] firm [in his] principle'? But at the same time Wise seems to believe that 'men are apt to understand [the term "atheism"] in this sense'. However, if this *is* the sense in which they do understand it, and in which it is 'generally used', then 'it' must surely refer to something more feasible, namely to just plain speculative atheism and not to Wise's attenuated 'absolute speculative atheism'. But then it will not be clear that Diagoras, Theodorus and Epicurus were not atheists in this feasible sense.

My conclusion, therefore, is that Wise wishes to conflate absolute and plain speculative atheism so as to suggest the impossibility of the latter as well as the former, and thereby eliminate Diagoras, Theodorus, etc. from the class of dangerous atheistic precedents. Thus as the passage proceeds the qualifiers 'absolute' and 'speculative' drop out, leaving the more general 'Atheists': the suggestion is that there have never been atheists in *any* respectable sense of the term.

But this is left at the level of suggestion. Wise never denies plain atheism, and he explicitly accepts partial speculative atheism under the title 'mixt atheism'. But if there can be *partial* speculative atheism, then why not also *complete* speculative atheism or just (plain) speculative atheism? Although Wise does not explicitly accept this class, much in his approach implies his acceptance. Not only does his book contain copious argumentation against atheism, but its very title indicates his implicit acceptance of plain speculative atheism: for it is 'a confutation of the *reason* and *philosophy* of atheism'.

Consequently, I do think that there is, in the final analysis, a clash in Wise: there is a tendency to deny speculative atheism and also to accept its existence. But neither the denial nor the acceptance is made entirely explicit. This could indicate that Wise couched his statements in guarded language to prevent them from clashing. I have already noted that he shows some awareness of the inhibitive possibilities of denying atheism; hence it should not surprise us to find him sensitive to the difficulties and suspicions that might arise from the crucial clash.

Some awareness of the inhibitive possibilities of the denial of speculative atheism can also be seen in Henry More, the Cambridge Platonist, who in the final chapter of his *Antidote against atheism* provides his readers with the following genetic account of atheism:

at first some famously-*learned* men being not so indiscreetly zealous and superstitious as others, have been mistaken by *Ideots*, and traduced for *Atheists*; and then ever after some vainglorious Fool or other hath affected, with what safety he could, to seem *Atheistical*, that he might thereby forsooth be reputed the more *learned*, or the *profounder Naturalist*.[14]

More, like Wise, is saying that *apparent* atheistic precedents have encouraged 'some vain-glorious fool or other' to affect atheism. Like the 'ignorant but wickedly inclined' of Wise, the 'vain-glorious fool' is said to be mistaken in thinking that his atheistic precedent is really an atheist. Again like Wise, the 'vain-glorious fool' is not himself accorded the dubiously honorific title of speculative atheist. In this More goes further than Wise; for he is not prepared to allow that the putative atheist is even a mixt atheist. For him atheism is not speculative; it is either practical or unthinking or both:

> And verily I think I have ransacked all the corners of every kind of Philosophy that can pretend to bear any stroke in this Controversy with that diligence, that I may safely pronounce, that it is mere brutish *Ignorance* or *Impudence*, no *Skill* in *Nature*, or the *Knowledge* of things, that can encourage any man to profess *Atheism*, or to embrace it at the proposal of those that make profession of it.
> ...if [any man] do but search into the bottom of this enormous *disease of the Soul*, as *Trismegist* truly calls it, he will find nothing to be the cause thereof but either *vanity* of mind, or brutish *sensuality* (p. 141)

These statements are from the penultimate section of More's *Antidote against atheism*, a book packed with arguments for theism and against atheism. Hence we find in More a crucial clash: affirming practical and unthinking atheism only, and in the same book arguing against speculative atheism. Hence his antidote is not appropriate to the atheistic disease he diagnoses and treats. Indeed he himself says that 'to such slow Constitutions as these [practical and/or unthinking atheists], I shall not wonder if, as the *first Part* of my Discourse must seem marvellous subtil, so the *last* appear ridiculously incredible'[15] He seems to recognise that his antidote may prove to be no antidote at all, for, since the atheists' sickness is not speculative atheism, they cannot respond to his argumentative cure.

More also believes, as we have seen above, that some have been encouraged to profess atheism because they (mistakenly) thought that certain 'famously-learned men' had done so before them. So atheism is not only an 'enormous disease of the soul', but a contagious disease as well. And it is so contagious that one can catch it even from those whom one may mistakenly believe to be suffering from it. More does not say, as Wise does, that the theistic cause would benefit if the famous men were not generally allowed to be atheists. He simply denies that the famous men were atheists, and he leaves it at that. I conclude that his awareness of the inhibitive possibilities of denying atheism lies even further below the surface than that of Wise; and that his denial of speculative atheism is more deeply repressive.

V. Indirect and inadvertent denials: Bentley and Cudworth

In the first of his Boyle Lectures Richard Bentley shows considerable interest in the question whether there are, and ever have been, any atheists.[16] He is aware of a tradition that denies the existence of speculative atheists. Commenting on his text from the fourteenth psalm: 'The fool hath said in his heart, there is no God', Bentley states: 'I know not any Interpreters that will allow it to be spoken of such as *flatly deny* the Being of God; but of them, believing his Existence, do yet seclude him from directing the affairs of the World, from observing and judging the actions of Men' (p. 4). A little later in his lecture he goes even further: he interprets these deniers of atheism to be saying that those who reject God's providence do not really reject it theoretically but practically. That is, 'those profane persons [the putative atheists] ... *do not, nor can* really doubt *in their Hearts* the *Being of God,* yet openly deny his Providence in the course of their lives' (p. 5). They are, in short, practical atheists.

Bentley provides us with an innatist account of why these un-named interpreters of Psalm 14 may have dismissed the existence of speculative atheists:

> I suppose they might be induced to this [denial] from the commonly received notion of an innate Idea of God, imprinted upon every Soul of Man at their Creation, in Characters that can never be defaced. Whence it will follow [according to these innatists and deniers of atheism] that Speculative Atheism does only subsist in *Our* [i.e. Bentley's] Speculation: whereas really Human Nature cannot be guilty of the Crime (p. 4).

This is one of the two explanations for the denial of atheism I have been able to find; the other — which I shall consider below in Section VIII — is offered by Arthur Schopenhauer. Bentley's innatist explanation may have been followed by the poet, physician and theologian Richard Blackmore, who held that those who believed that all people possessed an innate idea of God 'were led by this to another opinion, namely, that there never was in the world a real atheist in belief and speculation, how many soever there may have been in life and practice'.[17] Something very close to this movement of thought is to be found, as we shall see in Section IX, in the writings of two early seventeenth-century deniers of atheism, Lord Herbert of Cherbury and Bishop Martin Fotherby. It is difficult to know how common the innatist basis for the denial of atheism was in the seventeenth century, but it probably became much less popular in eighteenth-century Britain as a result of Locke's influential diatribe against innate ideas — which Bentley endorses — in Book I of the *Essay concerning human understanding* (London, 1690). Curteis, as we saw in Section III, is both a denier and an innatist. But his innatist theory is far less decided than either that of Herbert or of Fotherby; nor does he forge any direct link between his innatist theory and his denial of atheism.

On the whole, both Bentley and Blackmore rightly resist the tendency to doubt or deny the existence of speculative atheists. I say rightly because if there were no speculative atheists, or feasible speculative atheism, then their arguments against atheism would have little point. This simple though crucial insight is expressed by Ralph Cudworth in the Preface to his massive treatise against atheism, *The true intellectual system of the universe*. Cudworth not only adverts to the deniers of atheism, but he also gives them a title: he calls them 'exploders' of atheism.[18] Of these 'exploders of atheism' he writes: 'Some will be ready to condemn this whole labour of ours ... against atheism as altogether useless and superfluous upon this pretense, that an Atheist is a mere Chimera, and there is no such thing found anywhere in the world' (p. xxxix). But Cudworth does believe that there are atheists, and hence his arguments against atheism are not 'useless and superfluous'.

There is for Cudworth, as for Blackmore and Bentley, an enemy to be routed. Or more exactly, this is their considered view. For even these staunch resisters of the temptation to deny atheism do at times succumb to its enchantment. In the preface to the *True intellectual system* Cudworth outlines his programme, telling us that in Chapter 5 he will 'demonstrate the absolute impossibility of atheism, and the actual existence of God' (p. xxxvii). By the 'impossibility of atheism' he seems not to mean that there can be no atheists; but rather that atheism is false. At the same time, however, he admits that not everyone who understands his words will be convinced. For the 'appetite and passion' as well as the 'interest of carnality' of some will bias their minds against the truth of his demonstrations. Hence nonspeculative factors are operating to resist the belief in God and produce atheism. But then the atheism in question is either practical or unthinking or both, and not speculative atheism. Thus, one can infer from Cudworth's prefatory remarks that speculative atheism is untenable. At the most, mixt atheism is possible.

This inference is supported by related points made by Cudworth. While singling out his targets, he informs us that his book is not 'intended only for conversion of downright and professed Atheists (of which there is but little hope, they being sunk into so great a degree of sottishness); but for the confirmation of weak, staggering and sceptical Theists' (p. xi). But if the atheism of these professed atheists is caused largely by 'sottishness' then they are unthinking or mixt but not speculative atheists. Even more curiously Cudworth suggests that those who are completely moral do not need any proof of the existence of God; for they have an immediate or intuitive belief in God (p. xxvii). But the converse of this would seem to be that those who do *not* believe in God are prevented from doing so by some moral defect: they must be practical or mixt atheists.

Cudworth's apparent uncertainty as to whether there are speculative atheists recurs in a number of places in his book. The tension is fairly close to the surface in Chapter Three, Section XXXIX, where (on p. 134) he states:

> Besides these philosophical [or speculative] Atheists, whose several forms we have now described, it cannot be doubted, but that there have been in all ages many other Atheists that have not at all philosophized, nor pretended to maintain any particular atheistick system or hypothesis, in a way of reason, but were only led by a certain dull and sottish, though confident disbelief of whatever they could not see or feel: which kind of Atheists may therefore well be accounted enthusiastical or fanatical Atheists. Though it be true in the meantime, that even all manner of Atheists whatsoever, and those of them, who most of all pretend to reason and philosophy, may, in some sense, be justly styled also Enthusiasts and Fanaticks. Forasmuch as they are not led or carried on, into this way of atheizing, by any clear dictates of their reason ... but only by ... *a certain blind and irrational impetus.*

Here we find Cudworth in one long breath making the familiar distinction between speculative atheism and unthinking and practical atheism, and in the next breath withdrawing or annulling that distinction. All atheists, even those who 'most of all pretend to reason and philosophy', turn out to be non-speculative or mixt atheists; for the cause of their atheism is a 'certain blind and irrational impetus'.

In the Essay we found a direct denial of speculative atheism, and we inferred an indirect affirmation of speculative atheism. In Wise we encountered a direct denial of absolute speculative atheism and an acceptance of partial speculative atheism, i.e. mixt atheism. We then inferred an acceptance of plain speculative atheism and an intention to inhibit such atheism by means of the direct denial. This direct denial, we maintained, was more transparently and, indeed, consciously directed at the inhibition of speculative atheism than the denial in the Essay. With Cudworth we have a third kind of clash. Here, as in Wise, there is an inclination to allow some sort of speculative atheism, if only in order to justify the massive argumentation mobilised against it. This inclination expresses itself in Wise's affirmation of mixt atheism, and in Cudworth's repudiation of the exploders or deniers of speculative atheism. However, Cudworth himself follows this with an indirect denial of its existence: speculative atheism collapses into mixt atheism, at the most, and unthinking and/or practical atheism at the least. But speculative atheism is resurrected in the body of Cudworth's work; for, were this not the case, Cudworth's 'philosophical reasons' would be, by his own admission, 'altogether useless and superfluous'.

Of course in Cudworth's defence it might be said that his arguments may still have a point even though they are not intended for speculative atheists. For they may be intended, as he himself tells us, largely 'for the confirmation of weak, staggering and sceptical Theists'. But I do not think that this removes the conflict. For why are these theists weak and staggering? Surely they are staggering under the burden of factors either speculative or unspeculative. If the arguments in Cudworth's book are not to be superfluous, then the weak theist must be weak and staggering for speculative reasons. But then it will be feasible to suppose an even weaker theist also staggering as a result of speculative factors. In this way we will be able to move eventually from the very weak theist to the not-so-strong atheist, and hence to the downright speculative atheist. And if the first is allowed to be swayed by reasons, then why not the last? Yet since Cudworth believes that the downright speculative atheist is swayed by passion, irrational impetus, sottishness, carnality and so on, then surely it is plausible to infer that the weak theist is similarly — though to a lesser degree — swayed by these causes. But then the weak theist will not, despite Cudworth's claims to the contrary, be a fitting subject for argumentation. Hence I conclude that there are elements in Cudworth's thought that incline him to be a denier of speculative atheism. The fact that Cudworth is drawn to the denial of atheism, despite himself, indicates the underlying strength of the repressive tendency.

Bentley also inadvertently falls into the grip of the repressive tendency; he does so after having resisted its enchantment for some dozen pages. His words, like Cudworth's, indirectly imply the impossibility of speculative atheism. He tells us that the behaviour of atheists 'proclaims aloud, that they are not led astray by their reasonings, but led captive by their lusts to the denial of God.'[19] Thus after having opposed the view that 'speculative atheism does only consist in [the] speculations' of those — like himself — who oppose atheism, Bentley comes around to implicitly accepting this view. Once again atheism turns out to be unthinking and/or practical and not speculative atheism. But once again we are prompted to ask: 'If there are no speculative atheists, then why and against whom is Bentley arguing?' Bentley might have helped himself out of this difficulty (as I have helped Cudworth) by using Wise's class of mixt atheists. The atheists he is arguing against, Bentley might claim, *do* reason; but their atheism does not spring primarily from reasoning. Some compromise of this sort may have been at the back of Bentley's mind. Of course, as I have just tried to show, once one concedes partial speculative and partial non-speculative atheism one will find it difficult to resist the conclusion that there may also be plain speculative and plain non-speculative atheism. And how shall we know that what we call mixt atheism is not really plain speculative atheism? After all, the practical atheism of the atheist in question may be an *effect* of his speculative atheism.

It is worth mentioning that Bentley also denies (p. 34) the possibility of atheism in another, more sociological or anthropological, sense. According to him:

> No community ever was or can be begun or maintained, but upon the Basis of Religion. What Government can be imagined without judicial Proceedings? And what methods of Judicature without a religious oath? which implies and supposes an omniscient Being, as conscious to its falsehood or truth, and revenger of Perjury. So that the very nature of an Oath (and therefore society also) is subverted by the Atheist.

This is a more cautious and modest denial than that which would deny all speculative atheism. Here he is denying that a society could subsist if most of its members were atheists. This denial sometimes takes an even more modest, empirical form: it is stated that there are as a matter of fact no atheistic communities, be these communities ever so primitive (see below Sections IX and XI). The most famous opponent of both the empirical and conceptual forms of this kind of denial was Pierre Bayle.[20]

Richard Blackmore, who has much in common with Bentley, is more successful in resisting the repressive tendency. But even Blackmore, although he is convinced that there *are* speculative atheists, tends to doubt the existence of speculative atheism of former times. 'I am apt to think [he writes in the *Creation*, p. xix] that most who were reakon'd atheists in former reigns were rather unbridled libertines, than irreligious in principle; but now we are so far advanced, that the infection has seized the mind, the atheist in practice is become one in speculation.' But since Blackmore does allow that speculative atheism is to be found in his own time, there is nothing to clash with the arguments against atheism he presents in his various books.[21] Hence if we interpret his doubt concerning the atheism of former times as having an inhibitive aim, we should be inclined to say that it represents a very mild case of the repression of atheism.

VI. Freud and the crucial clash

I have argued that the crucial clash which is to be found in the statements of the anonymous Essayist, Balguy, Curteis, Wise, More, Cudworth, and Bentley, indicates a tendency to repress atheism. Before examining other denials of atheism, it may be helpful to look more closely at the nature of the clash and of repression, with the help of some illuminating observations made by Freud. In his *Introductory lectures on psychoanalysis* Freud says: 'Strangely enough, the people who deny the existence of sexuality in children do not on that account become milder in their educational efforts but pursue the manifestations with the utmost severity — describing them as "childish naughtiness".'[22] This account fits a number of our denials of atheism. Those who deny the existence of speculative atheism do not let the matter rest there; rather they argumentatively attack the sort of atheism of which they had denied the possibility. We have also seen in the case of Wise that the attacker explicitly attacks speculative atheism under a different name, 'mixt atheism'. And in most other cases, speculative atheism is assailed as being really practical and/or unthinking atheism in disguise.[23]

Judging from a note in one of Freud's case histories, the sort of clash we have been observing — as a sign of repression — may not be uncommon. Freud speaks of the following 'common type of reaction to repressed material which has become conscious: the "No" with which the fact is first denied is immediately followed by a confirmation of it, though, to begin with, only an indirect one'.[24] As far as I am aware, Freud never expressly elaborated on this — the direct no and indirect yes — as a *sign* of repression. For him, resistance is the primary sign of repression. He makes a number of valuable comments on negation and denial, especially in his essay 'Negation' (1925); but he tends to think of denial or negation as a technique whereby unconscious repressed material can be made conscious. He writes:

> the content of a repressed image or idea can make its way into consciousness, on condition that it is *negated*. Negation is a way of taking cognizance of what is repressed ... To negate something in a judgement is, at bottom, to say: 'This is something which I should prefer to repress.' With the help of the symbol of negation, thinking frees itself from the restrictions of repression and enriches itself with material that is indispensable for its proper functioning.[25]

Freud concentrates almost exclusively on one direction of negation. But some of his examples indicate that there is another side. Take, for instance, the following one:

> 'How nice not to have had one of my headaches for so long.' But this is in fact the first announcement of an attack, of whose approach the subject is already sensible, although he is as yet unwilling to believe it. (Ibid., p. 236, n.1)

The denial here (though Freud does not say so) seems to be a way of coping with the incipient pain of the headache. It is a way of keeping out of consciousness, if only for a few minutes longer, the recognition that a miserable headache must once again be endured. The mechanism whereby the negation hopes, as it were, to achieve this is a familiar one of self-suggestion. Hence there is another side to negation; it can also be a way of coping with painful ideas, of defending consciousness against unwanted ideas which are issuing from the unconscious. It is a way of sending such ideas back to the unconscious, of giving them a return ticket, so to speak.

But the question arises: How are we to identify cases of negation that are indicative of repression from those that are not? This question seems not to arise for Freud. He seems to have regarded all cases of negation or denial as indicative of previous repression — in other words, ideas have freed themselves from repression by being denied or negated. But I find it hard to accept his view that *all* negations allude to repression. I may deny, for example, that there are fifty-headed cats, or human beings who have lived for over a thousand years, or infinitely long snakes, or people who believe in these things; but I do not see that these denials indicate repression. They seem to be cases of mere, or asymptomatic, denials or negations. However, if I were to begin to argue vehemently that there are no fifty-headed cats, or infinite snakes, then I would be inclined to see my denials as having a repressive aim. This would be another instance of the crucial clash, which has been my chief touchstone for identifying repression. Where there is a denial *and* an affirmation the denial may be taken to be symptomatic of repression.

As I have interpreted the denial of atheism, the denier is unaware that his denial has the same aim as his indirect argumentative affirmation of atheism, namely to inhibit atheism. I would say the same of Freud's description of those who deny infantile sexuality; the denial itself was unconsciously designed to inhibit infantile sexuality. It is a less severe and obvious technique, but it has the same aim as the other educational efforts alluded to by Freud. I have also suggested that there are other signs that point to repression. If the denial is couched in highly abusive or emotive language we will be even more confident that it has a repressive aim. Of this we have instances in the Essay, Balguy and Curteis. We might also extend this to include the indirect affirmation: if it is couched in similarly abusive terms then we may suspect that the denial is repressive. I have mentioned (Section III) the example of a father saying to his son 'You are not a pessimist', and then angrily telling the son that if he ever hears him say he is, he will make the son regret it. The louder and more angry the father becomes, the more I should be inclined to interpret his denial as repressive. Similarly, the fact that the educational efforts of those who deny infantile sexuality are 'severe', according to Freud, also indicates that their denial is repressive.

Another sign that has led me to interpret a denial as repressive is some sort of awareness that affirming the undesirable thing may encourage it. This we found in Wise and More. Yet another indication of repression which we have encountered is the writer's trying to define the denied thing out of existence. (This might, however, be taken to be another form of arguing against the denied thing.) Of course, if the abusive language becomes too violent, and if there is a too-clear recognition that affirming the thing may only encourage it, then we may be tempted to see the denial as suppressive.

The crucial clash may, I should mention, be seen as a mild case of what Freud calls 'splitting of the ego in defence'.[26] But while there are similarities between this splitting and the crucial clash — especially in conflict of belief — there are also differences. In splitting of the ego, there is disavowal (*Verleugnung*): there is a rejection of reality (e.g. that the female has no penis). This is different from negation or denial (*Verneinung*), where an idea is expelled from consciousness, or, in my related sense, inhibited, discouraged or eliminated. But although it would be mistaken to try to *equate* disavowal and negation, the latter might be regarded as a weaker or partial form of the former. Thus the persons who deny sexuality do, nonetheless, witness behaviour such as masturbation; all their denial is able to accomplish is a reclassification of this as 'childish naughtiness'. If the repressive tendency were stronger, however, we might imagine their being unable even to recognise the masturbation. At the moment they are unable only to see it for what it is. On the other hand, there seems to be a certain amount of reinterpretation or reclassification in the fetishistic disavowers of the non-existence of the penis in females.[27] It is not clear that they actually hallucinate. They do not, according to Freud, see a penis attached to the female, nor do they see her foot, for example, as having the actual shape of a penis. The foot has the essential value or emotional valence associated with the penis. It has been grossly misinterpreted or misclassified; but there is still, I think, some element of reinterpretation.

VII. An atheist doubts his atheism

The next denial differs from those previously discussed in that it is made by a man who at one time seemed to have considered himself an atheist. This remarkable statement is to be found in an anonymous pamphlet entitled *The confessions of an atheist with a relation of the horrors he was in upon the death of one of his companions...*; it was printed in London and sold by John Applebee in 'Black-Fryers', and although it has no date it was probably published around 1735. Concerning his atheism the writer says:

> And openly avowing it was the most that ever I could do; let others determine for themselves, but this I know by my own heart, that I could never once, no not when surrounded by my

confederates, in the midst of mirth and wine, entirely divest myself of the belief of a God. ... I have often argued the cause of atheism, and a thousand times declared my assent to it; but God always asserted his existence, by the witness of my own conscience in his behalf; that ever checkt me, told me that all my conduct was one continued Lye.[28]

Here we have a man who was prepared over a long period to profess himself an atheist and who at one level seems to have held atheistic beliefs, but he is now denying that he ever was, or could have been, an atheist. But could the confessor really have meant what he says? How could he know that he was not an atheist if his talk and behaviour were expressive of atheistic belief? If he behaved in all respects like an atheist — that is, verbally, socially, etc. — then how could he (or we) distinguish himself from an atheist? His answer would seem to be that it was the 'witness of his conscience' which revealed his professions of atheism to be insincere. If we interpret this to mean that he felt guilty, or had qualms of conscience, when he said that he was an atheist, then we may have found a way of distinguishing his would-be atheism from authentic atheism. This interpretation does not quite fit, however, with his claim that '*all* my conduct was one continued Lye'; for if all his conduct was feigned, then the feelings of guilt were, too. On the other hand, perhaps he did not include these feelings within the realm of his conduct. Let us, in any case, ask: What did the confessor intend to effect by his confession (as quoted); and what would be the likely effect of his confession? Suppose that a man had set himself a goal but despite ideal conditions has failed: would not his confessed failure discourage others from following in his path? This will be especially so, I think, in cases where the potential atheists are isolated, where, unlike our confessor, they have no atheistic 'confederates' for companionship and support. How is a potential but lone atheist to know that he is an atheist? It is clear that his difficulties will be increased if he thinks that any vague feelings of guilt, or qualms, cast doubts on his atheism. He might have arguments for atheism; but then, he might tell himself, so did the confessor. He might say to himself: 'I am an atheist'; but so apparently did the confessor. How then could our potential atheist be sure that he was an atheist when the confessor was not? Once the confessor's sort of doubt is generated, it will be extremely difficult to lay it to rest.

This, I suggest, would be the likely effect of our confessor's statement, and indeed of most of the denials I have discussed. Whether they intended to or not, they would all be likely to discourage the growth of atheism. Something repeated often and confidently enough is bound to have some effect. The public mind is — like individual minds — suggestible. At the basis of the confessor's denial we can see a device which was also used by Curteis and Wise. Like Curteis and Wise, he is operating with an unrealistic conception of atheistic belief. Did the confessor intend to inhibit atheism? It is not out of the question that the confession is in the tradition of those edifying but fabricated death-bed conversions that were designed to weaken the resolve of infidels.[29] If this were so, then our confession would probably be an instance of the suppression, and not of the repression, of atheism.

VIII. Linguistic analogues and Schopenhauer's explanation

The denials of atheism may be helpfully compared to a general addressing troops: 'Men (he might say), I know that you are not cowards; I am convinced that none of you could commit a cowardly deed!' Now what the general seems to be doing here is trying to discourage cowardly behaviour in his army. Literally, of course, he is denying the possibility of cowardly behaviour in his soldiers. But we are inclined to see this denial as only a device for discouraging cowardice. And, if we were to listen further to the general's speech, we should probably hear the sort of indirect affirmation which we have found in some of the denials of atheism. We might, for example, hear him telling his men that they have nothing to fear from the enemy artillery, because he has certain knowledge that it consists only of small guns, and besides (he might add) the enemy has very little ammunition. He might also mention to his men that they greatly out-number the enemy who are, in any case, tired from long marching; and so on. He might also become quite angry and threaten the soldiers with harsh punishments if they behave in a cowardly manner. In all of this we can more plainly see the general's purpose: he wishes to encourage bravery in his men, and deter them from cowardly deeds. He does then believe that they *are* capable of cowardice; hence he did not literally mean what he said at first. From the indirect affirmations of the possibility of cowardice in the latter part of his address, we can be fairly confident that he denied cowardice in order to discourage it. Having observed a fairly transparent aim in the latter part of his address, we can in retrospect see a similar aim in the first part. This is also what I have done in the denials of atheism.

This sort of utterance is probably more common than one might at first imagine. Consider the case where a mother might say to her child: 'Daniel is a good boy; he is not naughty; he does not pull his mother's hair.' Very likely the mother is not uttering this in order to describe a state of affairs. She is using the quasi-descriptive statement to bring about or enforce a certain state of affairs. Once again, we should probably become convinced of this by what she might say after the initial utterance. (The context, the remarks and physical behaviour of both parties before and after would also, of course, have a bearing on the way we would interpret her initial utterance.) Hence if she were to say, 'Daniel does not pull his mother's hair, because he knows what happened to him the last time he did', we would have little doubt about the aim of the first utterance. Of course the indirect affirmation might be even more indirect. The mother might have followed her first utterance with: 'Daniel does not pull his mother's hair, because he will be punished if he does.' The latter part of this — beginning with 'because' — might just be construed as a reason or justification for the truth of the former part.

Similarly, those who after they have denied the existence of atheists, go on to argue that God evidently exists and that atheism is clearly preposterous, might just be interpreted as providing a reason for their denial. So the Essayist would, on this reading, be justifying his denial of speculative atheism when he shows the absurdity of atheism. But then we should have to say that what he is trying to show is not merely the falseness of atheism and the truth of theism, but the impossibility of believing in atheism. He would be saying something like this: 'No one could really believe that chance explains the world, for the chance-hypothesis is intrinsically absurd.'

This interpretation cannot be dismissed. Indeed it is, in some measure, advanced by Arthur Schopenhauer in the Appendix to his *World as will and representation* (1819):

> Until the time of Kant, there was a real and well-established dilemma between materialism and theism, in other words, between the assumption that blind chance, or an intelligence arranging from without according to purposes and concepts, had brought about the world, *neque dabatur tertium*. Therefore, atheism and materialism were the same thing; *hence the doubt whether there could in fact be an atheist*, in other words, a person who really could attribute to blind chance an arrangement of nature, especially of organic nature, which is immense, inexhaustible, and appropriate.[30]

27

For Kant the orderly arrangement of the sensible world is to be explained by the transcendental, categorial forms which are embedded in the human mind and which structure and order human experiences. Kant does therefore present a non-materialistic and non-blind-chance alternative to theism. Darwin's theory of evolution would be a later and more materialistic alternative to theism which does not resort to blind chance as a way of explaining the orderliness of the natural world.

Schopenhauer's claim that before Kant there was no feasible alternative to God as a way of explaining world-orderliness, is debatable — although I do not wish to argue the point in detail here. It should be noted, however, that, firstly, there were evolutionary theories in the air before Kant, and these could in some measure explain the orderliness of nature in a non-theistic and non-Kantian way without resorting to blind chance.[31] Secondly, there was also the non-theistic non-chance theory of Spinoza; for whom this eternal world is self-explicable.[32] It should also be noted that there is nothing self-evidently absurd about the Epicurean hypothesis of chance as the cause of the world and/or world-orderliness.[33] It may have been unreasonable — as it is in conflict with the principle of sufficient reason; but it was a thinkable and believable hypothesis, with a number of fairly coherent parts, e.g. the perpendicular fall of atoms.

But the important question for our study is this: Is the Essayist arguing for the impossibility of speculative atheism and hence the impossibility of believing in it; or is he arguing that speculative atheism is false; and thus, as I have maintained, indirectly affirming thinking believers in the Epicurean (or some other anti-theistic) hypothesis? Now one way of determining what the Essayist is doing will be by identifying the person or persons to whom his discourse is addressed. Consider our two analogues given above. If we found out that the mother was talking not to her child but to her husband, then we should be inclined to take her utterance literally — that Daniel is not naughty and he does not pull his mother's hair. Similarly with the second analogue: if the general were telling a fellow general that his men are not cowards — or if he had written this in his memoirs — then we should probably take his utterance as a factual claim rather than as a pep talk.

Whom, then, is the Essayist addressing? In part, no doubt, he is addressing his fellow theistic-believers. But *prima facie* he seems also to be addressing the atheists whom he denies. In the paragraph before the one which contains his denial of speculative atheists, he writes: 'Now think, thou *Patrons* to *Chance*, thou *Denyer* of thy *God*,

28

are these [various astronomical facts] the *blind Effect* of Chance? Could *Chance* produce such *Wonders*?' Of course, it could well be that this is a mere rhetorical device, and that we should not take it too literally. (After all, it might be said, the present writer is not taking literally other things the Essayist says.)

If the Essayist is addressing atheists, even in part, then we would hardly interpret him as arguing for the impossibility of atheism. But even if we suppose that he is directing his discourse to fellow theists alone, this would not necessarily show that he was arguing for the impossibility of atheism. For what other purpose would he have in addressing them on this subject but to reassure them? But if they need reassurance, then surely atheism must be at least a potential danger — and in that case it is not impossible. We saw in Cudworth that one of the primary aims in the *True intellectual system* was the 'confirmation of weak, staggering and sceptical Theists'. I have argued (in Section V) that Cudworth's attempts to confirm the weak theist are of a partly reasonable nature. It seems also to follow that if the weak believer's doubts are of a reasonable nature, then so must be the doubts of the weak unbeliever. Hence, if the Essayist is trying to reassure his fellow theists by reason, then there is a presumption that there is reason on the other side — that some degree of speculative atheism is, despite the claim of the Essayist to the contrary, possible.

I find it difficult to see the Essayist's argumentation as consistent with his denying the possibility of speculative atheism. This is not to say, however, that one *cannot* see them as consistent. It is possible that the Essayist was trying to allay by rational means the irrational fears and doubts of unthinking theists and atheists. If one takes this line, then one is retreating from the interpretation in which the Essayist's argumentation is designed to show the impossibility of speculative atheism to an earlier interpretation, which is also, I have argued, difficult to accept. Of course, most of the deniers we have examined deny (like the Essayist and Balguy) not the possibility of speculative atheism but only its actuality. The denial or doubt in Broughton, the *Encyclopedia*, Curteis and Wise takes a descriptive rather than a conceptual form: there have, as a matter of fact, been no speculative atheists. But these denials — with the possible exception of Curteis — are not defended in the way we should expect. The defence takes a conceptual rather than a descriptive form: putative atheists cannot be speculative because they must be practical or unthinking atheists (*Encyclopedia*); or they cannot be speculative atheists because the necessary conditions laid down make this impossible: atheists have been defined *out* of their speculative atheism and *into* mixt or unthinking atheism in Curteis and Wise. Thus even the descriptive doubts and denials tend towards denying the possibility of speculative atheism. But then their denials are in conflict, as we have seen, with their argumentation; for in their argumentation they indirectly affirm the atheism they originally denied. This is not to say that *all* argumentation must be taken in this way. Some, as we shall see in the following two cases, may be seen as justifying the impossibility of believing in atheism.

IX. Herbert and Fotherby

In perhaps the best-known chapter of his *De veritate* (1624) — Chapter 9, 'Common Notions Concerning Religion' — Lord Herbert of Cherbury denies that there are atheists. Some men, he allows, 'appear to be atheists'. Yet, he goes on to say:

> In reality they are not atheists; but because they have noticed that some people apply false and shocking attributes to God, they have preferred not to believe in God, than to believe in a God of such a character. When He is endowed with true attributes so far from not believing in Him they would pray that such a God might exist, if there were no such Being. If, however, you still maintain that irreligious persons and even atheists can be found (which I do not believe), reflect that there may be not a few madmen and fools included among those who maintain rationality is the final difference of man.[34]

Here we have a direct denial of the existence of atheists, which, on the surface, is similar to others we have already examined. There is, for instance, the familiar move of explaining away apparent or alleged atheists. The putative atheist really denies (like Socrates perhaps) false gods; he does not, and would not, deny the true God. Herbert's apparent atheist may remind us of More's 'famously-learned men' who were not as superstitious as others, and were thus 'traduced for atheists'; but Herbert seems to be saying that the apparent atheists also believed — although mistakenly — themselves to be atheists. But there are significant differences between Herbert's denial and those we have encountered. There is not, for example, the same crucial clash. This is not to say that Herbert does not argue for the existence of God, but rather that his argumentation does not so clearly suppose (even very indirectly) the existence of the atheism which he directly denied. For Herbert's denial, rather than being in conflict with his proof of God's existence, may be seen as an essential part of the proof. This is so because Herbert argues for the existence of God on the basis of universal assent: it is, he contends, a common notion which 'has been accepted by every normal person, and does not require any further justification' (p. 291). In this way his denial of atheists forms a necessary part or implication of his proof: if there were any atheists (or any normal persons who were atheists), then the belief would not be universal; but then — as universality is a sign of truth for Herbert — the belief in God would not be true. A modern reader might well wonder whether 'proof' is the correct term for a mode of reasoning which seems so question-begging. But Herbert does argue for universality by subjecting apparent falsifications to critical scrutiny. So he says (p. 295):

> It is no objection that temples or regions sacred to the Gods are not found among savages. For in their own fashion they consulted oracles and undertook no serious task without propitiating their Deity. I am aware that an author of reputation has said that in one remote region no religious practice can be observed. But this statement has been rejected by a later writer who pointed out that the author was ignorant of the language of that country.

Now, if there is no clash between denial and argument, then we have not the same grounds for positing repression. Hence we may have found in Herbert a descriptive denial, and argumentation which is aimed to justify that denial. As we have just seen, Herbert does try to argue against a claim that atheists have been discovered in a remote region. So this part of his argument does seem to be directed against the affirmers of atheism rather than against atheists themselves. But the question arises of why Herbert bothers to formulate his wider, consensus-of-opinion argument for the existence of God. Against whom is this argument being directed? Whom is he trying to convince? Clearly, there is a difficulty here; for why should he bother to convince fellow theists, especially since they cannot become atheists? It seems equally absurd to suggest that he is trying to argue with atheists. If he were, this would all too plainly disprove his whole argument; because to argue with an atheist would imply that the belief in God is not univeral.[35]

Now one way out of this dilemma is to suppose that Herbert is arguing against those who held that belief in God was derived from revelation and/or tradition, and was not in itself natural and reasonable. If this were so, then he would be arguing not about the validity of the belief, but about the manner in which it is known and justified. He would be opposing not atheists but those who question natural religion, whether they be fideists, fundamentalists, or believers in ecclesiastical tradition or authority. In this way he may be seen as arguing for the impossibility of atheism, rather than for its falsity. Consequently, we are not irresistibly drawn to interpret Herbert's denial as a device for repressing atheism. On the other hand, Herbert certainly wished that there were no atheists; for they would undermine his pioneer deistic system. Nor can we exclude the possibility that — despite its evident absurdity — he was also directing his denial and arguments against atheists. Hence I am inclined to think that his denial also contains a repressive element.

Bishop Martin Fotherby in his *Atheomastix* (London, 1622) denies, even more vehemently and frequently than Herbert, the existence of atheists. Fotherby allows that there are some who outwardly 'deny both God, and all Religion, yet according to him, such atheists are inwardly inforced to beleeve them, and to hold (even against their will) many notable points of the Christian Religion.'[36] Fotherby's denial, like Herbert's, is connected with the argument from universal assent. According to Fotherby: 'there is no particular person in the world, but that (in some degree) he beleeveth, there is a God' (p. 39). Fotherby differs from Herbert in the way he deals with potential falsification, or, as he puts it, 'objections against the universalite of consent in religion'. He discusses this subject in Chapter Ten, which begins with a rather lame and limited defence: if there *are* atheists, then they are very few in number. But he really holds a stronger position:

> But now he writes on p. 99 it may be doubted (yea, and that not without some probability of reason) whether those men, whom the Heathen have so branded for *Atheists*, were pure *Atheists* indeed, or no? For the pure *Atheist* (according to the propriety of that name) is he, which generally and constantly denieth all Divinity; and beleeveth as he saith.

Fotherby then considers various putative atheists, and finds that none of them satisfies his three necessary conditions for pure atheism: there is no atheist who (1) constantly and (2) sincerely rejects (3) all gods. So Diagoras of Melos, supposedly the first atheist, really only denied (according to Fotherby) the Athenian gods; he did not deny 'all Deitie' (p. 100). There may also have been some men who denied the existence of all gods; but their denial was not sincere; or it may not have been constant: it may have been caused by 'some sodaine passion', and hence lasted only a short time (p. 107). What appears to be pure atheism tends to collapse under Fotherby's scrutiny into unthinking and/or 'practical Atheisme' (p. 107). This tendency can be seen in a remarkable passage in which Fotherby formulates what I have called the crucial clash, while resisting the suggestion that he is himself guilty of it:

> And, whereas in divers passages of it [Fotherby's book], we affirme, that there be no *Atheists;* and yet, in other places, do we acknowledge many, and dispute against them: for the avoyding of offence by this seeming contradiction, I desire the reader to carry out with him this distinction: ... namely, that when we deny that there be any *Atheists,* as be properly so called, namely, which generally and constantly beleeve *There is no God,* and hold so unto the end: (of which sort There can be none...). ...When we confesse, *There be Atheists,* and dispute against them; wee understand only such as deny there is a God, rather by outward profession, than by inward perswasion: or, if they have indeed any such inward perswasion, it is but only upon some sodaine passion: which vanisheth as sodainly, as it was conceived fondly. (p. 107)

Of all those who both deny and attack atheism Fotherby is most clearly aware of the crucial clash. His attempts to evade the charge are similar to Wise's introduction of the class of mixt atheists. But the class of existent atheists which Fotherby introduces is wider, less defined, more inconsistent and confused than Wise's. On the whole, Fotherby tends to identify this class with unthinking and practical atheists. But sometimes, as we have seen, he suggests that a few pure atheists may exist; and he also allows that there are atheists who believe 'it [that there is no God] weakly'. He wishes to deny the existence of pure atheists, but he, like Cudworth, appreciates the importance of having enemies to justify his belligerent book: 'To what end, [he asks] this whole worke serveth, which is written against *Atheists,* if they be few, or none such?'

Fotherby's method of dealing with possible pure or speculative atheists is closer to Wise's than it is to Herbert's. Both Fotherby and Wise construct an ideal class: 'pure atheists' and 'absolute speculative atheists', by means of which they are able to reclassify atheists. Their method is analytic and conceptual; whereas Herbert's method tends to be empirical and anthropological. Fotherby, like Wise, emphasises the condition of constancy. But Fotherby and Herbert share a belief in the innateness of the idea of God. This is of some interest in that Bentley and Blackmore take this as the premise from which the denial of atheists is deduced. According to Fotherby, there is 'an inbred perswasion in the hearts of all men, That there is a God' (p. 15). And for Herbert all common notions are innate. Hence Fotherby's denial (like Herbert's) may have been a logical or descriptive consequence drawn from his innatist and consensus theories. There is in Fotherby, however, considerably more evidence of a repressive component to his denial. Despite his attempted evasions he is clearly guilty of the crucial clash; although his transparent vacillations, and admission of a 'seeming contradiction' may indicate that the clash is close to the surface. Also, unlike Herbert, Fotherby is not a champion of natural religion, fighting against the fideists, revelationists, and traditionalists. Although he says that he is disputing with non-speculative atheists, he also calls attention to speculative atheists, or, at least, atheists who pretend to speculate. In the Preface to the reader, he says: 'Now this is the worst kinde of Atheisme of all other, when as Atheisme is grounded, not so much upon *Ignorance*, as it is upon the opinion of knowledge. And yet such is the *Atheisme* of this our time.' Of course, this may be an expression of the attitude, sometimes expressed by churchmen, that their own age is the worst and most wicked. (We have also seen Blackmore, for example, deny that there was atheism in former times, but firmly attribute it to his own time.) However, I suspect that there is really something in Fotherby's claim that the atheism of his time is 'grounded upon the opinion of knowledge', for he spends a suspiciously large number of pages denying the existence of atheism and defending his denial. But it is hard to be sure about the nature of Fotherby's denial; this is so partly on account of his use of the full-blooded innatist and consensus arguments for God's existence, but also because we are ignorant of the nature and extent of the atheistic threat in his period.[37] For these reasons I am reluctant to pass confident judgement on his denials; whereas I did confidently judge Curteis's denial — which is in some respects quite similar — to be an example of repression; for, although Curteis makes use of the innatist and consensus arguments, they are both weaker and less directly connected with his denial of atheists. There is also more evidence of serious atheistic threats for Curteis's generation — for example, from Hobbes, Spinoza and their allegedly atheistic followers.

X. The 1697 Act for repressing atheism

There are, as we have seen, a number of ways of keeping something down. Perhaps the least effective way is openly to fight against it: when the thing comes up one shouts it down. Open opposition often provokes counter-opposition: oppression encourages revolt. The better way of keeping something down is to discourage it from rising up. And one technique for achieving that end is to persuade those likely to rise up that they really cannot. I have suggested that this is behind most of our denials. Like the denials of the general and mother (in Section VIII), our denials are designed to inhibit atheism. Of course, in the denials of the general and mother, we are inclined to see a consciously inhibitive aim. We are inclined to regard them as suppressive and not repressive. Rather than saying: 'You cannot be atheists' or 'Do not become atheists', the message of the deniers of atheism is: 'It is really most unlikely that one could (reasonably) become or be an atheist.' Their denials are subtle and cunning enough not to be directly addressed to those they wish to inhibit; so Balguy says: 'Atheism offers such violence to all our faculties, that it seems scarce credible it should ever really find any footing in human understanding.'

But there is an even more subtle way in which something can be prevented. Just as it is probably more effective not to take something seriously, rather than to fight directly against it, so it is wiser to refrain from even mentioning the thing one wants to keep down. We can see something of this tactic in Wise's suggestion that the term 'mixt atheism' should be substituted for 'speculative atheist'. We have also noted Freud's observation that those who denied infantile sexuality tried to inhibit or discourage it not under that name, but as 'childish naughtiness'.

I think that we can see this more subtle tactic in operation in the ingenious 1697 'Act for the effectual suppressing of blasphemy and profaneness', by which it was made punishable to 'deny any one of the persons in the holy Trinity to be God, or ... assert or maintain there are more Gods than one, or ... deny the Christian religion to be true, or the holy Scriptures of the Old and New Testament to be of divine authority.'[38] Now, there is nothing in this Act which makes atheism culpable; indeed, atheism, or the denial of the existence of God, is not even mentioned. What is legislated against is the denial of the Athanasian Creed, the truth of Christianity, and so on; all of which matters assume the existence of God. It seems to be implicit in the Act that no one could be so utterly depraved as to be an

35

atheist; hence what really has to be dealt with are lesser depravities. I suspect, however, that this is an Act not only for the 'suppressing of blasphemy' but also for the repressing of atheism.

If my suspicion is correct we can see in the 1697 Act the repressive tendency in an especially healthy and virulent form. The direct denials, such as in the *Encyclopedia*, the Essay and Balguy, while they are better than open hostility, may engender doubts. If there are no atheists, then why should theologians so often remind us of this? There are plenty of non-existent imaginary things, but few of us go around saying — sometimes with great warmth — that they do not exist. In the Act there is no such suspicious denial; but there is an implicit denial which is more eloquent for its being left unsaid. Of course it is difficult to argue from the conscious or verbal absence of something to its unconscious presence. The deeper the repression, the fewer the signs, and the more difficult it will be for us to be sure that such-and-such constitutes a case of repression. Thus the 1697 Act may show only that atheism was not thought to be a serious danger at that time. But because the Act does not make atheism punishable, we must not suppose that these legislators did not hold atheism in great abhorrence. Very few indeed did not regard atheism as a most frightful crime. Even such men as Thomas Hobbes and Anthony Collins could become extremely severe in their denunciation of atheism; although they were (with good reason) suspected of being atheists.[39] According to the received view of that day (see Chapter 7), atheism dissolved the bonds of society, because no atheist could be trusted to keep his oaths.

It is suggestive that during the eighteenth century no Act against atheism was passed, even though the danger must have become all too apparent towards the end of the century. Perhaps the unspoken policy was to hope that (as the Roman proverb has it) 'Without the word, without the thing': if one does not mention the crime, no one will think of committing it. This again would be a way of inhibiting atheism more subtle than our denials: they protest too much. Or to use Freud's model: in them the guard is finding it more and more difficult to prevent unwelcome guests from entering our house. We hear too much commotion. His tactics are becoming increasingly cruder: more like suppression than repression. Atheism can no longer be kept indirectly down. (Either the guard has lost some of his former power, or the interloper has gained in strength.) The guard is only half a preventer; for he is now also an ejector.

The direct denial of atheism, as in the *Encyclopedia*, the Essay, etc., may be located somewhere between deep repression and suppression.

Repression admits of degrees. As Freud writes: it 'is merely a question of the degree of his [the guard's] watchfulness, and of how early he carries out his act of recognition.'[40] Repression can be a function of both the guard and the policeman: both prevention and ejection; although it is more properly called repression the more the former is in operation. Repression and suppression shade into each other. This seems to be implied in Freud's official definition of repression: *'the essence of repression lies simply in turning something away, and keeping it at a distance, from the conscious'.*[41] The difference between expelling an idea from 'the conscious if it was previously conscious, or' holding it 'back from consciousness if it was about to become conscious' 'is not important; it amounts to much the same thing as the difference between my ordering an undesirable guest out of my drawing-room ... and my refusing, after recognizing him, to let him cross my threshold at all' (ibid., p. 153). As applied to our subject, it is a question of how little or how much the denier and his audience are aware that his denial of atheism is aimed at discouraging atheism.

XI. Repression and suppression

The more overt the danger of atheism, the more one would expect suppression rather than repression. Conversely, to the extent that one finds suppression one should expect to find atheism more formidable. A decisive date in this respect is 1770, the year d'Holbach published the first avowedly atheistic work, *The system of nature*. After this extensively argued defence of atheism, and detailed refutation of theistic arguments, no well-informed theologian could easily claim that there were no speculative atheists. Moreover, throughout the next twenty years or so a number of avowedly atheistic books were published by d'Holbach and others. And in 1782 the first work of that kind was published in Britain.

During and after this period, 1770–1790, one must suspect suppression rather than repression in any denial of atheism. But the formula or external appearance of the denial does not substantially change. Take the following statement by James Webb:

If I were asked the question: 'Are there real atheists?' I should answer, 'Yes, most certainly, but among animals only; not among men.' There have been, and still are persons impudent enough to say and even write that man is the work of chance;

and spontaneous production of nature, etc., that there are, or will be any stupid enough to believe it is impossible.[42]

We find here familiar features: some may say that man is the work of chance, but they cannot really believe it; such atheism is the result of animality, not rationality: it is unthinking atheism. If it were not that this statement was published in a pamphlet of 1889 — after Kant, Darwin, and such popularisers of atheism as Shelley, Richard Carlile, G. J. Holyoake, Charles Southwell and Charles Bradlaugh — one might be tempted to regard it as a case of repression. Indeed, if it were written in the early part of the seventeenth century, one would consider the possibility of its being a descriptive statement, like those of Herbert and Fotherby. But the date, together with the vituperative language, strongly suggest that by means of his denial Webb consciously designed to strike a blow against atheism.

This is also true, I think, of some expressions in Thomas Paine's *Discourse to the Society of Theophilanthropists,* first published in 1798. Here Paine speaks of 'pretenders to atheism' and 'the atheist who affects to reason'.[43] As Paine certainly knew of speculative atheists while living in Paris during the Revolution, one must suspect him of consciously using these expressions to discredit atheism. His suppressive expressions are not as frantic as those of Webb. Rather than bluntly saying: 'No one could be so stupid as to be an atheist', Paine more moderately abuses atheists by suggesting that there are no serious speculative atheists. The denial is no longer preventative: it is now a curative medicine, though of rather doubtful efficacy.

An example of how a denial of the seventeenth century could reach across nearly two centuries, and there be embraced by a fellow denier of the nineteenth century, can be seen in the case of Philip Baldaeus and J.A. St John. The former travelled in the Near East and recounted his experiences in a travel book which was first published in Dutch in 1672 and translated into English in Churchill's *Collection of voyages and travels* (London, 1704), vol. 3. The latter was the editor and annotator of the two-volume Bohn edition of the *Philosophical works of John Locke* (1854). In his *Essay concerning human understanding,* (I.iv.8), Locke had argued that as there are and have been atheists, the idea of God cannot be innate; because the idea of God is not universal it cannot be innate. In this chapter Locke is expressly arguing against Lord Herbert of Cherbury, and he does so by producing evidence from the growing body of travel literature.[44]

Locke's nineteenth-century editor, St John, treats Locke's claim —

that there are 'whole nations to which the most obvious of all truths [i.e. the existence of God] is unknown'[45] — with a mixture of pity and annoyance. St John tells us that it is a 'palpable error'; and says that 'This may serve to show how difficult it is even for the ablest minds, [such as Locke,] when supporting a favourite hypothesis [the non-existence of innate ideas], to guard against very palpable errors.'[46] For St John believes that 'man's mind is naturally fitted for the acquisition of certain ideas ... particularly the idea of God.' And to support his disagreement with Locke he quotes 'the testimony of Baldaeus, whose opinion on the general question [he says] exactly coincides with my own' (pp. 184–5). Here is the passage he quotes (p. 185) from Baldaeus:

> The existence of a God, or Supreme Being, is so firmly rooted in the heart of mankind, that there is no nation in the world but has acknowledged the same. What is alledged to the contrary of the *Chileses, Tapujars, Brasilians, Madagascarians,* as also the inhabitants of *Florida*, the Caribee Islands, and especially the Cape of Good Hope, must rather be attributed to the want of knowledge of those authors than real truth. Of this I was sufficiently convinced in 1666, when I tarried three months at the *Cape of Good Hope*, where I found these barbarians to perform their religious services in the night-time, which I had no opportunity to observe in 1665, when I came that way before.

Whatever the aim of Baldaeus's statement — which is in the tradition of Bentley, Herbert and the Act — there can be little doubt that St John's endorsement and implicit denials are likely to have had a suppressive aim, especially as they were written many years after the emergence of avowed atheism.[47] It is worth noting, however, that St John's anthropological denial is more resistant to falsification than most of the denials we have been discussing. The discovery of one or a number of atheists can be dismissed as freaks of nature — compare Herbert; a few exceptions need not affect the claim that there are no atheistic *societies*. Also, the anthropological denier can maintain — as St John and Herbert do — that those explorers who claimed to have observed atheistic societies were ignorant of the language and customs of the natives. St John also produces an interesting ulterior motive to explain why 'those credulous and hasty writers ... have libelled uncivilized nations [by describing them as atheistic, namely:] that they and their countrymen might have some excuse for plundering them' (p. 184).

St John's denial of atheistic societies should be seen as a weak restatement of those early seventeenth-century denials, by Herbert and Fotherby, whose justification was based on innateness and universal assent. In St John's case, these justifications have, of necessity, been watered down — even more so than in the case of Curteis. The claim is no longer that *everyone* has a belief in God — which is the view of Herbert — but that 'No language whatever, of which a complete vocabulary has been published, is found to want such a substantive [signifying God]; nor do I believe that any thus imperfect exists in the world' (p. 164). In the same way, St John does not maintain (as Herbert did) that all normal people have an explicit innate idea of God, but rather that 'man's mind is naturally fitted for the acquisition of certain ideas and principles ... particularly the idea of God' (p. 184). But although St John's denial is as weak and diluted as his justifications, it is suppressive none the less.

After the 1770s the denial of atheism took various watered-down forms. Consider, for example, this statement from Edmund Burke's *Reflections on the revolution in France* (8th edn, Dublin, 1791):

> We know, and it is our pride to know, that man is by his constitution a religious animal; *that atheism is against, not only our reason but our instincts; and that it cannot prevail long.* But if, in the moment of riot, and in a drunken delirium from the hot spirit drawn out of the alembic of hell, which in France is now so furiously boiling, we should uncover our nakedness by throwing off that Christian religion ... we are apprehensive (being well aware that the mind will not endure a void) that some uncouth, pernicious, and degrading superstition might take place of it.[48]

Burke does not deny the existence of atheism; he openly recognises that it exists in France. But he does deny that it has any basis in human nature, and that it can long prevail. The sociological denial has, of necessity, been weakened: it is not – as in Bentley, Herbert and Baldaeus – that no atheistic society is possible or has ever existed; but that it cannot exist for any appreciable period of time. The temporal criterion, which in Curteis, Wise and the Confessor we have seen applied to individual atheists, is now being applied sociologically. Burke is also using a blunted version of the familiar innatist justification for the denial; and it is fairly clear that he is using it suppressively – to rationalise his denial of atheism. Atheism 'cannot prevail long'! It need not be taken very seriously!

But then why is Burke allowing himself to become so alarmed by it? His alarm and angry condemnation of what he takes to be a Jacobin atheism — or 'atheism by establishment' as he calls it in the *Letters on a regicide peace* (1796) — correspond to the (argumentative) indirect affirmation of previous denials. It seems likely that Burke was aware of the conflict; for in the latter part of this statement he provides us with an explanation for his alarm. It is not that he is fearful of Jacobin atheism, it would seem, but of that 'pernicious and degrading superstition [which] is likely to take the place of it'. Atheism is not being taken seriously for what it is in itself — since it is only a transient thing, a freak of the moment — but because when it passes it will create a void which will be filled by some form of debased religion. This attempt to explain away the apparent conflict supports a largely suppressive interpretation of Burke's qualified denial of atheism. When we observe an attempt to reconcile a conflict, we suspect the conscious mind at work. The unconscious mind attacks in every possible way that which it wishes to destroy; its disregard for consistency enables us to distinguish its repressive activity from that of the more consistent conscious mind.

XII. Conclusion

How successful was the repressive denial of atheism? To what extent did it help to inhibit and discourage the emergence of speculative atheism? This is a difficult question, but one we can hardly avoid.

I must first emphasise yet again that avowed speculative atheism did emerge surprisingly late: in Europe it is hardly more than 200 years old and in Britain it is even younger. This striking chronological fact stands in need of explanation. No doubt part of the explanation must be sought in economic and scientific developments, the growing acceptance of non-religious morality and so on; but here I shall focus on the part played by the repressive denial. For I think that it did help to retard the rise of speculative atheism. In order to assess its influence, we must seek to determine how widespread the denial of atheism was in Britain in the seventeenth and eighteenth centuries.

We have seen in the course of our examination that many of the deniers themselves — as, for example, Cudworth and Bentley — allude to the popularity of the denial and disbelief, and Schopenhauer suggests that it was widespread, especially in Britain.[49] According to the anonymous author of *The materiality of the soul* (London, 1729): 'As to *Atheism*, it is now justly and pretty generally understood that there neither is, nor ever was or can be, really an Atheist' (p. 15). This picture is supported by well-known writers such as Sir Thomas Browne, Anthony Collins, George Berkeley and David Hume. Browne states in his treatise on *Vulgar errors* (1645) that 'many there are who cannot conceive that there was ever any absolute Atheist'.[50] And in his *Discourse of free-thinking* (London, 1713), Collins asserts: 'many Divines maintain that there never was a real *Atheist* in the world'.[51] This is in accord with Berkeley, who states in the Advertisement to *Alciphron* (London, 1732) that 'it hath often been said, there is no such thing as a speculative Atheist ...'. And writing some 15 years later, Hume remarks: 'the most religious Philosophers still dispute whether any Man can be so blinded as to be a speculative Atheist'.[52]

Judging from the following temperate assertion of John Evans, the disbelief in atheists had somewhat dwindled by the beginning of the nineteenth century. Writing in 1804, he says:

> It is to be hoped that *direct* Atheists are few. Some persons indeed, question the reality of such a character, and others insist, that pretensions to Atheism have their origin in pride, or are adopted as a cloak for licentiousness.[53]

But it was still necessary for Robert Flint in his *Baird lecture* of 1877 to spend nearly four pages in proving the existence of avowed atheists (so that he could then refute them). According to Flint: 'The existence of atheism has often been doubted. It has been held to be absolutely impossible for a man entirely to throw off belief in God.'[54]

I conclude from this evidence, and also from the denials and doubts examined, that the disbelief in atheists was widely held in Britain in the seventeenth and eighteenth centuries.[55] And since its tendency was, I have maintained, to inhibit and discourage atheism, there can be little doubt that it did help to retard its emergence. The repressive denial of atheism was a potent preventative medicine.

Additional and even more striking evidence in support of this conclusion is to be found in the first avowedly atheistic book published in Britain — the *Answer to Priestley* — and an early review of it. In the Prefatory Address to this book the writer, William Hammon, shows himself to be aware — like his atheistic forerunner d'Holbach — of the denials of, and disbelief in, speculative atheism.[56] He also seems to have been sensitive to its repressive power, for he is anxious to explode the disbelief once and for all:

as to the question whether there is such an existent Being as
an atheist, to put that out of all manner of doubt, I do declare
upon my honour that I am one. Be it therefore for the future
remembered, that in London in the kingdom of England, in
the year of our Lord one thousand seven hundred and eighty-
one, a man publicly declared himself to be an atheist. (p. xvii)

One might imagine that this straightforward avowal of atheism
would settle the matter. But not so with such a deep-seated repressive
tendency. One of the few reviewers of the book dwells with considerable fury on Hammon's avowal of atheism; he says:

The writer of this letter [i.e. Prefatory Address] is an avowed
atheist; and lest his simple declaration should not be credited,
he swears to the truth of it. But what doth he swear by? Whom
doth he appeal to? not to God: for he believes there is none.
And as he thinks he can swear by nothing greater, he swears
by his HONOUR![57]

The reviewer then quotes Hammon's avowal of atheism and concludes in this way: 'Was ever honour so pledged! When it "fell
among *gamblers,* it was stripped and wounded, and left half dead."
It remained only for the *atheist* to finish the date of its shame and
wretchedness!'

In short, the reviewer seems unwilling to trust the word of an
atheist. An atheist's honour is really no honour. His oath is worthless
because, as Locke, Bentley and others had maintained, only God
could give meaning and force to oaths (see Chapter 7). This apparent refusal to accept the word of an atheist that he is an atheist must
be considered one of the most insidious and revealing expressions of
the tendency to repress atheism. In some ways it is a fitting reaction
to the first published avowal of atheism in Britain; for in the
reviewer's paradoxical contortions we can almost see the repressive
tendency in its death throes.

Notes

1. Vol. 1, p. 97. The following is an index of the denials, in order of appearance:

Encyclopedia, 1771	Cudworth, 1678	Act, 1697
Essayist, *London Magazine*, 1734	Cudworth, 1678	Webb, 1889
Balguy, 1749	Bentley, 1692	Paine, 1798
Balguy, 1749	Bentley, 1692	Baldaeus, 1672
Curteis, 1726	Confessor, *c.* 1735	St John, 1854
Wise, 1706	Herbert, 1624	Burke, 1791
More, 1653	Fotherby, 1622	

2. *Encyclopedia Britannica; or, a dictionary of arts and sciences*, vol. 1, p. 501.

3. *London Magazine: or gentleman's monthly intelligencer* (June) p. 309. The essay was originally printed in the *Universal Spectator*, no. 296 (8 June 1734).

4. *A discourse concerning the being and attributes of God*, 6th edn (London, 1725), pp. 2–3.

5. *Some thoughts concerning the several causes and occasions of atheism especially in the present age ...* , especially pp. 4–61; also see J.M. Robertson, *Dynamics of religion: an essay in English culture history* (London, 1926), Chapters 3 and 4.

6. That is, Baron d'Holbach's *La Système de la nature, ou des lois du monde physique et du monde moral* (London imprint, though actually printed in Amsterdam, 1770) and *An answer to Dr Priestley's letters to a philosophical unbeliever* (London, 1782) by William Hammon and Matthew Turner. For an examination of the *Answer to Priestley*, see below, Chapter 5.

7. *London Magazine*, p. 308.

8. *A discourse*, p. 3. This was also Ralph Cudworth's considered opinion; see below, Section V.

9. Freud uses this topological analogy with slight variations in at least three works. Firstly, in the second of the *Five lectures on psychoanalysis* (1910), he compares a repressed idea to the ejection of some disturbing person from his lecture hall; see the *Standard edition of the complete works of Sigmund Freud*, revised and edited by James Strachey (London, 1966–74), vol. 11, pp. 25–7; (referred to hereafter as the *Standard edition*). Secondly, it is used in the essay 'Repression' (1915), his fullest account of the topic, where he speaks of setting a guard at the door to his drawing-room in order to keep out an unwanted guest; (*Standard edition*, vol. 14, p. 153). Thirdly, in the *Introductory lectures on psychoanalysis* (1916–17), Lecture 19, the guard becomes a watchman; (*Standard edition*, vol. 16, p. 295).

10. Sermon on 'The folly and wretchedness of an atheistic inclination', in *Twenty-one sermons* (London, 1749), Part 2, p. 1.

11. The example seems to have been a common one. We find it in one of the long notes to the Creech translation of Lucretius' *Of the nature of things* (London, 1714). Commenting on the lines:

By CHANCE to that convenient ORDER hurl'd,
Which frames the BEINGS, that compose the WORLD.

the annotator tells us that 'the meer Consideration even of a Gnat, or the Eye of a paultry fly' should convince the atheist of the falsity of his position; see pp. 81 and 83.

12. 'The folly and wretchedness of an atheistic inclination', p. 2. The

following quotation is from p. 3.

13. *Dissertation,* p. 35. Curteis may have had Lord Rochester's famous 'death-bed' conversion in mind here, see below Chapter 2, Section IV.

14. *A collection of several philosophical writings of Henry More,* 4th edn (London, 1712); *Antidote,* p. 141.

15. Ibid. More began his book on quite a different note. In the Preface to the *Antidote,* he tells of the lengths to which he has gone to accommodate himself to the atheist, in order that he 'might, if it were possible, win him off from down-right Atheism.' He writes: 'that he [the atheist] might not be shie of me, I have conform'd my self as near his own *Garb* as I might, without partaking of his Folly or Wickedness' (Section 12). So the atheist *has* a (rational) garb, distinct from that of folly and wickedness.

16. *Eight sermons preach'd at the Honourable Robert Boyle's lecture, in the first year MDCXII,* 6th edn (Cambridge, 1735); the first lecture or sermon is called 'Folly of atheism, and (what is now called) deism: even with respect to the present life'.

17. *The Creation: a philosophical poem* (London, 1712) p. iv.

18. *The true intellectual system of the universe: the first part, wherein all the reason and philosophy of atheism is confuted, and its impossibility demonstrated* was first published in London, 1678; no further parts were published. I quote from the 2nd edn (London, 1743), edited by Birch; see pp. xxxix–xl.

19. *Eight sermons,* pp. 15–16.

20. See Bayle's *Miscellaneous reflexions, occasion'd by the comet* (London, 1708), especially Section CLXI.

21. See the extensive essay 'Of atheism' in his *Essays upon several subjects* (London, 1717), vol. 2, pp. 3–163 and *Natural theology* (London, 1728), pp. 2–25.

22. *Standard edition,* vol. 16, p. 312.

23. This may be compared with William Wilberforce's persecution of free-thought as 'vice'. It was 'the constant maxim' of Wilberforce 'that no man should be prosecuted for his attacks on religion'. But this did not prevent him from prosecuting the publishers and sellers of Paine's *The age of reason,* when he was Vice-President of the Society for Suppressing Vice. Wilberforce, according to Robertson, apparently 'supposed that by calling free-thought "vice" he was excluding it from the category of "attacks upon religion" '; see *Dynamics,* pp. 185–6.

24. See 'Notes upon a case of obsessional neurosis' (1909), in *Standard edition,* vol. 10, p. 183, note 2.

25. *Standard edition,* vol. 19, pp. 235–6.

26. See 'Splitting of the ego in the process of defence' (1940); in *Standard edition,* vol. 23.

27. See 'Fetishism' (1927), in *Standard edition,* vol. 21.

28. Pages 10–11. The only copy of this pamphlet known to me is an imperfect one in the New York Public Library, 42nd St, New York.

29. Compare a correspondent in *The Athenian oracle,* who mentions an unnamed 'man ... of debauch'd conversation; who in my hearing affirm'd that he did not believe that there was either God nor Devil'; yet 'condemned ... to be hanged ... he did with many tears bewail his former delusions ... and told me ... that when he had formerly said ... there was no God, yet he did not then heartily believe what he said'. The correspondent then asks: 'do you

think there ever was a real atheist?', to which the *Oracle* replies: 'there may be a drunken injudicious Atheist, but not a sober thinking *Atheist*'. Another questionable confession of atheism is Richard Sault's *The second Spira: being a fearful example of an atheist* ... (London, 1693), especially p. 35; also see G.W. Foote's *Infidel death-beds* (London, 1886).

30. *The world as will and representation* trans. E.F. J. Payne (New York, 1966), vol. 1, p. 512. The second italics are mine.

31. Denis Diderot, David Hume and Baron d'Holbach presented early evolutionary theories; see Diderot's *Early philosophical works* (Chicago, 1916), pp. 111–12, Hume's *Dialogues concerning natural religion* (1777), Section VIII, and d'Holbach's *System of nature* (Boston, 1868), trans. H.D. Robinson, vol. 1, ch. VI. All references to the *System* are to this edition, a facsimilie of which was published by Burt Franklin (New York) in 1970.

32. See his *Ethics* I, especially propositions vi, xviii–xix; also see III, proposition ii scholium. John Toland also expressed views similar to Spinoza's in his *Letters to Serena* (1704) and *Pantheisticon* (1720); see my articles on Tindal and Toland in G. Stein (ed.), *The Encyclopedia of Unbelief* (New York, 1985), pp. 667–70.

33. There is some doubt whether Epicurus and his followers really held the chance theory that was attributed to them. They did not think of chance as an actual entity or force. For many seventeenth- and eighteenth-century writers atheism seems to have been essentially connected with this almost animistic chance theory.

34. *De veritate* (Bristol, 1937), introduced and translated by Meyrick H. Carré, p. 295.

35. See Locke's *Reply* (1699) to Stillingfleet, in which he writes: 'Were there ever in the world any *Atheists* or no? If there were not, what need is there about raising a question about the Being of God, when nobody questions it?' — *Works of John Locke*, 2nd edn (1722), vol. 1, p. 574.

36. *Atheomastix: clearing foure truthes, against atheists and infidels* (London, 1622), p. 129.

37. See G.T. Buckley's *Atheism in the English Renaissance* (Chicago, 1932). Despite his title, Buckley is unable to find any atheism during the period. A similar judgement can be passed on John Redwood's study of the period 1660 to 1750, *Reason, ridicule and religion* (London, 1976). Throughout the book we read of the 'atheist scare', 'atheist question', 'atheist plot'; but the author never examines the simple but central question: Were they any avowedly atheistic books published in the seventeenth or eighteenth centuries?

38. See *The thirty-nine articles* ... *together with several acts of Parliament* ... (London, 1739), p. 120.

39. See Hobbes's *Answer to Bramhall*, in the *English works of Hobbes* (London 1840), vol. 4, p. 294, and Collins's essays in the *Independent Whig* 6th edn (London, 1732), especially 'Of high-church atheism, part 5', p. 283. A possible analogue here is homosexuality. Although male homosexuality has been legally culpable in Britain, the law does not mention female homosexuality. Why? Possibly because such activity amongst the 'gentle sex' was felt to be unthinkable.

40. *Introductory lectures, Standard edition*, vol. 16, p. 295.

41. 'Repression', *Standard edition*, vol. 14, p. 147; italics in text.

42. *Are there any real atheists?* (London, 1889), p. 3.

43. See the *Theological works of Thomas Paine* (London, 1818) pp. 5 and 7; each tract in this collection is separately paginated.

44. Like Cudworth and Bentley, even Locke sometimes falls inadvertently into the repressive tendency; see my 'Theoretical/practical distinction as applied to the existence of God from Locke to Kant', in *Trivium* 12 (1977), pp. 93–5.

45. See *Essay concerning human understanding*, I.iv.8; in *Philosophical works of Locke*, vol. 1, pp. 183–7.

46. *Philosophical works of Locke*, vol. 1, p. 184.

47. A repressive interpretation of Baldaeus is supported by the following statement of Baldaeus's which is not quoted by St John: 'What is said of *Diagoras, Theodorus* ... and their denial of the existence of God, being to be understood only of the plurality of Gods, which was always rejected by the wiser sort among the Pagans; whence it is that we meet with the titles of *Ens entium*, the *Being of Beings* ... *the first Being* ... in their [pagan] writings.' (See Churchill's *Collection of voyages*, vol. 3, p. 830.) This more conceptual non-empirical denial also casts doubts on Baldaeus's disinterestedness in observing and reporting the non-existence of atheists.

48. See p. 135; my italics.

49. *The world as will and representation*, vol. 1, pp. 512–13.

50. See J.M. Robertson's *A history of freethought* (London, 1936), vol. 2, p. 654. Browne, too, was 'of opinion there was never any' atheism; ibid., p. 653.

51. See *Discourse*, p. 104. Collins quotes Bacon's essay 'Of atheism': 'The contemplative Atheist is rare.'

52. *Philosophical essays concerning human understanding* (London, 1748), Essay xii. And yet, as Hume also notes in the same opening paragraph, 'there is not a greater Number of philosophical Reasonings ... than those which ... refute the Fallacies of *Atheists'.*

53. *A sketch of the denominations of the Christian world*, 9th edn (London, 1804), p. 3.

54. *Anti-theistic theories: being the Baird lecture for 1877*, 6th edn (London, 1899), p. 5.

55. For more denials, or evidence of their popularity, see *A defence of ... religion: being a collection of sermons at the lecture founded by Robert Boyle* (London, 1739), vol. 1, p. 365 and vol. 2, p. 202; John Dunton's Dedication to the thirtieth edition of Sault's *The Second Spira* (London, n.d.); Edward Synge's *Gentleman's religion*, 6th edn (Dublin, 1730), p. 15; and Benjamin Martin's *General magazine of arts and sciences* (London, 1755), p. 8.

56. According to d'Holbach: 'many theologians, in despite of those invectives with which they attempt to overwhelm atheists, appear frequently to have doubted whether any existed in the world'. *System of nature* (1868 edition), vol. 2, p. 303. (One wonders to what extent d'Holbach and Hume [see note 52] were aware of the crucial clash.)

57. *The Monthly Review* (1783), p. 129. The review is not signed, but it is the work of Samuel Badcock; see B.C. Nangle, *The Monthly Review* (Oxford, 1934), p. 53.

2

Restoration Atheists: Foundling Followers of Hobbes

I. Acts against atheism

In Section XI of the last chapter I proposed the formula: when repression of atheism gives way to suppression, one should assume that atheism has become more formidable. If one finds an armed guard in place of the old watchman, one would naturally suppose that the intruders have become more threatening. Because the Blasphemy Act of 1697 did not make atheism criminal, I inferred repression. Atheism was not felt to be a serious danger at the time; it could be contained by subtle, repressive, tactics.

A reader of this and other histories might gain the impression that there was a gradual emergence of atheism, and hence a gradual movement from repression to suppression. I hope to show that this is a false representation, for the evidence indicates that in the late seventeenth century atheism in Britain was more prevalent than in the middle of the eighteenth century. There was, particularly in the Restoration period, an explosion of atheism, largely confined to the upper classes and based primarily on the thought of Hobbes. This upper-class Hobbesian atheism was not published or publicly avowed in any straightforward manner; hence it is difficult to identify. But it existed, and the failure to recognise it must distort any intellectual history of the seventeenth century in Britain.

Let us begin by considering two draft acts of Parliament for discouraging irreligion. The first is dated 31 January 1666–7; the second 29 January 1677–8:

> Engrossment of an Act for punishing and suppressing of atheism, prophaness... Any person who denies or derides the essence, persons, or attributes of God the Father, Son or Holy

Ghost given in the Scriptures, or the omnipotency, wisdom, justice, mercy, goodness, or providence of God in the creation … shall upon conviction … be committed to the common gaol until payment of fine … not exceeding 50s[1]

(For the better punishing of those crying sins of atheism and blasphemy) If any person, *being of the age of 16 years or more* not being visibly and apparently distracted out of his wits by sickness or natural infirmity, or not a mere natural fool, void of common sense, shall, *after the day whereon the Royal Assent shall be given to,* by word or writing deny that there is a God … [that person] shall be committed to prison.[2]

It can be immediately seen that these draft bills are far more suppressive of atheism than the later Act of 1697 (see above Chapter 1, Section X). The 1666/7 bill comes close to criminalising the denial of God, the 1677/8 does it openly. A tentative conclusion is that atheism was more threatening around 1677 than it was in 1697 or in 1666. More overt tactics indicate a more overt atheistic threat. Of course, it is possible that the framers of the two earlier draft bills were over-reacting. And as George Hickes remarked in a letter of 17 February 1677/8: 'I would fain know why the bill against atheism was thrown aside.'[3]

II. Robertson and Bentley

An interesting insight into the state of unbelief in the late seventeenth-century Britain is provided by a letter of Richard Bentley, dated 1692, to his friend Professor Bernard, in which he discusses his Boyle Lectures:

And then for Theists you say, they have books written, but Atheists have only talk. Must we then pass by the Atheists, against the judgement and command of my Honble Benefactor [Boyle], who hath put them in the very first place as the most dangerous enemies? Atheism is so much the worse that it is not buried in books, but is gotten [into life]; that taverns and coffee-houses, nay Westminister-hall and the very churches, are full of it…But are the Atheists of your mind, that they have no books written for them? Not one of them but believes Tom Hobbes to be a rank one; and that his corporeal God is a meer

> sham to get his book printed. They understand that Cabbala
> well enough: that all that is but juggle; and that a corporeal
> infinite God is downright nonsense. I have said something to
> this in my first sermon, and I know it to be true by the conver-
> sation I have had with them. There may be some Spinosists,
> or immaterial Fatalists, beyond seas; but not one English
> Infidel in a hundred is any other than a Hobbist; which I know
> to be rank Atheism in the private study and select conversation
> of these men; whatever it may appear to be abroad[4]

Bentley's confident assertion that the taverns and churches are full of
atheism must be taken with caution. So must his claim that he has
had 'conversation' with Hobbesian atheists, who have acquainted
him with the atheistic meaning of Hobbes. What Hobbesian atheist,
or any other sort of atheist, would avow atheism in the company of
Richard Bentley, the belligerent champion of orthodoxy? On the
other hand, why would Bentley wish to prevaricate in a private letter
to his friend? I agree with J.M. Robertson, who quotes this letter,
that Bentley 'must have had some basis for his assertion that in
private certain Hobbists avowed themselves Atheists'.[5]

Robertson is one of the few writers who deals in a forthright
manner with the question of when and in what form atheism first
appeared. His view seems to be that atheism emerged in Restoration
England, but remained dormant until the end of the eighteenth century. As evidence for the latter claim he writes:

> In 1765 ... we find Diderot recounting, on the authority of
> d'Holbach, who had just returned from a visit to this country,
> that 'the Christian religion is nearly extinct in England. The
> deists are innumerable; there are almost no atheists; those who
> are conceal it. An atheist and scoundrel are almost
> synonymous terms for them.'[6]

Robertson sometimes seems to suggest — although not very clearly
— that seventeenth-century Hobbesian atheism was deflected or ab-
sorbed into eighteenth-century constructive deism, and that consequently atheism in Britain emerged twice.[7] However, there is much
that is unsatisfactory in Robertson's discussion. For example, with
little justification he claims (see below, Chapter 3) that Anthony
Collins could not possibly have been an atheist, as feasible atheism
had not been formulated in Collins's time. But as Collins published
his works in the early eighteenth century, this claim is hardly consis-

tent with the affirmation of late seventeenth century Hobbesian atheism. In the *Dynamics of religion,* Robertson writes: 'Almost all ascriptions of Atheism in England before his Hobbes's time are to be looked on with suspicion, as being probably mere theological expletives' (p. 74). I am inclined to agree with Robertson's judgement; but he provides virtually no justification for it. Since he allows that Restoration atheism was unpublished and unavowed, and must therefore be inferred largely from theological critics, how can he be sure that these ascriptions are not also theological expletives? In other words, by what criteria are we to distinguish valid ascriptions from theological expletives? Robertson is silent on this. He also provides far too little concrete evidence to support his inference that there was Hobbesian atheism during the Restoration. In the following sections I hope to fill in some of these gaps.

III. Informers of atheism

First we must ascertain whether there were Hobbesian atheists from 1660 to 1690. We have inferred such atheism from Bentley's letter to Bernard and from the two draft blasphemy bills of 1666 and 1677, but the inference is by no means certain. Even less certain is the confession mentioned in the *Athenian oracle,* or that by 'the Second Spira' (Richard Sault) in 1693 that his atheism was based on the 'creed of *Spinosa* and the *Leviathan*', i.e. Hobbes; for it is likely that both confessions were pious frauds.[8] What we should like is some authentic avowal by an Hobbesian atheist, possibly in a letter or diary. Now to some extent we have something like this from Charles Gildon, who asserted the existence of speculative atheists. As a radical free-thinker who associated with the most prominent free-thinkers of the 1690s, Gildon was in an excellent position to know the real beliefs of those suspected of atheism. Therefore we must take very seriously his statement in *The Deist's manual* (1705), in which he states that his 'conversation has frequently afforded [him] proofs of the *Hobbists* of the times; the very foundation of whose *system* is *atheism* in speculation'.[9] Of course, Gildon never himself confessed, as far as I am aware, to being a Hobbesian atheist. However, on balance, I think we should accept his claims: the ascriptions of a former free-thinker are preferable to the evidence of a hostile outsider such as Bentley.

IV. Lord Rochester, apostate atheist

The next witness I wish to call is another apostate free-thinker: the poet and wit John Wilmot, Earl of Rochester. Rochester differs from Gildon in being not only more famous but also a self-confessed atheist; at any rate, he comes very close to such a confession. He is also less interested than Gildon in accusing others than in accusing himself. The two most important accounts of Rochester's religious and irreligious beliefs are recorded by Robert Parsons in his *Sermon preached at the funeral of* ... *Rochester* (Oxford, 1680), and by Gilbert Burnet in his *Some passages of the life and death of* ... *Rochester* ... *written by his own direction on his death-bed* (Dublin, 1681). Both accounts were based on personal acquaintance with Rochester — although late in his life, and at a time when severe disease was painfully drawing his life (and irreligion) to a close.

Parsons was the chaplain of Rochester's mother, and in his *Sermon* we find Rochester's 'dying remonstrance, sufficiently attested and signed by his own hand' — as well as by his mother and her chaplain — in which he declares: 'I think I can never sufficiently admire the goodness of God, who has given me a true sense of my pernicious Opinions and vile practices, by which I have hitherto lived without Hope, and without God in the world' (p. 32). Can we take the last clause as a confession of past atheism? I think we can, but it is not unambiguous — for it might be construed as a confession of practical atheism. A practical atheist behaves as though God does not exist. Hence he may be described, or may describe himself, as godless. But the more likely interpretation, I think, is that Rochester is confessing to both practical and theoretical atheism, the latter being one of his 'pernicious Opinions'. Fewer ambiguities surround the following recollection by Rochester of an incident which he took to be a premonition of his future conversion:

One day, at an Atheistical Meeting, at a person of quality's, I undertook to manage the Cause, and was the principal disputant against God and Piety, and for my performance received the applause of the whole company; upon which my mind was terribly struck, and I immediately reply'd thus to myself: Good God! that a man that walks upright, that sees the wonderful works of God, and has the use of his senses and reason, should use them to the defying of his Creator! (p. 23)

Parsons does not throw much light on the theoretical basis of
Rochester's disbelief. We should like to know more about the 'Cause
... against God', and how Rochester managed it at the 'Atheistical
Meeting'. We do learn from Parsons of the influence of Hobbes.
Rochester is recorded as saying that the 'absurd and foolish
Philosophy, which the world so much admired, propagated by the
late Mr. Hobbs, and others, had undone him, and many more of the
best parts of the Nation'.[10] The general impression given by
Parsons, however, is that Rochester was less interested in justifying
irreligion than in abusing religion. Thus we find him talking about
'defying ... his Creator', rather than denying God's existence. The
latter formula is used in his 'dying remonstrance', but Rochester does
not *quite* say that *he* has denied the existence of God. He warns 'those
whom I may have drawn into sin by my example and encouragement
... no more to deny his being, or his Providence or to despise his
Goodness' (p. 32).

I have now quoted the relevant portions from Parsons's *Sermon*.
The picture they sketch is not very distinct, but the broad outline of
an atheist, or at least of an extreme unbeliever, is fairly plain. Of
course, we are seeing the virulent young heretic through the weary
eyes of the dying penitent, and the words of the latter are being
recorded by an interested observer whose perfect veracity and
discrimination cannot be taken for granted. Hence it is useful to have
a second witness in Gilbert Burnet, an author and theologian in his
own right. Burnet is more perceptive and sensitive to the problematic
aspects of Rochester's theoretical position. It is more complex than
Parsons's narration suggests. There are three relevant passages; the
first is from p. 7:

> As to the Supream Being [writes Burnet], he had always some
> Impression of one; and professed often to me, That he had
> never known an entire *Atheist*, who fully believed there was no
> God. Yet when he explained his Notion of this Being, it
> amounted to no more than a vast power, that had none of the
> Attributes of Goodness or Justice, we ascribe to the Deity.

> He believed there was a Supream Being: He could not think
> the World was made by chance, and the regular course of
> Nature seemed to demonstrate the Eternal Power of its Author.
> This, he said, he could never shake off; but when he came to
> explain his Notion of the Deity, he said, he looked on it as a
> vast Power that wrought everything by the necessity of its

Nature; and thought that God had none of those Affections of Love or Hatred, which bred perturbation in us, and by consequence he could not see that there was to be either Reward or Punishment. He thought our Conceptions of God were so low, that we had better not think much of him: and to love God seemed to him a presumptuous thing, and the heat of fanciful men. Therefore he believed there should be no other Religious Worship, but a general celebration of that Being, in some short Hymn: All the other parts of Worship he esteemed the Inventions of Priests, to make the World believe they had a secret of Incensing and appeasing God as they pleased. In a word, he was neither persuaded that there was a special Providence about humane Affairs; nor that prayers were of much use, since that was to look on God as a weak Being, that would be overcome with importunities. (p. 23)

After telling us that 'This was the substance of his speculations about God and Religion', Burnet provides the following gloss on these speculations:

> I told him his Notion of God was so low, that the Supream Being seemed to be nothing but Nature, For if that Being had no freedom nor choice of its own actions, nor operated by Wisdom or Goodness, all those reasons which led him to acknowledge a God, were contrary to this Conceit. (Ibid.)

Let us begin with the first passage from Burnet, where we find a familiar denial. Clearly this denial of atheism cannot be taken — as some commentators have — at its face value.[11] For one thing, it is in conflict with Rochester's 'dying remonstrance', in which he implored his fellow wits 'no more to deny [God's] being or providence'. If he was serious in this exhortation, then he must have been aware of some atheists. Of course, Rochester does qualify his denial. But what is an 'entire atheist', and what does it mean to 'fully ... believe that there is no God'? Does it not imply that there are plain atheists who believe (although not fully) that there is no God? We encountered qualifications of this kind in Chapter 1, for example, in the repressive denials of Curteis and Wise. Certain of Rochester's remarks seem to fit into this mould. His denial also resembles that by the Confessor, which exhibits the failure of a would-be atheist to deny God entirely. Indeed, his statement may well have been derived from Rochester.

However, there are serious obstacles which oppose our interpreting Rochester as we have interpreted Bentley and the Confessor, the most formidable of which is Rochester's characterisation of God as 'a vast power' devoid of freedom, goodness and wisdom. We should hardly expect to find this conception of God accepted by any of the repressors of atheism. They would be likely to hold that such a conception saves the name 'God' but subverts the thing. To say that a vast self-determined eternal power exists is not to say that the Christian or even the deistic God exists. Rochester is most unlikely to ever have regarded himself — as some have regarded him — as a deist.[12] For a deist must believe in a God that possesses at least wisdom and goodness, attributes which, according to Burnet, were lacking in Rochester's God. And it is worth pointing out that it was in Burnet's polemical interest that Rochester should acquiesce to some attenuated notion of God, since Burnet's subsequent argument for the Christian God (based on parity of reasoning) depends on such a concession. But Rochester never allows that his former conception of God included intellectual or moral attributes; he only concedes that God was for him a non-chance principle capable of explaining the world. The more difficult question is whether Rochester thought of himself as an atheist. Did he realise that his conception of God was closer to the notions of the atheist (or to those who were thought to be atheists) than to the beliefs of their theistic opponents?

The two arch-atheists of the period were Hobbes and Spinoza. Neither of them denied the existence of God, but their portrayals of God were generally thought to be atheistic. Although Rochester's sketch of God is not quite a copy of the idiosyncratic God of Hobbes or of Spinoza, it has clear resemblances to both. The emphasis on power recalls Hobbes, for whom God is an essentially powerful being.[13] And the description of the vast power bringing everything about 'by the necessity of its nature' recalls Spinoza, according to whom 'God exists only from the necessity of his nature' (*Ethics* I, proposition XVII, corollary 2). Burnet seems to have been aware of Rochester's Spinozism, for in his gloss he says that Rochester's God 'seemed to be nothing but nature'. Spinoza, as is well known, speaks of '*Deus sive natura*' in *Ethics* IV, Preface. Burnet's gloss may also allude to Hobbes, since in his *History of my own time* (Dublin, 1724) Burnet states that Hobbes 'seemed to think that the universe was God'.[14]

In short, Rochester's God has far more in common with the surrogate Gods of the atheistic suppressors of 'atheism' (see below Chapter 4) than with the theistic repressors of atheism. Like Radicati and

Hume, Rochester expands the class of non-atheists as he contracts the class of atheists. His assertion that 'our conceptions of God were so low, that we had better not think much of him' is just the sort of dismissive remark which we would expect from someone who wishes to bury the debate between atheist and theist, and thereby protect the atheists. On the other hand, this interpretation supposes some bad faith on Rochester's part when we should least expect it. His conversations with Burnet were conducted at his own request, and there is good reason to believe that his avowals were sincere and that they were faithfully recorded by Burnet. But why then should Rochester say he was *not* an atheist if he believed he was? One way of meeting this difficulty, and saving his sincerity, would be to suppose that he wished to eliminate atheism, and also desired to blunt the emotive force of 'atheism'; the two desiderata might dimly coexist in the weary mind of a repentent atheist. What seems clear, I think, is that Rochester's verbal denial of atheists points to the existence of atheists rather than their non-existence.

Perhaps the closest that Rochester came to avowing his past atheism was in a revealing encounter with 'his great friend' William Fanshaw, Master of Requests in the King's Household. Fanshaw came to see Rochester shortly before his death, and, hearing Rochester pray, he is supposed to have said to Dr Radcliff — the attending physician and our informant — that Rochester 'was certainly delireous, for to his knowledge ... he believed neither in God nor Jesus Christ'. When Radcliff told Rochester what Fanshaw had said, Rochester 'addressed himself to Mr F to this effect; S^r It is true you and I have been very lewd and profane together, and then I was of the opinion you mention; but now I am quite of another mind ... I am sensible how miserable I was whilst of another.'[15] The 'opinion you mention' must surely refer to Fanshaw's statement that Rochester 'believed neither in God nor Jesus Christ'. It is interesting that Rochester uses this circumlocution, since it may suggest an unwillingness to admit openly his previous disbelief in God.

My conclusion is that Rochester was not only an atheist but an avowed atheist who associated with other avowed atheists, such as Fanshaw. But the oral and second-hand nature of his surviving statements preclude a conclusive judgement. The unpublished, non-permanent nature of his avowals, and those of other Restoration atheists, may also have hindered the Restoration atheists from forming a firm and settled belief in the non-existence of God. The atheists, as Bernard nicely put it, had only talk. It was only when they came to recant their former atheistic talk that their statements were published, with suitable condemnation.

V. Hobbes's denial of atheism and Scargill's confession of atheism

Probably the most elaborate and sensational recantation of the Restoration period was issued by Daniel Scargill. With Scargill we are able to move from the tenuousness of oral testimony to a printed and published statement. His *Recantation ... publickly made before the University of Cambridge (of which he was formerly a member) ... 25 July 1669* (Cambridge, 1669) contains an emphatic statement that there were Hobbesian atheists and that Scargill himself had been one of them. To be sure, the circumstances surrounding the composition and publication of Scargill's *Recantation* do not inspire complete confidence in all its assertions; yet we are none the less on firmer ground than we were with Rochester. But before quoting Scargill's confession of Hobbesian atheism it will be helpful to examine a passage from Hobbes himself, which intimately relates to the Scargill case, and also to two of the principal themes of this study: the emergence and the denial of atheism.

Did Hobbes deny the existence of atheists? It might seem so; for as John Laird notes in his *Hobbes* (New York, 1968): ' "constant and resolved atheists" probably did not exist' for Hobbes (p. 225). However, as in the case of most of Hobbes's views on religion, the issue is somewhat complicated. The main source here is Hobbes's posthumously published *An Answer to Bishop Bramhall*. In this late work, from which Laird's quotation is taken, Hobbes defends himself against the charge of excusing or encouraging atheism. He felt obliged to answer Bramhall's atheistic accusations 'because [as he says] the word *Atheism, Impiety* and the like, are words of the greatest defamation possible'.[16] His discussion concerns two kinds of atheism: speculative atheism, and at least one sort of non-speculative atheism — namely, where a 'man that thinks there is a God, dares deliberately deny it'. It is this 'malicious' atheism that Hobbes definitely rejects the existence of. His reason is: 'upon what confidence dares any man, deliberately I say, oppose the Omnipotent?' (p. 15).

Did Hobbes also deny, as many of his contemporaries did, the existence of *speculative* atheism? I do not think so; for he allows that some persons do reason, or misreason, themselves into atheism. He says that atheism 'proceedeth from opinion of reason without fear'. He also asks: 'is not Atheism Boldness grounded on false reasoning, such as is this, *the wicked prosper, therefore there is no God?*' (p. 13). Hobbes's formula is that 'Atheism is a sin of ignorance': 'denying

God is a sin of ignorance proceeding from misreasoning'. But the difficulty comes in the following crucial passage, which follows immediately upon Hobbes's denial of 'malacious' atheism:

> *David* saith of himself, *My feet were ready to slip when I saw the pros-*
> *perity of the wicked*. Therefore it is likely the feet of men less holy
> slip oftener. But I think no man living is so daring, being out
> of passion, as to hold it as his opinion. Those wicked men that
> for a long time proceeded so successfully in the late horrid
> Rebellion, may perhaps make *some* think *they* were constant and
> resolved Atheists, but I think rather that *they* forgot God, than
> believed there was none. He that believes there is such an
> Atheist, comes a little too near that opinion himself; Never-
> theless, if words spoken in passion signifie a denial of God, no
> punishment preordained by Law, can be too great for such an
> insolence; because there is no living in a Commonwealth with
> men, to whose oaths we cannot reasonably give credit. (p. 15)

This passage contains not a few ambiguities. The most striking instances are in the fourth sentence, where there are three pronouns:
'some', and 'they' (used twice) — which I have italicised. Now on
one reading, the two 'they's could refer to 'those wicked men', the
Puritan fanatics; thus the sustained and successful wickedness of the
Puritans made some people think that the Puritans were 'constant
and resolved atheists'. This is the most plausible interpretation if we
read the sentence as a single unit. The interpretation is also helped
by the balance between wickedness lasting a 'long time' and the
atheism being 'constant and resolved'.

But that is not the only possible interpretation: for the pronouns
might refer not to the Puritans but to the Royalists who became, or
thought they had become, atheists by observing the sustained success
of the wicked Puritans. This interpretation is enforced by the first
two sentences quoted above: it was his seeing the prosperity of the
wicked that momentarily inclined King David to atheism; hence the
same thing is likely to occur even more often to those — the Royalists
— less holy than David. But which of the two interpretations should
we prefer? Neither interpretation perfectly fits the text. For why —
to take the first — should the wicked and successful Puritans make
some think that the Puritans were 'constant and resolved atheists'?
Yet why — to consider the alternative interpretation — should the
wicked and successful Puritans make some Royalists *now* think they
themselves were 'constant and resolved atheists'? The first

interpretation transforms the crucial sentence into a *non sequitur*; the second interpretation is at odds with its tense. In short, the two interpretations are equally plausible or implausible. We are presented with something like an ambiguous visual illusion, for example the well-known duck/rabbit (Figure 1). Depending on how one looks at the figure, one may see either a duck or a rabbit:

Figure 1

Our perplexity is not alleviated by the context. Indeed, Hobbes's next sentence only aggravates it. For leaving aside the question of whether he is referring to malicious or speculative atheism, we must enquire what he could mean by saying that he who believes there are constant and resolved atheists comes very close to atheism himself. And what are we to make of the strongly worded condemnation of atheism?

These ambiguities would be puzzling in nearly any writer, but they are particularly so in Hobbes. For as one commentator has noted: his 'style seems to be the very perfection of didactic language. Short, clear, precise, pithy, *his language never has more than one meaning,* which never requires a second thought to find.'[17] I believe that our striking ambiguities are explicable if they are put in the context of Daniel Scargill's sensational 1669 *Recantation*. Here Scargill confesses that he has 'lately vented and publicly asserted in the said University [of Cambridge], divers, wicked, blasphemous and Atheistic possitions' (p. 1) and that he has found 'by the grace of that God whom I had deny'd, that they [the so-called five 'positions'] are ... of dangerous and malicious consequence, inconsistent with the Being of God' (p. 2). One of these positions is 'That there is a desirable glory in being, and being reputed, an Atheist; which I implied when I expressly affirmed that I gloried to be an *Hobbist* and an Atheist' (p. 4). Scargill speaks of 'the accursed Atheism of this age, acknowledging myself to be highly guilty of the growth and spreading thereof... I do profess [he goes on to say] ... that the openly professed atheism of some, and the secret atheism of others, is the accursed root of all the abounding wickedness ... in the present age' (p. 4).

When Hobbes mentions those who mistakenly thought they were

constant and resolved atheists, he is alluding, I believe, to Scargill and those like him. He is saying something like this: 'You may think (or may have thought), that you were atheists; but you are mistaken. You were either temporarily misled by some passion or forgot God amidst the wickedness of the Puritan regime. Your atheism was not based on my philosophy. And if you, or those who are encouraging you, say that there is such a thing as constant and resolved atheism — and that I hold such a position — then beware! Hobbes might then have said (what he is supposed to have said when someone asked him his opinion of Spinoza's *Tractatus*) 'Judge not that ye be not judged!'[18]

In the passage quoted Hobbes is trying not only to protect himself against the accusation that he is an atheist and a spreader of atheism; he is also trying to discourage avowed atheism. His denial points to the existence of atheists. He is against anyone 'so daring ... as to hold it as his opinion'; he is even opposed to the verbal 'denial of God'. Scargill, as we have seen, makes much of his two-fold profession: his having 'expressly affirmed that I gloried to be an *Hobbist* and an Atheist'. Hence, according to my interpretation, Hobbes is saying to Scargill *et al*: firstly, 'You are really not full-blooded atheists': secondly, 'Your atheism, such as it is, or was, can be excused on account of the bad effects of the late horrid rebellion'; thirdly, 'You really only forgot God.' This is the kindly part of his message. He then begins to threaten: fourthly, 'If you accuse me of atheism, or claim that atheism is feasible, beware! for that indicates that *you* may indeed be full-blooded atheists.' And fifthly he declares: 'But if anyone has denied God — as you Daniel Scargill have apparently done — then no punishment preordained by law can be too great for such an insolence.'

Hobbes's justification for this severity — that 'there is no living in a commonwealth with men, to whose oaths we cannot reasonably give credit' — is not altogether consistent with his position on oaths in *De corpore politico;* for (in Part 1, Chapter 2, Section 17) he maintains that an oath does not oblige any more than a covenant, and that a covenant is sanctioned naturally and not supernaturally. An oath, he writes, 'addeth not a greater Obligation to perform the Covenant sworn, than the Covenant carrieth in itself, but it putteth a Man into greater Danger, and of greater Punishment [i.e. from God]'.[19] Thus Hobbes is exaggerating when he says, in the *Answer to Bramhall*, that there is 'no living in a commonwealth' with someone who can not swear oaths; and such exaggeration confirms my construing his words as a threat.

Two bits of external evidence should be mentioned. One bit goes against, the other supports, my interpretation. Against it is the date generally assigned by scholars to Hobbes's *Answer to Bramhall*. He is supposed to have written it in 1668.[20] For in the preface 'To the Reader', Hobbes mentions that Bramhall's *The catching of Leviathan* (London, 1658), to which he is replying, was published 'ten years since', whereas Scargill's *Recantation* took place on 25 July 1669. In favour of my interpretation is the fact that Hobbes wrote an essay concerning Scargill's *Recantation*. Hobbes, according to Aubrey, gave this work to Sir John Birkenhead 'to be licensed, which he refused to do (to ... flatter the bishops), and would not returne it nor give a copie. Mr. Hobbes kept no copie, for which he was sorry. He told me he liked it well himself.'[21] Considering the weight of evidence *for* my interpretation, I think the chronological difficultly can be overcome. These suggestions seem plausible: firstly, that Hobbes wrote the *Answer* in late 1669; (ten years is, after all, a round number); secondly, that he revised it in 1669 — or later — and inserted the passage I have quoted; thirdly, that he knew about the Scargill affair in 1668 or earlier, and wrote with the intention of *preventing* a scandal.

However the problem of dating is to be resolved, it should not be allowed to obscure the import of Hobbes's *double entendre*. The first, exoteric, message was: there are no malicious atheists; some may think the Puritan fanatics were constant and resolved (malicious) atheists, but this is unlikely. The second, esoteric, message was addressed to Scargill, Scargill's old atheistic associates, and his new orthodox acquaintances who were encouraging him to denounce Hobbesian atheism. This message pointed to what Hobbes considered the real cause of Scargill's mild (and excusable) atheism: the prosperity of the wicked Puritans.[22] As with the duck/rabbit, we can see either one thing or the other. Having failed to publish his open defence (against Scargill's *Recantation*), Hobbes attempted to slip a more subtle message into print. If I am right, in this esoteric message we have the main points of Hobbes's lost apologia.

VI. The atheistic exploitation of the anti-Hobbes literature

There can be little doubt that — despite his protests — Hobbes provided the main theoretical basis for Restoration atheism. This was the opinion not only of orthodox critics such as Bramhall and Bentley, but of some of the alleged Restoration atheists themselves — Rochester and Scargill. But this is not to say that Hobbes was himself an atheist, or even that his writings were directly used by the Restoration wits. In *The character of a town gallant*, published in 1675, we read:

> His religion (for now and then he will be prattling of that too) is pretendedly Hobbian, and he swears *The Leviathan* may supply all the lost leaves of Solomon, yet he never saw it in his life, and for ought he knows it may be a treatise about catching of sprats, or new regulating the Greenland fishing trade. However, the rattle of it at coffee-houses has taught him to laugh at spirits, and maintain that there are no angels but those in petticoats.[23]

There is also evidence that the more serious atheists took much of their Hobbesian atheism from the books written *against* Hobbes, particularly those books by Archbishop Tenison, Lord Clarendon, Seth Ward and Ralph Cudworth. According to James Axtell, Scargill drew his Hobbism not from Hobbes's scarce and expensive books but from the extensive anti-Hobbes literature, especially Tenison's *Creed of Hobbes* (1670).[24]

Critics such as Tenison and Ralph Cudworth saved the wits the trouble of finding the atheistic passages and meaning in Hobbes's books. Although this may seem odd, there are comparable cases. For example, Reginald Scot's *Discoverie of witchcraft* (1665), which was designed to expose the folly of witchcraft persecutions, became almost a textbook on witchcraft, popularising the very beliefs it aimed to explode. A more recent analogue may be found in some books written against pornography which reprint the most lascivious passages in order to show how offensive the allegedly pornographic works are. But in doing so they can assist those people who relish pornography. Rather than buying the books in which there are occasional pornographic passages, the relishers of pornography need only buy the anti-pornographic work.

Thus the Restoration atheists did not have to write atheistical books, since they were, in a sense, written for them by men like Tenison and Cudworth. It is difficult to say how far these critics of Hobbes were responsible for producing Hobbesian atheism. Hobbes obviously had some share in the engendering of such bastard offspring as Scargill. What seems clear in this early development of British atheism is that the parents cared neither for each other nor for the foundling atheism. Apparently Cudworth so resented the suggestion that he had helped to engender atheism by his *True intellectual system* that he would not publish a second part of that already vast work.[25] It was certainly felt by some that Cudworth had stated the case for atheism more strongly than it had previously been stated. So Dryden remarked that Cudworth 'has raised such strong objections against the being of a God and Providence, that many think he has not answered them'.[26] Shaftesbury also notes that Cudworth 'was accused of giving the upper hand to the Atheists' (ibid.). Here the suggestion is that Cudworth not only presented the atheistic side of the argument fairly, but actually favoured it, despite his clear statements to the contrary. This suggestion can hardly be taken very seriously. But a similar technique was certainly used later by the free-thinkers, who sometimes reprinted extracts from free-thinking works with introductions in which the free-thinking beliefs were attacked in an obviously weak way; such subterfuge enabled them to achieve their ends with less risk of legal prosecution. One such work was a compendium of d'Holbach's *System* which was first printed in Glasgow in 1799. In his publisher's preface to the second edition of this little work, Richard Carlile pointed out that in the previous edition 'the translator found it necessary to prefix and affix a few pages of abuse on his own work, by way of cheating the persecuting Christians. The present publisher has no fears or scruples to put forth such a work in its pure and naked form'.[27]

Once again we are dealing with the duck/rabbit phenomenon. Looked at in one way Tenison's *Creed of Hobbes* would show the foolishness of Hobbes and atheism. Looked at in another way, by those who were, like the younger Rochester, sympathetic to Hobbes and atheism, and this book could be an inspiring text. Hence it was, to use a phrase William Warburton applied to Cudworth, dangerous 'to strip *Atheism* of all its Disguises'.[28] For to some the stripping revealed a thing of beauty and not something ugly. When Charles Blount published his broadsheet of quotations extracted from Hobbes's writing, some readers believed that the design was to show the weakness and falsity of Hobbes's doctrines, or, as Sir Walter Scott apparently thought, to 'expose the deistical doctrines of Hobbes, by concentrating them into one focus.'[29]

It is sometimes said that our understanding of the deists or free-thinkers has been distorted because we tend to see them through the eyes of their critics.[30] There may be some truth in this observation; but it is still of the last importance to pay close attention to the critics of irreligion; for these critics not only described the views of their opponents but, in some cases, created or constructed, their irreligious views. According to the author of the first avowedly atheistic book published in Britain, critics such as John Leland and Thomas

Stackhouse converted more people to deism than the deists themselves; and this author was himself encouraged to become an open atheist by reading Joseph Priestley's book against atheism. The fact that it proved dangerous to write against Hobbes may help to explain why some of the most formidable eighteenth-century books — for example those by Radicati and Hume — were largely ignored. Eighteenth-century theologians may have learned this lesson from their seventeenth-century anti-Hobbes colleagues. On the whole, they wisely refrained from drawing attention to, or removing the esoteric disguise from, atheistic books. They did what Bernard apparently advised Bentley to do: leave atheists to their talk.

VII. Hobbes's atheism

Although Hobbes was thought to be a covert atheist in his own time — indeed almost *the* atheist — scholars are now evenly divided on his actual religious beliefs. Whereas Hobbes's contemporaries employed depth interpretation, there has been a growing tendency to accept the surface meaning of Hobbes's statements and, hence, the sincerity of his Christian professions. One of the most popular arguments for this view is stated by Anthony Quinton as follows: 'Yet, finally, Hobbes does constantly refer to God, and that cannot be brushed aside as verbiage insincerely scattered about to obstruct potentially dangerous opponents.'[31] Similarly, Bernard Willms says that 'at least half of *Leviathan* constitutes a contradiction to this approach' — of 'taking Hobbes as an enlightener and atheist'.[32] Again, Angelo Campodonico writes of 'Hobbes's many references to Scripture ... [which] it is impossible to think of ... as merely some sort of practical device or stratagem'.[33] One might call this the quantity argument for Hobbes's Christian belief. Is it compelling?

Consider first a plain historical fact: atheism and irreligion were viewed with the greatest fear and horror in Hobbes's time and later. Indeed, atheism was felt to be so subversive that, as we have seen in Chapter 1, it was often said that no rational person could actually believe it. I would suggest that, until the late eighteenth century, atheism was Europe's most fearful, threatening belief, and that this is shown in its surprisingly late appearance. In Hobbes's time, a man could lose his life for heresy or infidelity, and Hobbes's life, we are told by John Aubrey, was seriously threatened.[34] Of course, this does not show that Hobbes *was* a secret atheist. That a dangerous idea could not be openly expressed does not prove that the idea was being indirectly expressed in a certain work. But if we find purposeful signs of esoteric techniques in the *Leviathan* (or any other putative radical work), then the hypothesis must be taken seriously.

At the outset, it should be clear that the quantity argument cannot preclude esotericism, because Hobbes may have wished to hide his irreligious statements in a forest of orthodoxy. I should also mention that there is something misleading in the way the quantity argument is usually stated. Thus W.B. Glover attacks the view that Hobbes 'cluttered his works with theistic suggestions and pronouncements in order to protect himself from persecution'[35] and Quinton speaks of 'verbiage insincerely scattered'. Now such statements seem to indicate that according to the crypto-atheistic hypothesis — which I shall be defending — Hobbes's orthodox utterances are thrown about in a random and pointless manner. In fact, as I shall argue, Hobbes's orthodox pronouncements make up a more or less orderly story in which the irreligious thought or story is embedded and camouflaged.

Obviously, I cannot argue this for the whole of the *Leviathan*. Instead I shall look at one chapter — Chapter 6 — of that great work, where, in eight (folio) pages, Hobbes soberly describes nearly 50 emotions. In the middle of this psychological chapter, however, is the following paragraph:

> *Feare* of power invisible, feigned by the mind, or imagined from tales, publiquely allowed, RELIGION, not allowed, SUPERSTI-TION. And when the power imagined, is truly such as we imagine, TRUE RELIGION.

Prima facie, this paragraph does not particularly stand out from its surrounding text. Like the paragraphs around it, it begins with an emotion printed in italics. Just before Hobbes had considered: *'Jealousie', 'Revengefulness',* and *'Curiosity',* just after: *'Panique Terror', 'Admiration'* and *'Glory'.* Yet the first sentence can be and was read as a superbly condensed statement of unbelief. Hobbes's epigrammatic gem can be seen alone, even though it is embedded in a different, duller story. It is also hidden in the sense that the last sentence (about true religion) covers up and effectively denies the first provocative statement. Yet Hobbes's real or latent meaning was in the daring first sentence, rather than in the forest of psychological description or cover-up sentence. Clearly, this interpretation will not satisfy all Hobbes scholars; for a critic will probably deny, firstly, that Hobbes intended to hide his epigram and, secondly, that his final sentence was a cover-up.

Let us, however, consider how Hobbes could, if he wanted, have hidden a dangerous atheist gem from some readers, while revealing it to others. He would probably have known of Cicero's injunction that the good orator will choose 'the strongest points for the opening and closing, and insert the weaker points in between'.[36] By implication, the middle of a work (like the middle of a thicket) would be an ideal place to hide something. And Hobbes's gem could hardly be more in the middle of Chapter 6.[37]

Yet is there evidence that Hobbes intended the paragraph's final sentence as a cover-up? I think there is on page 51, where we find virtually the same epigram, although less tersely and provocatively stated and *without* the final sentence or caveat: 'And this Feare of things invisible, is the naturall Seed of that, which everyone in himself calleth religion; and in them that worship, or feare that Power otherwise then they do, Superstition.'

Of course, a critic will probably reply that by here omitting the caveat on true religion Hobbes has hardly repudiated it. Yet consider the previous paragraph on page 51, where Hobbes says that men 'cannot have any idea of him [God] in their mind, answerable to his nature':

> For as a man that is born blind, hearing men talk of warming themselves by the fire, and being brought to warm himself by the flame, may easily conceive, and assure himself, there is somewhat there, which men call *Fire,* and is the cause of the heat he feels; but cannot *imagine* what it is like; nor have an Idea of it in his mind, such as they have that see it: so also, by the visible things of this world, and their admirable order, a man may conceive there is a cause of them, which men call God; and yet not have an *Idea or Image* of him in his mind. (My italics.)

Note Hobbes's words: we 'cannot imagine' or have 'an Idea or Image' of God. Yet if that is so, then no 'invisible power' *can* be 'truly such as we imagine'. Nothing could count as true (or false) religion. Hobbes's clear criterion, or necessary condition, for TRUE RELIGION — that 'the power imagined, is truly such as we imagine' — cannot be met, given his extreme negative theology.[38] Surely this *does* constitute a denial both of the final sentence and of true religion.

Some critics will, I imagine, regard my interpretation of Hobbes as far-fetched. Could he really have intended to embed his irreligious gem in the middle of Chapter 6 in order to hide it from the vulgar and, at the same time, reveal it to the learned – especially to a potential king-philosopher? Could he also have intended to use the final sentence – which seems to constitute the *Leviathan's* only formal criterion for true religion – first as a cover-up, then as a way of denying true religion? It seems just too clever and too conspiratorial. Yet surely Hobbes *was* clever enough. And how else could he safely insinuate his atheism?

In a helpful essay, 'Hobbes on the Knowledge of God', Ronald Hepburn rejects the thesis that Hobbes was a covert, 'oblique sceptic'. If Hobbes intended to attack theism obliquely, Hepburn writes, 'he missed many chances of sharpening the sceptically tending side of his theological writing.'[39] Yet Hepburn does not specify how and where Hobbes could have done this, while still protecting himself. If we suppose that Hobbes wished to express and disguise his atheism in *Leviathan*, I cannot see how he could have done it more effectively than by the esoteric technique I have tried to exhibit here.

Notes

1. *Eighth Report of the Royal Commission of Historical Manuscripts*, Appendix, part 2, (London, 1881), 31 January 1666/7, 111a. The great London fire of 1666 is generally thought to have produced a religious reaction.
2. *House of Lords Calendar 1677–8. Ninth Report of ... Historical Manuscripts*, Appendix, part 2 (London, 1884), p. 98. The words in italics were added after the original draft; the words in parentheses were subsequently deleted.
3. *Thirteenth Report*, Appendix, part 2, vol. 2 (London, 1893), p. 46. Hickes was to become one of the leading non-jurors.
4. The letter is printed in the *Museum criticum* (Cambridge, 1826), vol. 2, pp. 557–8.
5. *Dynamics of religion*, p. 74.
6. *A history of freethought*, 4th edn (London, 1936), p. 780. A note in *The System of nature* (Robinson translation, 1868) states that atheists are rare in England; see vol. 2, Chapter X.
7. See *Dynamics*, pp. 81 and 90–3.
8. See Chapter 1, note 29.
9. See 'Epistle dedicatory', and below, Chapter 4, Section II.
10. Parsons's *Sermon*, p. 26. According to another account, 'During his last illness [Rochester] often exclaimed, "Mr Hobbes and the philosophers have been my ruin" '; quoted in Johannes Prinz's *John Wilmot, Earl of Rochester, his life and writings* (Leipzig, 1927), p. 232. On this and the previous remark see Samuel Mintz's *Hunting of Leviathan* (Cambridge, 1962), pp. 141–2. Mintz tends to play down Hobbes's influence on Rochester, and, in general, the existence of Restoration atheism; see p. 51.
11. See, for example, Prinz's *John Wilmot*, p. 220.
12. See Charles Williams, *Rochester* (London, 1935), pp. 234 and 248.

13. See *The English works of Hobbes,* edited by William Molesworth (London, 1841), vol. 5, p. 116, where God is described as having 'Power irresistible'; also see Richard Peters's *Hobbes* (London, 1967), p. 231. One of the (supposed) *Last sayings, or dying legacy of ... Hobbs,* published by Charles Blount in 1680, was: 'That God is almighty matter'; in *Somers collection of tracts,* 2nd edn (London, 1812) p. 370. This *'saying'* is to be found in Thomas Tenison's *The creed of Mr Hobbes* (2nd edn London, 1671), p. 7.

It is worth noting that in his play *Valentinian,* Rochester has one of the characters declare: 'Why then I see there is no God — but Power.' The innocent Lucina utters this line after being raped by the Emperor Valentinian; see *Works of Rochester* (London, 1714), p. 268.

14. See vol. i, p. 106. On this topic, it is helpful to compare F.A. Lange's description of Hobbes's conception of God: 'The quintessence of Hobbes's whole theology is probably ... most clearly expressed in a passage in the *De homine,* iii. 15 ... where it is bluntly said that *God rules only through nature ...* We must not indeed conclude from this that Hobbes identified God with the *sum* of nature — pantheistically. He seems rather to have conceived as God a *part* of the universe — controlling, universally spread, uniform, and by its motion determining mechanistically the motion of the whole.': *History of materialism,* vol. I, p. 290 n.

15. See J. Prinz (ed.) *Rochesteriana* (Leipzig, 1926), p. 51. We learn from a letter by Rochester's mother that during this visit Rochester told Fanshaw: 'Believe what I say to you; there is a God.' This clearly implies that Fanshaw, and perhaps Rochester himself, had denied or doubted God's existence. The letter is quoted in Graham Greene's *Lord Rochester's monkey* (London, 1974), p. 216.

16. The *Answer* was published in *Tracts of ... Hobbs ... containing I. Behemoth ... II. An Answer to Arch-Bishop Bramhall's book, called the Catching of the Leviathan ...* (London, 1682). My quotations are from this 1682 edition; see 'To the Reader'.

17. Sir James Mackintosh, *On the progress of ethical philosophy,* 4th edn (Edinburgh, 1872) p. 58; my italics.

18. The story is reported by Aubrey: 'When Spinoza's *Tractatus theologico-politicus* first came out [1670], Mr Edmund Waller sent it to my Lord Devonshire and desired him to send him word what Mr Hobbes said of it. Mr H. told his lordship: *"Ne Judicate ne judicemini"* '; *Brief lives,* edited by Andrew Clark (Oxford, 1898), vol. 1, p. 357. Hobbes's reply may itself contain a double meaning; for it was said at the time that Spinoza had taken some of his ideas from Hobbes.

19. *Hobbes's tripos in three discourses* (London, 1684), pp. 112–13.

20. G.C. Robertson, in his *Hobbes* (Edinburgh, 1886), says that the *Answer* 'can be definitely referred to the year 1668' (p. 197).

21. John Aubrey, *Brief Lives,* vol. 1, pp. 360–1; also see S.I. Mintz, *Hunting of the Leviathan* p. 152.

22. It is interesting that Hobbes's own (alleged) atheism was accounted for in a similar way in d'Holbach's *System,* according to which: 'the horrors produced in England by fanaticism, which cost Charles I his head, pushed Hobbes on to atheism' (1868 Robinson ed.) vol. 2, p. 314 note. There is also some evidence in Rochester's *Valentinian* that the triumph of fanatical wickedness was in the background of Rochester's atheism; see above note 13.

23. Quoted in Greene's *Lord Rochester's monkey*, p. 205. According to Greene, 'It is difficult to exaggerate Hobbes's popularity, even among those who had not read his works' (p. 204).

24. See Axtell's 'The mechanics of opposition, restoration Cambridge vs. Daniel Scargill', in *Bulletin of the Institute of historical research*, vol. 38 (1965), pp. 108–9.

25. See William Warburton's *Divine legation of Moses*, vol. 2, 2nd edn (London, 1742), p. xii.

26. Quoted in Thomas Birch's 'Account of the life and writings of ... Cudworth', prefaced to his edition of the *True intellectual system* (1743), p. xiii.

27. *The true meaning of the System of nature, translated from the French of Helvetius* (London, circa 1825).

28. *Divine legation of Moses,* vol. 2, p. x.

29. *Somers collection of tracts,* 2nd edn (London, 1812), p. 368; 'revised, augmented and arranged' by Walter Scott; also see Anthony Wood's *Athenae Oxonienses* (1691), vol. 2, p. 481.

30. See, for example, G. Gawlick's 'Hume and the deists: a reconsideration', in *David Hume* (Edinburgh, 1977), pp. 132–3.

31. Quinton, 'Hobbes' in *Thoughts and thinkers* (London, 1982), p. 158.

32. Willms, 'Tendencies of Recent Hobbes Research' in J.G. van der Bend (ed.), *Thomas Hobbes: his view of man* (Amsterdam, 1982), p. 148.

33. A. Campodonico, 'Secularization in Thomas Hobbes's Anthropology', in *Thomas Hobbes* (see note 32), p. 121.

34. Aubrey writes: 'There was a report (and surely true) that in Parliament, not long after the King Charles II was setled, some of the Bishops made a Motion to have the good old Gentleman Hobbes burn't for a Heretique. Which, he hearing, feared that his papers might be search't by their order, and he told me he had burnt part of them'; Aubrey's *Brief lives* (Oxford, 1898), edited by A. Clark, vol. 1, p. 339.

35. Glover, 'God and Thomas Hobbes' in K.C. Brown (ed.), *Hobbes studies* (Oxford, 1967), p. 146.

36. Cicero, *Orator* XV. 50; in Loeb Classical Library (London, 1939), with an English translation by H.M. Hubbell, p. 343.

37. In the first 1651 folio edition, which I shall be using here, it is 166 lines from the beginning of the chapter and 174 lines from its end.

38. Hobbes presents his negative theology throughout the *Leviathan;* thus in Chapter 31 he says that it is wrong 'to say we conceive, and imagine, or have any *Idea* of him God , in our mind' (p. 190); even 'existence' cannot be *literally* attributed to God (pp. 189–90). For other statements of his negative theology, see *Leviathan* Ch. 3, p. 11; Ch. 12, p. 53, Ch. 46, pp. 371–4.

39. The essay is included in M. Cranston and R.S. Peters (eds.), *Hobbes and Rousseau* (Garden City, 1972), p. 88.

3

Anthony Collins's Atheology

I. The deist interpretation

In the preceding chapter I tried to identify the covert Hobbesian atheism of the seventeenth century. In this chapter I shall be concentrating on one early eighteenth-century thinker — 'the Goliath of Freethinking', as T.H. Huxley called Anthony Collins. I shall first argue, in opposition to modern scholarly opinion, that Collins was not a deist but a speculative atheist. This case is made specifically against James O'Higgins's *Anthony Collins, the man and his works* (The Hague, 1970), the first full-length study of Collins. I shall then go on to determine the form or forms Collins's atheism took.

Like many controversial figures Collins was called by a variety of names; among them were 'infidel', 'minute philosopher', 'free-thinker', 'deist', 'man of matter', and 'atheist'. For O'Higgins, Collins is to be seen somewhere on the border between very Low Church Christianity and Deism. The tendency of Collins's thought, according to O'Higgins, is away from revelation and organised religion and towards a reasoned belief in a very few theological doctrines. 'He believed in God and in a future life.'[1] In his account of Collins's various works, O'Higgins carries on a running debate with himself about the extent of Collins's allegiance to a watered-down Christianity on the one hand, and pure deism on the other. At times one is unsure as to whether it is Collins who is uncertain of his position or O'Higgins who is uncertain of Collins's position. For example, in commenting on the *Discourse of free-thinking* (1713), O'Higgins asserts that 'Taken at its face value it seems to be an extreme anti-clerical protestant insistence on private judgement' (pp. 88–9). However, O'Higgins then asks:

Was this his true position? A good deal of what he wrote [in the *Discourse*] can be interpreted as the writing of an anti-clerical protestant, insisting on private judgement for the laity. A few other passages ... seem to imply a bias against Christianity itself, or at least against Revelation. (p. 89)

Finally, in the last chapter, he states that Collins 'was just on or just over the fringe of Christianity'. But this is immediately followed by a note of uncertainty: 'In spite of his books against Revelation and his defence of natural religion, it is doubtful if he had ever really analysed and defined his position' (p. 234).[2] But, whatever position Collins really held, O'Higgins is entirely confident of one thing: Collins was not an atheist. For example: 'Collins himself never abandoned his belief in God' (p. 15); and the *Discourse* 'poses the question of Collins's real position, which, whatever it was, was not that of the atheism with which Bentley credited him' (p. 81; for similar statements see pp. 22, 74, 76, 221, 234–5). O'Higgins often-repeated judgement that Collins was not an atheist is no doubt based on the, apparently straightforward, statements which Collins makes to that effect throughout his writings.

II. Collins's atheism: the external evidence

But against O'Higgins's judgement, I shall try to show that there is considerable evidence — of both an internal and external nature — that Collins was very far from a watered-down Christianity or deism but was in fact a strong-minded atheist, with a demonstration of the non-existence of God. I do not claim to be able to prove this. But I do hope to show that it is highly probable. As even the possibility seems to have been ignored — not only by O'Higgins, but by most scholars of deism and free-thinking — there is surely a need at least to present the evidence, and make a case. Even such a careful scholar as Robertson, who was both a champion of Collins and a friend of atheism, dismisses out of hand the possibility that Collins was an atheist: 'It was [Richard] Bentley's cue to represent Collins as an atheist, though he was a very pronounced deist... "Ignorance", Collins writes, is the foundation of Atheism and free-thinking the cure of it.' (*Discourse of free-thinking*, p. 105). Like Newton, he contemplated only an impossible atheism, never formulated by any writer'. This statement from Robertson's *History of freethought* is especially surprising since in his *Dynamics of religion* Robertson holds that there were Hobbesian atheists (see above, Chapter 2). In the *Dynamics* (which contains a chapter on the Collins/Bentley debate), Robertson describes Collins as 'undoubtedly a Deist' (p. 74).

The external evidence for Collins's atheism is drawn primarily from the writings of George Berkeley. In the Advertisement to *Alciphron* (London, 1732), Berkeley asserts that he 'is well assured, that one of the most noted writers against Christianity in our Times, declared, he had found out a Demonstration against the Being of a God'. This charge is again made in Dialogue One, Section 12, and also in Dialogue Four, Section 16. In both of these places the deviser of the proof is aptly given the name Diagoras, no doubt after Diagoras the Melian, reputedly the earliest atheist. The passage in Dialogue One, in which the accusation is made, consists of a catalogue of the 'discoveries' of free-thinking. The catalogue concludes with the following:

> But the Master-piece and finishing Stroke [of modern free-thinking] is a learned Anecdote of our great *Diagoras*, containing a Demonstration against the Being of a God, which it is conceived the Public is not yet ripe for. But I am assured by some judicious Friends who have seen it, that it is clear as Daylight, and will do a world of Good, at one blow demolishing the whole System of Religion. (Section 12)

It is certain, for various reasons, that Berkeley meant Diagoras to stand for Collins. In establishing this, we will also be able to see more fully the extent of Berkeley's charge.

In Dialogue Four we learn more about Diagoras. He is described as 'a Man of much Reading and Inquiry', who

> had discovered, that once upon a time the most profound and speculative Divines finding it impossible to reconcile the Attributes of God, taken in the common Sense, or in any known Sense, with Human Reason, and the Appearances of things, taught that the words Knowledge, Wisdom, Goodness, and such like, when spoken of the Deity, must be understood in a quite different Sense, from what they signify in the vulgar Acceptation, or from any thing that we can form a Notion of, or conceive. (Section 17)

Diagoras is said to have been 'wonderfully delighted' with this way of understanding the divine nature, because of its atheistic implications. For if the new sense is such that we can form no notion or conception of the divine nature, then the term 'God' is virtually deprived of any cognitive meaning. Indeed, if such a conception, or non-conception, of God were widely held there would have been little reason for Diagoras to have taken such 'pains to find out a Demonstration that there was no God' (Section 16). For such a conception denies the existence of God, while merely retaining the name.

In his account and criticism of this version of negative theology (in *Alciphron* IV, 16–22) Berkeley has two targets in view: an unwary friend of religion, and a wary enemy. The unwary friend is Archbishop King, who, in his *Sermon on predestination* (1709), developed the theory summarised above. The wary enemy was Collins, who attacked King's *Sermon* of 1709 in a vigorous pamphlet entitled *A vindication of the divine attributes, in some remarks on ... the Archbishop of Dublin's Sermon ...* (London, 1710). Collins's interest in King's *Sermon* did not end there. Three years later, in the *Discourse*, he juxtaposed King's conception of God with Archbishop Tillotson's opposing anthropomorphic conception of God. The apparent intention of Collins's sceptical juxtaposition was to cast doubt on accepting a theological doctrine on the authority of a churchman: for here are two illustrious archbishops disagreeing with one another on a fundamental doctrine of religion.

Berkeley, however, suspected that Collins had a more sinister motive. He expressed his suspicions in a work published one year after *Alciphron,* the *Theory of vision vindicated and explained* (London, 1733), where he also goes some way towards identifying Collins with Diagoras; for Collins's atheism is associated, like Diagoras's, with an interest in King's version of negative theology:

> the author of a book intituled *A Discourse of Free-thinking...*, who, having insinuated his infidelity from men's various pretences and opinions concerning revealed religion, in like manner appears to insinuate his atheism from the differing notions of men concerning the nature and attributes of God,[3] particularly as it hath been misunderstood and misinterpreted by some of late years. Such is the ill effect of untoward defences and explanations of our faith; and such advantage do incautious friends give its enemies ... instead of causing scandal to good men and triumph to atheists [such friends should] return to speak of God and his attributes in the style of other Christians, allowing that knowledge and wisdom do, in the proper sense of words, belong to God.[4]

Apart from this circumstantial evidence identifying Collins with Diagoras — the inventor of an atheistic demonstration — we also have more direct evidence from Samuel Johnson, Berkeley's American friend. In *A Letter to Mr. Jonathan Dickenson* (Boston, 1747), Johnson remarks that Collins 'gave out in conversation, as I was informed by one present, that he had found a demonstration against the being of a God'.[5] That Berkeley was the 'one present' is clear not only by Johnson's citation of the Advertisement of *Alciphron* as support for his remark, but by the following passage in Johnson's autobiography:

> He [Berkeley] had, as he told Mr. Johnson, been several times in their [free-thinking] Clubs in quality of a learner... On one of these occasions (as he told Mr. Johnson) he heard Collens [*sic*] declare that he had found a demonstration against the being of a God... (*Samuel Johnson, his career...*, vol. I, p. 26)

There can be no doubt, then, that Berkeley meant Diagoras to stand for Collins. It should be noted, however, that Berkeley was well aware that the charge of atheism was repudiated publicly:

> if they [the free-thinkers] own it [i.e., being infidels and atheists] in their conversation, if their ideas imply it, if their ends are not answered but by supposing it, if their leading author hath pretended to demonstrate atheism, but thought fit to conceal his demonstration from the public; if this was known in their clubs, and yet that author was nonetheless followed, and represented to the world as a believer of natural religion — if these things are so (and I know them to be so)...[6]

Before examining more particularly Berkeley's testimony — which is largely completed by the above quotation — I shall quote a further piece of external evidence for Collins's atheism. Among the many interesting memoranda made by John Percival, Earl of Egmont, is the following note: 'Of Collins Esq. deceased December 1729 ... [he] is a Speculative Atheist and has been for many years, as he owned to Archibald Hutchinson Esq. who told it to Dr. Dod M.D. and he to me.'[7]

III. Difficulties in identifying atheism

We have, then, two quite different statements that Collins was a speculative atheist. Admittedly, both witnesses claim to know this not from any written or published work by Collins, but from word of mouth; in Berkeley's case, from Collins's own mouth. However, if word of mouth was the only means available to testify the fact, then we can hardly demand more. Moreover, if it is ascertained that the charge is true, and Collins was an atheist, then this will mean more than a mere change in label. It should, and must, have an effect on our reading of Collins's writings. For if the fact is established, we will be obliged to look in his works for hints and suggestions which might reveal the form his atheism took; and we will also pay close attention to those 'ideas [as Berkeley puts it, which] imply it'.

That there is a hidden meaning or message in the writings of some of the early eighteenth-century free-thinkers is definitely suggested by Collins's acquaintance, John Toland, particularly in his essay 'Clidophorus', which makes up a part of *Tetradymus* (London, 1720). This essay deals with the esoteric and exoteric distinction. Although Toland examines the esoteric, or, as he sometimes calls it, the 'internal doctrine', mostly in the context of ancient writers, he affirms that his contemporaries, also, are obliged to say one thing but mean something else. 'I have [he writes] more than once hinted that the external and internal doctrines are as much in use as ever' (p. 94).[8] Again: 'In fine, daily experience sufficiently evinces, that there is no discovering, at least no declaring of TRUTH in most places, but at the hazard of man's reputation, employment or life' (p. 67).

My thesis — that for prudential reasons Collins held back from exoterically publishing his atheism — is supported by a number of factors, both from Collins's life and times. As O'Higgins shows (Chapter VIII) Collins had a genuine interest in his position as a county justice and treasurer, a position which he conscientiously fulfilled. Hence he would have been reluctant to put either his 'reputation' or 'employment' in jeopardy. But it would have been extremely awkward for an atheist magistrate to take oaths. Indeed, 'application was said to have been made by [William Whiston, one of Collins's theological opponents] to the Lord Chancellor King to remove Mr. Collins from the Commission of Peace, but without success'. The reason for the legal action, according to Whiston, was that Collins had 'taken superabundant care not to be suspected of believing so much as the Apostles' Creed, or the Books of either the Old or New Testament, or indeed *any Divine Providence at all*: Yet

[Whiston goes on to charge] does he [Collins] claim a right to be admitted to take an oath upon the Bible ... and in virtue thereof is in Commission of the oath'.[9] The time was hardly right for Collins to avow his atheism, even anonymously, when as late as 1729 his fellow free-thinker, Thomas Woolston, was sentenced to prison for the alleged blasphemy in his *Discourses on the miracles of our saviour* (London 1727–9); and this was no token punishment, for Woolston died in prison. Even in the polite *Spectator* we read: 'In my opinion , a solemn judicial Death is too great an honour for an Atheist'.[10] It would, then, have been most imprudent and uncharacteristic for an urbane gentleman, such as Collins, to have risked his reputation, to say nothing of his neck. As Toland remarked, 'considering how dangerous it is made to tell the truth, 'tis difficult to know when any man declares his real sentiments of things.'[11]

IV. The existence of atheists: opposing tendencies

There is, however, another side to the question of whether Collins was an atheist. It was not uncommon at the time for a theological writer to accuse his opponent of atheism. The suggestion of atheism was a popular way of discrediting the opposing point of view. Moreover, theologians in Collins's day did not often make the distinction between views that *tended* towards socinianism, deism or atheism, and views which *were* socinian, deistic or atheistic. As a clerical versifier innocently wrote:

> *Atheist* I stile him; for he's much the same,
> Tho' chusing Deist's somewhat milder Name.[12]

For polemical purposes, grey often became black. The frequency of unwarranted accusations of atheism may also have been facilitated by the lingering use of 'atheism' to signify both theoretical and practical atheism. Hence one must be careful about trusting the judgement of eighteenth-century theologians on their contemporaries. And it may well be such caution which lies behind O'Higgins's frequent and off-hand dismissals of the charges of atheism levelled against Collins by, for example, Bentley (p. 81), Swift and Bolingbroke.[13]

That there was an obsessive tendency to shout atheism on the barest grounds cannot be denied.[14] But one can hardly believe that Berkeley was in the grips of such an obsessive tendency when he informed his clerical friend Johnson that Collins had claimed to have found a demonstration against the existence of a God. What polemical purpose could be served? Nor, I think, would such a tendency apply to Percival's private note. Admittedly, the weight of my case — thus far — for Collins's atheism depends very much on how reliable and truthful Berkeley's testimony is. Yet what more reliable witness could one find in the whole eighteenth century? All the evidence we have strongly indicates that Berkeley — who had, according to Pope, every virtue under heaven — is an unimpeachable witness.

There is a final piece of external evidence that should be examined. It is from the second edition of the *Biographia Britannica* (London, 1778–1793), edited by Andrew Kippis. This edition of the *Biographia* does not seem to be as well known as the first edition, perhaps because it was left incomplete, reaching only the fifth volume and the letter 'F'. Kippis added a few things to the first-edition article on Collins. The following is of most interest for our discussion:

> It has not been uncommon to connect his [Collins's] name with authors of atheistic principles; but this is doing a manifest injustice to his character. A worthy and respectable clergyman put a paper into our hands, containing two anecdotes which represent Mr. Collins as an Atheist and as having introduced a young gentleman to a club of such persons in London. The paper, by some accident, has been mislaid.[15]

It is curious that Kippis's judgement — that Collins was not an atheist — is made not on account of, but in spite of, the evidence he mentions. One way of accounting for this is by means of the deep-seated repressive tendency. Thus Kippis, like the theologians we discussed in Chapter 1, may have been unwilling to believe in the existence of atheists (and his so-called 'accident', in which the counter-evidence was mislaid, may have been no accident). There are, then, two opposing tendencies: in one atheism is seen lurking nearly everywhere, in the other the very possibility of atheism is denied. We can, I think, see these tendencies reflected in various attitudes and practices. For instance, on the one hand we find a powerful desire to expose the absurdity and falsehood of atheism; but on the other hand, there is an unwillingness to display too much of any positive atheistic position, apparently out of fear that it may appear plausible to some.

It is interesting that Collins is aware of both tendencies. In the

Discourse he makes much of the obsessive tendency, and obviously took some pleasure in recording that such distinguished men as Locke, Tillotson and Cudworth had been called atheists (pp. 84–5). But he is also aware of the opposing tendency; for again in the *Discourse* he remarks that 'many divines maintain that there never was a real Atheist in the world' (p. 104).[16]

There is another way of explaining Kippis's unwillingness to ascribe atheism to Collins. Collins was celebrated for his honesty, integrity — in short his moral character. As one versifier put it:

> Ev'n the Superstitious own
> His public, private, virtues shone.[17]

But according to the prevailing view, an atheist should be immoral, and a theist moral (see below, Chapter 7). Kippis may have been influenced by this view; it would explain why attributing 'atheistic principles' to Collins would be doing an injustice to his character. It is suggestive that Kippis opens his account of Collins with the remark: 'Whatever may be thought of [his] writings, that he was a most respectable man in private life seems to be found upon evidence which cannot be contradicted.' But if his morality could not be contradicted, his atheism could. With some belief in religious theory the moral Collins might be less of an embarrassment to believers than such moral atheists as Epicurus and Spinoza.

We must be guarded, then, about refusing to believe that there were eighteenth-century atheists; and we should, I contend, be prepared to read between the lines. In an age where it could not openly be published, it had to be insinuated. That Collins, for one, had a hidden message, or internal doctrine, is asserted not only by Berkeley, but by others such as Dr John Mitchell. In a letter to Professor Charles Mackie, dated 27 July, 1728, Mitchell says: 'Colins [*sic*] and all that tribe are mere fools and cowards to him [Woolston]; *for they mask, as much as they can, what they say*; but he never minces any expression whatsoever.'[18] I shall now try to look behind the mask. In doing this I shall be guided by the hypothesis that what we will find is a speculative atheist.

V. The atheistic argument from the eternity of matter

We are naturally much in the dark as to the precise nature of Collins's atheistic demonstration, since it was never published. One suspects, however, that it was among the manuscripts that Demaizeaux inherited from Collins. If this suspicion is correct, then it would help to explain why Demaizeaux became so upset after he sold or gave the manuscripts to Collins's wife; and why he thought that he had 'betrayed the trust' of his friend, as he expressed it, when he learned that some of the manuscripts — the 'several important pieces' — had been lent to the Bishop of London, Edmund Gibson.[19] (Gibson, it was rumoured, destroyed the manuscript of the second part of *Christianity as old as creation* (1730), by Collins's friend Matthew Tindal.[20]) Gibson was also in close touch with Berkeley in the early 1730s.[21]

Laying this conjecture aside, however, let us examine Collins's writings for hints or insinuations of atheism or, as Berkeley puts it, those ideas that 'imply it'. This need not be as difficult a task as one might at first imagine. For although we are looking for something which is hidden, there would be little point in a writer hiding it so deeply that few or no one could find it. On the contrary, there is much evidence (some of it we have seen above) which suggests that the esoteric message was hidden only deeply enough to protect the free-thinking authors, e.g. from legal prosecution. But, as Bishop Gastrell, one of Collins's early critics, remarked: 'every Body understands their meaning'.[22] And, indeed, there would hardly be much point in publishing if some persons did not understand the intended meaning, and were not able to be influenced by it.

Let us begin our search of Collins's writings with one of his most philosophical pieces, his *Answer to Mr. Clarke's third defence* (2nd edn, London, 1711). In this last of four pamphlets against Samuel Clarke, Collins examines such questions as the distinction between adequate and inadequate ideas (pp. 4–14), personal identity (pp. 56–66), the nature of substance (pp. 68–72), and the creation of matter *ex nihilo* (pp. 75–9). This last topic will now be considered.

In his influential Boyle Lectures Clarke had inferred, according to Collins, from the assumption that there exist 'two beings of different kinds', that God created matter (*Answer*, p. 75). Collins argues, however, that even if we grant that there are two different beings, it might be that neither created the other, for both may have existed from eternity. There is, at any rate, nothing in the assumption that implies that one of the two existing beings created the other. Hence creation *ex nihilo* is a problem for those theologians, like Clarke and the other Boyle lecturers, who believe that the question of the existence of God is really a question, 'which otherwise [as Collins mischievously notes] would be with few any Question at all' (p. 76).

Collins then rather ostentatiously asserts that 'out of the inclination I have to see the foundation of all religion established on demonstration... I shall conclude this debate with an essay, showing a way how to demonstrate the *existence of God*' (p. 76).

In order to do this, and answer atheists such as Strato, 'the *Literati* in China', and particularly Spinoza — who has 'endeavoured to reduce Atheism into a system' — it is absolutely necessary, Collins claims, to 'prove the creation of matter *ex nihilo*; or which is all one, that matter is not a self-existent being' (p. 77). For if matter 'be allowed to be a self-existent being, we Christians who believe in one self-existing being, are obliged by our reasoning to allow matter all possible perfections... Because it is from the idea of self-existence, that we infer the perfections of God' (p. 78). In short, the theist's logic leads — once matter is allowed to be a substance — to pantheistic materialism. On the other hand, Collins suggests, one might maintain that there are two self-existing beings, namely spirit and matter. But if this is allowed, it will be plausible to argue that there are — for all we know — three, or indeed any number of, self-existing beings. We will then have a world in which there is, in effect, a plurality of gods. The question is: If matter, which evidently exists, is not sufficient, then why should *two* beings be sufficient?

Thus, if we are to withstand pantheistic materialism, on the one hand, and polytheism, on the other hand, we must, Collins contends, give some sense to or — in his terminology — 'have an idea of the *creation of matter ex nihilo*' (p. 78). Having shown the crucial importance of doing this, and the dire consequences if we cannot, Collins then, surprisingly, goes on to tell his reader that

> to get an Idea of Creation, or a Conception how Matter might begin to exist, *we must* (as the incomparable Mr. *Locke, Essay of H.U.B.* 4.c.10.§18 with great modesty expresses himself) *emancipate our selves from vulgar Notions, and raise our Thoughts as far as they can reach to a closer contemplation of things; and then we may be able to aim at some dim and seeming Conception, how Matter might at first be made, and begin to exist by the Power of the External First Being.* But as he thought that *this would lead him too far from the Notions, on which the Philosophy now in the World is built,* and that it *would not be pardonable to deviate so far from them;* so the small compass of this Treatise, and the great labour of shewing the falshood of so many receiv'd Prejudices and Opinions as is necessary to give an Idea of *Creation ex nihilo*, must make it more pardonable in me (who own myself to be infinitely below him

in Abilities) if I omit for the present so useful a Design, or should leave it intirely to some of those Gentlemen that are appointed annually to preach at the Lecture founded by the Honourable Robert Boyle. (p. 79)

This is surely a most surprising conclusion! After promising a proof for the existence of God, Collins presents the reader with what is, in effect, an argument *against* being able to prove the existence of God. Admittedly, he does say that although 'demonstration is thought so necessary in the case... I should think probability enough to determine any man' (pp. 76–7). But it is not at all clear what he means, or could mean, by 'probability'. Certainly he would not hold that, while we cannot form an idea of creation *ex nihilo*, or the nonexistence of matter, it is nonetheless probable that God did create matter in this way. Because, for Collins, it is strictly meaningless to speak about something if we can form no idea of the supposed thing. So I am apt to suspect that the talk of probability was mere dust thrown up to obscure the atheistic argument and conclusion. But the dust did not stop one early reviewer of Collins's *Answer* from describing Collins's discussion of the creation of matter as 'bare-faced Atheism'.[23]

This is not the only place in Collins's writings where, claiming to strike a blow *against* atheism, he succeeds in striking one *for* atheism. In the *Philosophical inquiry concerning human liberty* (3rd edn, London, 1735), he defends determinism by pointing out that indeterminism provides the basis for Epicurean atheism, which holds that 'chance may have produced an orderly system' (p. 53). This position, Collins asserts, is atheistic, and should be rejected. But what he does not point out is that the deterministic alternative for which he is arguing is at the heart of the far more formidable atheism of Spinoza. Thus it is interesting to find Richard Blackmore declaring, in a work published at roughly the same time as the *Philosophical inquiry* that... 'I am told by those, who are very capable of informing me, that the modern Atheist [in England] has given up the system of *Epicurus* as absurd and indefensible, and adheres to that of the Fatalists'; and Spinoza, according to Blackmore, 'is plainly a Fatalist' ('Of Atheism', pp. 90–1). For both Collins and Spinoza, God is a necessary being. But a being whose nature is necessary, or who must exist, cannot be free; and an unfree God is really no God. Collins does not say this openly. Rather he mainly makes the point by the following quotation from Bishop Burnet: 'it is not easy [writes Burnet] to imagine how they [God's supposed free actions] should be one with the divine essence, to which necessary existence does most certainly belong' (p. 67). In other words, if God can act freely then He might have acted differently. But then His nature or essence might have been different, and if this is the case, His nature is not necessary but contingent. Hence 'God' is necessary and not free.[24]

Our suspicions that Collins accepted this Spinozistic line of argument is enforced by the passage in Johnson's autobiography, from which I quoted a portion above (Section II). After stating that Collins had found a demonstration against the being of a God, Johnson adds that Collins 'soon after published [it] in a pretended demonstration that all is fate, and necessity'. Johnson is no doubt referring to the *Philosophical inquiry* which was published early in 1717. This suggests that Berkeley heard Collins talk of an atheistic demonstration sometime in 1716.[25]

VI. Second approach to Collins's atheism: his 'vindication' of the divine attributes and Christian prophecies

It seems to have been a part of Collins's general strategy to attack religion and Christianity through the eccentric theories of prominent churchmen and theologians. Thus we find him capitalising (1) on Henry Dodwell's odd theory that the soul is naturally mortal, but that by his grace God 'immortalises' the infant's soul by baptism, (2) on Archbishop King's theory that we can as little believe that God is good or wise as that He has arms and is occasionally jealous, (3) on William Whiston's theory that the text of the Old Testament was corrupted by the Jews in their attempt to cast doubt on Jesus's fulfilment of the prophecies, and, as a part of the same controversy, (4) on W. Surenhusius's Rabbinical rules for finding in the Scriptures such meanings as could never be derived from any normal rules or procedures of interpretation.

Now, by comparing Collins's attack on (2), King's theory, with his criticism of the theories of (3), Whiston, and (4), Surenhusius, we should be able to throw a good deal of light on the nature of Collins's atheism. Our discussion will also reveal how all-embracing his attack on religion is. In both these controversies — the first on our knowledge of the divine attributes, the second on the fulfilment of the prophecies — Collins identifies crucial problems for theism and Christianity, respectively. The theories which he attacks were designed to solve these problems.

In his *Vindication* against King, Collins considers what may be called the Manichean problems. These fundamental problems had been recently raised by Pierre Bayle in his famous *Historical and critical dictionary*, from which Collins quotes at length on the classic problem: How can God be both omnipotent and all good, since there is evil in the world? (pp. 6–7). (Other problems are also mentioned, such as the one King specifically deals with: How can men have free will if God knows everything that will happen?) Bayle's apparent solution to the Manichean problems was fideism: 'captivating the Understanding to the obedience of faith' (p. 10). But it is clear that Collins does not take Bayle's fideistic solution seriously, and he shows that the solution is not acceptable to the most distinguished theologians of the day (pp. 10–12).

But if Bayle's solution is unacceptable, then how are the Manichean problems to be solved? King's 1709 *Sermon on predestination* is, according to Collins, the latest attempt at a solution. He points out that King recognised that the standard theistic conception of God contains formidable internal difficulties, supporting his claim with a number of quotations from King, e.g. 'if the Attributes of God are understood literally and in the same way as we find them in us, absurd and intolerable consequences will follow' (*Vindication*, p. 15). Now, King's solution to any conflict in the divine attributes is to deny that the attributes are like anything in man: human and divine goodness, for example, differ in kind, and not merely in degree. Hence, if we do not know what the divine goodness really is, we cannot know that it is in conflict with evil in the world, or with the attribute of omnipotence, of which we are, again, ignorant.

In his *Vindication*, Collins shows that King's solution will not work. If we have no proper or literal knowledge of the divine attributes, then we can only be saying when we speak of God that He is '*rabba*' (p. 25). But as '*rabba*' in English is meaningless — in Hebrew it means 'great' — so must the concept of God be either meaningless, or, at the most, equivalent to 'a Being that is a general Cause of Effects'. But if the latter meaning is held, says Collins, 'I see not why atheists should not come into the belief of such a Deity' (pp. 19–20). In short, King's theory renders the divine attributes invulnerable to attack, but at far too high a price; for it deprives the attributes of any determinate, cognitive meaning. Consequently, Collins contends, if King's theory were true, atheism would be unavoidable.

Collins's avowed opinion, as stated in the *Vindication*, is that King's theory is mistaken, and that atheism is avoidable. We do, he says, have literal knowledge of the divine attributes, such as goodness and wisdom. He writes: 'Our conceptions indeed of those attributes do not reach the full extent of them as they are in God, but yet as far as our conceptions go, they correspond to the wisdom, goodness, holiness, justice, will and foreknowledge, of God' (p. 10). We have already considered a number of things which should make us suspicious of this avowal; but let us, for the moment, work on the assumption that Collins did believe, in opposition to King, that we have literal knowledge of the divine attributes. Supposing he did, then what — we should ask — is the actual conclusion of the *Vindication*? It is, simply, that there are very formidable, or insuperable, difficulties in the theistic conception of God — revealed by the Manichean problems — and that the latest attempt to cope with, or solve, these difficulties, i.e. King's theory, has failed; for the medicine is as bad as the disease. But the disease remains!

So, as in the case of matter's creation *ex nihilo*, Collins calls attention to a fundamental problem for theism. He has done this, on the face of it, in the interest of theism: to prove the existence of God and to vindicate the divine attributes. But this, I maintain, is the exoteric message. For he leaves us with what appears to be an insuperable problem. And for Collins that which appears to be a problem is a problem; and we must act on what appears to us to be true.[26] In short, he has woken the patient up, not to give him his sleeping pill, but to remind him of his incurable illness.

As the *Vindication* is, in my opinion, aimed at the heart of natural religion, so Collins's *A discourse on the grounds and reasons of the Christian religion* (London, 1724) is aimed directly against revealed religion, i.e. Christianity. Not only, however, is the attack more direct than in the *Vindication,* but it is also less heavily disguised. Collins's line of attack may be outlined in the following way:

(1) The New Testament depends for its truth on its connection with the Old Testament.
(2) That connection is the fulfilment of the Old Testament prophecies by Jesus.
(3) It is necessary, therefore, that the prophecies relating to a messiah in the Old Testament were indeed fulfilled by Jesus, as described in the New Testament.
(4) But there are serious difficulties in (3), as pointed out by Surenhusius and Whiston, e.g., that there are discrepancies between the quotations of the prophecies in the New Testament and the same prophecies in the Old Testament.
(5) Furthermore, as Collins points out, the prophecies in the

Old Testament cannot have been literally fulfilled by Jesus, because some of them had been literally fulfilled in the Old Testament, and others are about events which occurred many years before the birth of Jesus.

(6) All that remains, then, is non-literal fulfilment of the prophecies.

(7) Hence the Old Testament prophecies were non-literally, i.e., typologically, fulfilled by Jesus; and so Christianity is true.

(8) But typological fulfilment is absurd, as nearly anything could be fulfilled by its means.

(9) Therefore since the Old Testament prophecies have not been literally fulfilled by Jesus, there is no connection between the Old and New Testaments, and Christianity is groundless.

Now Collins does not explicitly assert (8) and, *a fortiori*, (9). But his account of (7) is such that it is universally agreed that he believed, and expected his readers to believe, that (7) is false, and (8) is true, and by implication (9) is also the case.[27]

Let us now look back at the argument in the *Vindication*. As (1) – (3) state the conditions necessary for the truth of Christianity, so Collins holds in the *Vindication* that theism would be meaningless if we had no literal knowledge of the divine attributes.[28] He quotes Archbishop Tillotson's necessary condition for the truth of religion. This is: 'if we had no certain and settled Notion of the Goodness and Justice and Truth of God, he would be altogether an unintelligible Being; and Religion, which consists in the Imitation of him, would be utterly lost.' This is the motto on the title-page of the *Vindication;* it is also quoted in the *Discourse* (p.51). The difficulties of (4) and (5) are paralleled by the Manichean problems. But, whereas, in the prophecy debate, Collins dismisses a literal solution and pays lip-service to a non-literal solution, in the *Vindication* he rejects a non-literal solution and, apparently, supports a literal solution. But it is a solution which does not solve anything: the Manichean problems remain. In both cases he shows that the latest attempts to solve the legitimate problems are unsatisfactory.[29]

The question which we must then ask is this: was Collins as insincere in his saying that we have literal knowledge of the divine attributes as he was in claiming to believe in typological fulfilment of the prophecies? The preponderance of evidence, if we take Collins's statements in a straightforward exoteric way, certainly argues for a negative answer. But since it is allowed by all commentators that Collins was *not* being straightforward about typological fulfilment (7), then there is certainly a serious possibility that he was acting in the same way concerning our knowledge of the divine attributes. To concede that Collins did not really mean (7) is tantamount to admitting that he had an esoteric or internal doctrine.

There is an important discussion of the nature of thinking in Collins's *Answer* which is relevant to our discussion. Collins maintains there that thinking follows the action of bodies on our senses (p.27); and that human thinking, and all of its modes, 'has Succession and Parts, as all material Actions have' (p.28). But, although he holds that human thinking is essentially tied up with matter, he claims that God, alone, is totally unconnected with matter. As the passage in which he asserts this is of considerable importance I shall quote it in full:

> It is evident to me that God must be an Immaterial Being, that is, a proper Immaterial Being, a Being without any of the Propertys of Matter, without Solidity, Extension or Motion, and that exists in no place; and not a Being that has Extension (and consequently exists in Place and has Parts) according to Mr. *Clark's* idea of Immaterial Being. Now Thinking in God cannot be founded on any Objects acting upon him, nor is Thinking in him suppos'd to be successive, or to consist of Parts, or to have any Modes, because Modes of Thinking are distinct Acts of Thinking. But as his Essence is eternal and immutable, without any the least Variation or Alteration, so his Thinking is suppos'd to be one numerical individual Act, comprehending all things and all the Possibilitys of things at one View, and as is fixt, and permanent and unvariable, and as much without Succession and Parts, as his Essence. So that if we can form any Judgement of the nature of Thinking in Man, from its perfect Conformity with the Powers of Matter, and its intire and total Disagreement with Thinking, in that only Immaterial Being which, we are satisfy'd, exists; we may reasonably conclude Human Thinking a Power or Affection of Matter (p.29).

There is, I think, a direct conflict between Collins's statement here and his assertions in the *Vindication* against King. If human thinking has an 'intire and total Disagreement with Thinking, in that only Immaterial being,' how can any of the intellectual or moral perfections be literally applied to man and God? Collins allows that thinking is the genus from which all the particular mental modes are derived, or at least upon which they depend. He says: 'Thinking has its Modes, such as Doubting, Willing, Knowing, Pleasure, Pain, etc.' (p.28).

How then are we to account for, and deal with, the conflict between his non-anthropomorphic description of God in the *Answer* and his anthropomorphic account in the *Vindication*? Toland has provided us with a suggestion in his 'Clidophorus'. The fact that *'the same men do not always seem to say the same things on the same subjects...* can only be solved [he says] by *the distinction of the external and internal doctrine.'*[30] When we meet with an evident contradiction in such men as Collins, we must be on our guard and be prepared to look more deeply. My proposal, in short, is that Collins's internal doctrine was the negative argument of the *Vindication* combined with the immaterial conception of God in the *Answer*. Taken together they make up an argument for atheism. This interpretation is in general accord, I think, with the rule which Toland lays down for determining when a writer is sincere: If someone, he says, *'seriously maintains the contrary of what's by law established, and openly declares for what most others oppose, then there is a strong presumption that he utters his mind'* (p.96).

In his conception of an immaterial being, Collins is making as great and as unbridgeable a gap between things divine and human as did Archbishop King. An immaterial being must have a completely different psychology from all material beings. But we can only have ideas of material beings and their psychology; we have no idea what an intellect is like which is utterly different from ours. Hence talk of divine attributes is without content and meaningless. As Collins emphatically, although conditionally, puts it in the *Philosophical inquiry* in an utterance worthy of Spinoza: 'When we use the term *God*, the Idea signified thereby, ought to be as distinct and determinate in us, as the Idea of a triangle or square is, when we discourse of either of them; otherwise, the term *God* is an empty sound' (pp.11-12).

I might summarise my reconstruction of Collins's atheistic argument in the following way: (1) God is an immaterial being, and His identity is like nothing that we can conceive; (2) but what we cannot conceive is meaningless; (3) supposing, however, that we can conceive His attributes, then they are observed to be contradictory; (4) hence, as the conception of such a being is either meaningless or contradictory, that being cannot exist.

Such a reconstruction supposes that Collins's *Vindication* plays a central role in his atheism; and this agrees with Berkeley's association of Collins's atheism and King's theory in *Alciphron* IV.16-22.

Another piece of evidence which supports my reconstruction is that one very early critic of the *Vindication* interpreted Collins's true intentions in generally the same way I have done. The reason why Collins recorded Bayle's Manichean problems, according to a reviewer in *Censura temporum*, was

> to shew that *Bayle* must be in the right, if the Bishop's [King's] solution of the difficulties relating to the matter be wrong and indefensible, and then as far as he is able to prove it so, and substitute a contrary principle in the place of it, which it is impossible should be true.[31]

The 'contrary principle', I take it, is Collins's apparently anthropomorphic conception of the divine attributes. Hence the reviewer calls Collins 'this mock Vindicator.' For what is really being vindicated is the Manichean difficulties in the theist's conception of God. Other difficulties which might be brought in by Collins to support the atheistic claim in (3) – that there are conflicts in the theist's conception of God – have been considered above. These are (a) the problem of conceiving the creation of matter *ex nihilo* (Section V), (b) the difficulty of retaining both the necessity and the freedom of God (Section V), and (c) the problem of how an eternal Being can act in time (note 30).

Notes

1. James O'Higgins, *Anthony Collins, the man and his works* (The Hague, 1970), p. 234; all quotations from, or references to, O'Higgins, will be to this work. I shall also be using the following editions, and abbreviated titles, of Collins's works: *An essay concerning the use of reason in propositions*, 2nd edn (London, 1709) — *Essay; An answer to Mr. Clarke's third defence of his letter to Mr. Dodwell*, 2nd edn (London, 1711) — *Answer; A vindication of the divine attributes, in some remarks on his grace the Archbishop of Dublin's sermon intituled Divine predestination* ... (London, 1710) — *Vindication; A discourse of free-thinking* (London, 1713) — *Discourse; A philosophical inquiry concerning human liberty* (3rd edn, 1735) — *Philosophical inquiry; A discourse on the grounds and reasons of the Christian religion* (London, 1724) — *Grounds.*

2. See also pp. 81–4, 173, 191–2 and 234–5.

3. Compare *Alciphron* 1.8, where Berkeley traces, and explains, the development of free-thinking. It starts from latitudinarianism and ends with atheism, progressing by continually cancelling the differences in theological positions, and retaining that which is held in common. Eventually nothing is held in common. This is the beginning of atheism, and the end of

religion. Compare *Answer to Priestley*, p. xxv, for a similar account by an atheist.

4. *The works of George Berkeley,* (London, 1948–57) edited by Luce and Jessop; vol. i, p. 254; hereafter referred to as *Works*.

5. *Samuel Johnson, his career and writings* (New York, 1929), H. and C. Schneider (eds.), vol. iii, p. 191; see also T.E. Jessop's Introduction to *Alciphron*, in *Works*, vol. iii, p. 23.

6. See *Theory of vision vindicated*, in *Works*, vol. i, p. 255.

7. In the British Museum, Add. MS 47126, fol. 166. In *The religious, rational, and moral conduct of Mathew Tindal, LL.D. late Fellow of All Souls College in Oxford* (London, 1735); the author, who styles himself 'a member of the same College' as Tindal, speaks of 'Dr. Dodd, a very sober, and pious, and worthy physician, formerly one of the fellows of the College' (p. 26).

8. In his *Pantheisticon* (1720) Toland offers an intriguing (although questionable) account of societies of pantheists, flourishing especially in London, that made use of the esoteric/exoteric distinction. The pantheists, according to Toland — who was, incidently, the first to use the word — believe that God is the universe.

9. Quoted in the article 'Collins', in *A general, historical and critical dictionary* (London, 1734–41), vol. iv, p. 402. One can understand Whiston's annoyance at Collins's duplicity, since Whiston had been forced to give up his Cambridge professorship because he would not subscribe to articles in which he did not believe. Lord Chancellor King was the nephew of Locke, and through him a friend of Collins.

10. No. 389, 27 May 1712; by Eustace Budgell. For an account of those prosecuted for irreligion, see Charles Bradlaugh's *The laws relating to blasphemy and heresy* (London, 1878).

11. *Tetradymus* (London, 1720), p. 95. In *An essay towards preventing the ruin of Great Britain* (1721), Berkeley says that 'the public safety requireth that the avowed contemners of all religion should be severely chastised' (in *Works*, vol. vi, pp. 70–1).

12. This is Joseph Trapp; see his *Thoughts upon the four last things ... a poem* 2nd edn (London, 1745), p. 10.

13. In his forceful satire, *Mr C——ns's Discourse ... put into plain English ...* (London, 1713), Swift writes: 'a brief complete body of Atheology seemed yet wanting, till this irrefragable Discourse of free-thinking appeared' (Introduction). (The word 'atheology' had been introduced by Cudworth.) Swift's friend Bolingbroke, who was himself charged with atheism, also ascribed atheism to Collins. 'Both of them', i.e. the atheist and theist, writes Bolingbroke, 'reason *a priori* from assumed moral attributes of divinity. So they call their method of reasoning... [but it is false, because] their ideas of these attributes are very human ideas, applied arbitrarily to the divine nature... Both of them pretend to be led from proposition down to their different conclusions ... a COLLINS concludes, that there is no God; and a CLARK, that there is a future state of rewards and punishments.' — *Works of Bolingbroke* (London, 1754), vol. 5, p. 331. Of course, the antipathy of Swift and Bolingbroke to Collins would no doubt have been helped by their Tory hatred of an extreme Whig.

14. Two books which clearly illustrate the obsessive tendency are *Some discourses upon Dr. Burnett and Dr. Tillotson...* (London, 1695) by George Hickes

(see pp. 39–40, 48); and *Spinoza reviv'd* (London, 1709) by William Carroll, with a preliminary discourse by Hickes. A brief extract from Hickes's discourse may serve as a sample of the whole: 'one of the *Deists*, or *Atheists*, so little difference there is between them'. In his *Reflexions on atheism*, J. Edwards remarks: 'At this day *Atheism* itself is slily called Deism by those who indeed are *Atheists* (p. 136). Also see above Chapter 1, Section 3 for Curteis's obsessive statements.

15. *Biographia Britannica* (London, 1789), vol. iv, p. 27. It is a pity that Kippis mislaid the anecdotes, for we have very little information about the free-thinking clubs. Berkeley refers to them in his *Guardian* essays, and in J.H. Monck's *Life of Bentley* (London, 1830) Collins is said to have been at the centre of a club which met 'at the Grecian coffee-house, near Temple-bar' (p. 268). One meets the suggestion that some of the free-thinking books, e.g. Toland's *Christianity not mysterious* (1696), were written in free-thinking clubs. This charge was made by Peter Browne in his *Letter in answer to Christianity not mysterious* 3rd edn (London, 1703): 'And therefore [writes Browne] I hope he [Toland] won't take it ill of the world, if they believe me when I inform them, that this Book, which goes under his name, was the *joynt Endeavours* of a Secret Club' (p. 143). In the Preface to a later deistic work, *The moral philosopher* (1737), Thomas Morgan acknowledges that the book arose from discussions 'many years ago by a Society, or Club of Gentlemen in the Country, who met once a Fortnight at a Gentleman's House in a pleasant retired village, with a Design to enter impartially into the Consideration of the Grounds and Principles of Religion in General' (pp. vi–vii).

16. David Hume was also aware of the two opposing tendencies, as we can observe from the opening remarks in his *Enquiry concerning human understanding*, Section XII; see below, Chapter 4. In Chapter 1, Section III, we saw that Curteis manages to be caught within both opposing tendencies in one and the same pamphlet.

17. See *The fall of priestcraft ... a burlesque poem* (London, 1732), p. 41.

18. See *Historical manuscript commission report*, Laing II (London, 1925), p. 223; my italics.

19. This strange incident is described in I. Disraeli's *Curiosities of literature* (London, 1858), 'Des Maizeaux and Anthony Collins's MSS', vol. 3, pp. 13ff, where the relevant letters are conveniently reprinted.

20. See D. Berman and S. Lalor, 'The Suppression of *Christianity as old as the Creation*, vol. 2', *Notes and Queries* (March, 1984), pp. 3–6.

21. See two letters of Gibson to Berkeley, printed in A.C. Fraser's *The works of George Berkeley* (Oxford, 1871), vol. iv, pp. 238 and 244. Both letters were written in the mid-1730s, and they show that Berkeley and Gibson conferred on the problem of the free-thinkers. For example, in the second letter of 7 February 1735–6, Gibson writes: 'Here we have now little trouble from professed infidels, but a great deal from semi-infidels.' One wonders whether Gibson either showed or mentioned to Berkeley the atheistic proof. Speaking of it in *Alciphron* 1.12, one dialogist remarks: 'I am assured by some judicious friends who have seen it.' In the same passage the proof is called 'a learned *Anecdote*', which suggests that it was written out, although not published (see Johnson's *Dictionary*). Berkeley met Gibson in London — in 1731/2 — before the publication of *Alciphron*.

22. See *Principles of deism, set in a clear light* (London, 1708), p. 32.

23. Samuel Parker, *Censura temporum: the good and evil tendencies of books, sermons...* (London, 1708), vol. i, no. iv, p. 117. The review runs from pp. 117–26; and, like all the reviewers in this periodical, it is written in a loose dialogue form. It is not mentioned by O'Higgins. Nor does O'Higgins mention the following statement from Warburton's 'Dedication to free-thinkers' in his *Divine legation of Moses*: 'No sooner had he [Locke] gone to rest, than Mr Collins publickly [in his *Answer* to Clarke] insults a notion of his *honoured* Friend's concerning the *possibility of conceiving how matter may first be made and begin to be:* And goes affectedly out of his way to it' (pp. xxiv–xxv). In a letter of 18 April, 1693 William Molyneux had asked Locke to address himself to this problem. In *Essay* IV. x. Locke had, according to Molyneux, provided 'a most exact demonstration of the *existence of a God*. But perhaps [Molyneux added] it might be more full, by an addition against the *eternity of the world*, and that all things have not been going on in the same manner, as we now see them *ab aeterno*. I have known a pack of philosophical atheists, that rely on this *hypothesis*' (*Works of Locke* (1722), vol. iii, p. 514–15). That this hypothesis did represent a serious threat at the time may also be seen in remarks such as that of Wise, who calls the hypothesis 'the Achilles, or pretended invincible objection of the atheist' (p. 520). For an account of what Locke is supposed to have had in mind in *Essay* IV.x.18, see Hamilton's edition of the *Works of Reid* (6th edn., Edinburgh, 1863), vol. 2, note F.

24. See pp. 66–7; compare Spinoza's *Ethics* Part I, prop. 33. Concerning Spinoza's influence on Collins, see my review of O'Higgins's edition of the *Philosophical inquiry*, in *Studies: an Irish quarterly review* (1977), no. 262, pp. 252–3. In the *Pantheisticon*, Toland notes that the Pantheists are called by that name 'upon account of an opinion concerning God and the *Universe*, peculiar to themselves; but diametrically opposed to the *Epicureans*' There is in Corry's *Reflexions upon liberty and necessity* (London, 1761) an interesting discussion concerning the alleged atheism of Collins's *Philosophical inquiry*. According to Corry in Samuel Clarke's 'Answer to Mr Collins's second argument [Clarke] insinuates, or rather indeed, asserts, that Mr. Collins has an atheistical meaning in the argument... and that Mr. Collins means to insinuate that there is no such thing as a self-moving principle in the universe, and consequently no God' (pp. 82–3). In his long chapter (pp. 61–106) Corry tries to defend Collins against this and other criticisms. After briefly defending Collins on this point, he writes: 'but I must likewise declare, that if Mr. Collins should be thought to have a latent atheistical meaning, I look upon such meaning to affect himself only, and apprehend that the question of human liberty is no ways connected with his manner of discussing it' (p. 83). It is noteworthy that as late as 1761 this was still an issue.

25. In a paper published in 1975, 'Anthony Collins and the question of atheism in the early part of the 18th century', from which much of the material in this part is taken, I had conjectured that the meeting took place in 1713; but (as O'Higgins has pointed out to me) Collins was probably on the Continent at that time.

26. See *Essay,* pp. 4–41; for an examination of this point, see my 'Anthony Collins: aspects of his thought and writings' in *Hermathena* (1975), no. CXIX, pp. 57–61.

27. See, for example, John Leland's *A view of the principal deistical writers...*

(London, 1754), pp. 108–10; Stephen, *History of English thought*, iv. 32–3; and O'Higgins, pp. 168–71.

28. O'Higgins goes even further, and claims that Collins makes 'God's intellect univocal with ours'; see p. 63, note 7.

29. Logically, of course, the option of Manicheanism in the one case and Judaism in the other remain open. But Collins's readers would hardly have considered these as serious possibilities or solutions.

30. See *Tetradymus*, p. 85; and also see p. 77. O'Higgins does not draw attention to the conflict between Collins's negative conception of the divine attributes in the *Answer* and his positive conception in the *Vindication*; although he does mention another doctrinal conflict, first identified by Samuel Clarke, which is connected with the first (pp. 71–2). In the *Essay* Collins had asserted that God acts in time, and there is succession in the divine nature. In the long passage from the *Answer*, which I have just quoted, Collins denies that thinking in God is successive. Clarke pounced on this apparent contradiction, and in his next pamphlet the *Fourth defence* (1708) printed the opposing statements in opposite columns (pp. 17–19). Collins never answered Clarke's charge of contradiction, although there is no doubt that he was aware of it. He did slightly alter the passage in the second edition of the *Answer* in such a way as to suggest that the denial of succession in God was the received view rather than his own particular view. In the first edition the second sentence contained the words 'nor can thinking in him be successive'; and in the next sentence the words 'supposed to be' were added in the second edition. In this way he very slightly lessened the conflict between the *Essay* and the *Answer*. But the conflict between the *Answer* and the *Vindication* remains unaffected. Certainly, it is very surprising that in the *Vindication* of 1710, he should contradict the very same statement from the *Answer*, which Clarke had pounced on with such alacrity as in contradiction to the *Essay*.

31. *Censura temporum* (1710), vol. iii, no. 2; p. 36.

4

The Suppression of 'Atheism'

I. Count Radicati

In Chapter 1 I examined a number of denials of the existence of atheism, most of which I described as repressive. Yet there are other denials of atheism which resist such classification. Nor can these denials be categorised as suppressive with those of Webb, Paine, or Burke; or as partly descriptive with Herbert and perhaps Fotherby. Consider the following statement from Albert Radicati, Count of Passeron, who, though Italian, published most of his works in England where he for a time resided. One such work was the *Twelve discourses concerning Religion and Government* (2nd edn, 1734):

> to say that Deists are Atheists is false; for they that are so called by the Vulgar, and by those whose interest it is to decry them, admit a first cause under the names of God, Nature, Eternal Being, Matter, universal Motion or Soul. Such were Democritus, Epicurus, Diagoras, Lucian, Socrates, Anaxagoras, Seneca, Hobbes, Blount, Spinosa, Vanini, St Evremond, Bayle, Collins, and in general all that go under the name of Speculative Atheists; and none but fools or madmen can ever deny it. So that the word Atheist must signify Deist, or nothing. There being no such thing as an Atheist in the world as the Ignorant imagine, and the crafty Priests would have believed, when they brand with this odious name such as detect their impostures. (pp. 11–12)

Although this statement resembles the denials in Chapter 1, it differs significantly in tone and point of view. Whereas putative atheists are castigated by the anonymous essayist as pretenders or practical atheists, Radicati *defends* those who have been *accused* of atheism. It is either the vulgar or fools and madmen who decry Democritus, Epicurus *et al.* as speculative atheists. Nor does Radicati suggest that the so-called atheists are motivated by non-rational or immoral causes. He is sympathetic to those who have been accused of atheism, referring to one of them (who, I have argued, was indeed a covert speculative atheist) as 'that great and good man Mr. Collins'[1]

Yet the significance of Radicati's statement is not primarily in his sympathy for those who have been branded speculative atheists, but, as I shall argue, in his suppressing the emotive *name* 'atheist'. One way of redeeming something which suffers from a bad name is to dispute that it truly possesses, or deserves to possess, that label. This is Radicati's strategy: he wants to relieve atheism of its 'odious name'. His concept of God is so expanded that virtually every account of the world must be deistic or theistic. As long as a philosopher is willing to posit some kind of absolute — whether it be nature or matter or motion — Radicati will call him a deist. (The only theory which might, perhaps, count as atheistic would be an anti-metaphysical position — like that of scepticism, agnosticism or logical positivism — which resists committing itself on the question of a First or Ultimate Cause.) The main reason, however, for believing that Radicati's denial has an altogether different aim from that of the essayist is that he was not only a free-thinker but an atheist, as appears in his brilliant though little-known *Philosophical dissertation upon death* (1732). Though it contains no denial of God's existence or avowal of atheism, the *Philosophical dissertation* is atheistic in all but name. In its first ten or so pages a materialistic version of pantheism clearly replaces theism or deism. '*By the Universe*', writes Radicati, 'I comprehend the infinite Space which contains the immense Matter'.[2] Radicati argues that matter and motion 'are inseparable' (p. 5), 'of eternal co-existence' and 'exist necessarily' (p. 9). Because motion is essential to matter, and since both are necessary and eternal, no God is needed to superadd motion to matter or create the world. But Radicati makes God not merely superfluous, but equivalent to the material world: 'This *Matter*, modified by *Motion* into an infinite Number of various forms, is that which I call NATURE. Of this the qualities and attributes are, *Power, Wisdom* and *Perfection*, all of which she possesses in the highest degree (p. 10).'

Radicati's version of pantheism is even more evidently atheistic than Spinoza's, and it was described as such by one of the few contemporary writers who took notice of it. In the Preface to a *Summary account of the deist's religion* (1745) the editor calls the *Philosophical dissertation* a 'truly *Atheistic* Book'. The *Philosophical dissertation* is, even by present-day standards, a work of devastating and thorough naturalism, and its radical point of view is proved by its being attacked by deists and moderate free-thinkers.[3] Radicati's atheological position may be described as pantheistic materialism. It combines Spinoza's central insight that the whole world is god because it alone is perfect and necessarily existent, with Hobbes's main doctrine that the world consists entirely of matter in motion.

Of course, to my interpretation of Radicati's denial of atheists one can object that it supposes the existence not only of a secret code but of bad faith on Radicati's part; and that it does so without any direct evidence. But in fact there *is* evidence for both the secret code and bad faith. The broad outlines of the code were known and made public by, among others, Richard Blackmore and Bishop Berkeley. They provide us with a key for explaining Radicati's denial of atheism. Of course, Radicati never assented to the explanation which Blackmore or Berkeley offered; in this sense we have no direct evidence that there was an esoteric code, or — if we allow that there was a code — how it is to be decoded. But we should hardly expect Radicati to endanger his safety by openly revealing the thing he intended to mask. If, however, their key explains more than any rival explanation, then surely it should be accepted.

II. Charles Gildon

Before describing this key I should like to show the need for it by establishing that at least one noted free-thinker did deny in bad faith the existence of atheists. This was Charles Gildon, who started life as a Roman Catholic, then became a friend of Charles Blount and one of the leading free-thinkers of the 1690s, and finally, as a result of Charles Leslie's *Short and easie method with the deists* (London, 1698), a militant Christian.[4] In 1705 Gildon published *The Deist's manual*, in which he defends his recently acquired religious beliefs. He also categorically asserts the existence of speculative atheists of a Hobbesian type. In the 'Epistle dedicatory' to the Archbishop of Canterbury he states:

> I know, my Lord, that many have asserted, that there are no *Speculative Atheists,* yet, my Lord, I cannot agree with those

Gentlemen, because my Conversation has frequently afforded me Proofs of the contrary in the *Hobbists* of the Times; the very Foundation of whose *System* is *Atheism* in Speculation, which I am confident, is entirely defeated, in the following Treatise [*The Deist's manual*]. There are besides, my Lord, a very numerous Party of *Practical Atheists,* who (whatever they pretend, like Mr *Hobbs,* of Magnificent Expressions of *God*) are really Atheists in their Opinions, as well, as Practice.

But this was not always Gildon's opinion. Indeed, some ten years earlier he himself had been one of 'those gentlemen' who staunchly denied the existence of atheists. His extensive denial is to be found at the beginning of his essay entitled 'To Dr R.B. — of a God', which was published in *The oracles of reason* (1693), a free-thinking miscellany which he himself edited:

I have perus'd your Arguments for the proof of a Deity [Gildon writes to R.B.], but think that you undertook a needless trouble since I am confident there's no man of sense that doubts whether there be a God or no. The Philosophers of Old of the *Theodorean sect,* that had spent all their time and study to establish the contrary as truth, when they came to dye confuted all their Arguments by imploring some Deity; as *Bion* in particular. I know not whether the *Idea* of a God be *Innate* or no, but I'm sure that it is very soon imprinted on the minds of Men; and I must beg Mr. *Lock's* pardon, if I very much question those Authorities he quotes from the Travels of some men, who affirm some Nations to have no notions of a Deity, since the same has been said of the Inhabitants of the *Cape of Good Hope*, which the last account of that place proves to be false.[5]

This dismissal of the putative atheist on the grounds that he will renounce his atheism when death approaches is typical of the repressive denials. The latter, anthropological, part of the denial is also by no means novel. But in the light of his strong affirmation of speculative atheists in *The Deist's manual* it is difficult to take his earlier denial at its face value. The letter 'To Dr. R.B.' first appeared in 1693 and was republished in 1695 in *Miscellaneous works of Charles Blount.* As Gildon edited the *Miscellaneous works* we may assume that he stood by his essay in 1695. But he must surely by that time have held some of those frequent conversations which convinced him that there were speculative atheists; for he is more likely to have held such conversations while a free-thinker than after his conversion to Christianity. So we are led to the conclusion that his denial of atheists in 1693 (and 1695) was in bad faith.

The letter 'To R.B.' itself supports the charge of bad faith. While it is avowedly pro-theistic, its actual arguments are anti-theistic. Dr R.B. had apparently based a proof for the existence of God on the finite duration of man's habitation on earth. But Gildon tries to undermine this basis by casting doubt on the Biblical account of creation: e.g. 'the *Chinese*... in a traditional account tell us, that the Posterity of *Panzon* and *Panzona,* inhabited the Earth 90,000 years.'[6] Gildon insinuates that men have always inhabited the earth. For the eternity of the world would undermine not only R.B.'s but any causal argument for God's existence. Of course, Gildon's *avowed* purpose is to help and not to harm theism; he concludes his letter by advising R.B.: 'build your Demonstration ... on a firmer Basis, else instead of promoting the cause, you espouse, you only give advantages to those who would be thought at least to be what they are not' (p. 184). Here again we have a (somewhat oblique) denial of atheism. There are some who mistakenly think that they are atheists, and R.B.'s infirm proof (which Gildon has shown to be infirm) may unwittingly help to confirm such deluded persons in their atheistic delusion.

When we find an essay in which the arguments are anti-theistic but the avowals pro-theistic, we must be suspicious. Blackmore and Berkeley encourage us to be suspicious, as we shall see. However, in this remarkable case we do not have to appeal to outsiders for our key; for Gildon himself has provided it in the part of his *Deist's manual* where he argues against the eternity of the world. Contending against his former self, he writes:

> that all Records of time [refer] to a Beginning, is a Proof that the World, and Man are not Eternal, is in force, till you bring better convictions of it, than all your *Peradventures, Maybe's, Supposes,* etc. borrow'd from the *Oracles of Reason* and from a Letter there.[7]

The 'Letter there' is clearly Gildon's own to Dr R.B. The only possible alternative would be Blount's letter to Gildon[8]; but it does not agree with Gildon's allusions. It is Gildon's letter to R.B. which contains a 'sequel' that tries to 'render at least doubtful' divine creation (pp. 179–180) and providence (pp. 181–2). Here is one of Gildon's 'maybes' with regard to divine creation:

But since our Correspondence with *China*, we have found they have Records & Histories of four or six thousand years date before our Creation of the World; and who knows but some other Nations may be [!] found out hereafter, that may go further. (p. 182)

III. Blackmore and Berkeley

Gildon's revealing essay to R.B. also deals with the subject of divine providence; but before we examine this topic it will be helpful to consider Blackmore's key in the prose introduction to his philosophical poem *The Creation* (1712):

there are two sorts of Men, who without Injustice have been call'd Atheists; those who frankly and in plain terms have deny'd the Being of a God; and those, who tho' they asserted his Being, denied those Attributes and Perfections, which the Idea of a God includes; and so while they acknowledge the name, subverted the thing. These are as real Atheists, as the former, but less sincere. If any Man should declare he believes a Deity, but affirms that this Deity is of human shape, and not Eternal ... or though he allowed him to be Eternal, should maintain, that he showed no Wisdom, Design, or Prudence in the Formation, and no Care or Providence in the government of the world ... nor interests himself in human Affairs ... such a Person is indeed, and in Effect, as much an Atheist as the former. ...such Notions of a Deity [who is indifferent to man] lay the Axe to the root of all Religion.[9]

For Blackmore the assertion 'God exists' is not a sufficient condition for regarding the writer as a theist or even a deist, since he may be allowing the name 'God' but by extracting essential attributes from the concept of God denying His reality. So, if God is said to exist but all we know of Him is that He is eternal, then we should not, Blackmore holds, think that such a being is God. For matter or space are thought by many to be eternal, and they would, according to this definition of God, be Gods. Hence those, or some of those, who argue in this way are atheists; while their atheism is covert rather than open, it is atheism none the less. Their unwillingness to call themselves atheists is bound up, Blackmore believes, with their desire to propagate atheism. He exemplifies this in his poetic characterisation of Spinoza:

Spinosa next, to hide his black Design,
And to his Side th' unwary to incline,
For Heav'n his Ensigns treacherous displays,
Declares for God, while he that God betrays:
For whom he's pleas'd such Evidence to bring,
As saves the Name, while it subverts the Thing. (p. 154)

I do not wish to go into the question of whether Spinoza, in particular, was a covert atheist; but I do argue that Gildon and Radicati intended to save the name 'God' while subverting the thing.

Consider the following passage from Gildon's letter to R.B.; it follows his denial of the existence of atheists:

> And if there be a God, the necessary Qualities that must be
> granted to him, will not permit a man that Reasons right of
> things to question his Care and Providence over humane
> Affairs. Tho' I confess it a superficial way of Dispute; the
> *Epicureans* may seem to have some Reason to conclude, that the
> Deity has no care of mankind, because the confusion of
> humane Affairs, and general triumph of Wrong over Right ...
> would perswade it, and almost make one think, if what the
> *Pythagoreans* and *Chaldeans* held of Souls were true, viz. that they
> were created in Heaven, and thence transmitted to the Bodies
> for punishment, that we are Devils. ...(pp. 178–9)

Here we have once again an orthodox avowal and an unorthodox argument. Gildon asserts that God must be concerned with human affairs; like Blackmore he says that providence is an essential attribute of God. But Gildon insinuates that the Epicurean rejection of providence is more credible than the Christian affirmation. He does not deny God's providence, but the *evidence he brings,* to use Blackmore's formula, does *subvert the thing.*

Gildon twice hypothetically posits God's existence. The first instance I have quoted above; the second is: 'if they confess a God, they must not deprive Him of his necessary perfections, and certainly a Providence over his Works is one'.[10] Here, as in the case of the eternity of man, Gildon is trying 'to render at least doubtful' — to use his own description in *The Deist's manual* — the existence of God. His method is, first, to protect himself by a caveat denying atheism; secondly, to lay down in plain language a necessary condition for God's existence; thirdly, to confusedly and sceptically insinuate that the condition is not met. In other words, we have a sort of atheistic enthymeme.

Berkeley's identification of covert atheism is to be found, as we have seen, at length in *Alciphron,* Dialogue Four, where he criticises a version of negative theology in which God's attributes are said to be qualitatively different from anything we can know in this world.[11] This version of negative theology had been developed in Berkeley's time by Archbishop King and Bishop Browne. Although Berkeley did not question the good intentions of these two prelates, he believed that their theory tended ineluctably towards atheism. For if we can have no literal knowledge of God's attributes, then 'these Attributes themselves are in every intelligible Sense denied; and consequently the very Notion of God taken away, and nothing left but the Name, without any meaning annexed to it.' (Section XVII). An intelligible belief in God must affirm something more than that 'there is something in general without any proper Notion, though never so inadequate, of any of its Qualities or Attributes: for this may be Fate, or Chaos, or Plastic Nature, or anything else as well as God. Nor will it avail to say, [as King and Browne did say] there is something in this unknown Being analogous to Knowledge and Goodness... For this is in Fact to give up the Point in dispute between Theists and Atheists' (Section XVIII), since atheists never denied that *something* produced the world, or that the world has some cause or reason. Thus the atheistic dialogist, who is exploiting the view of the two prelates, concludes his speech significantly: 'and, not to be singular, we will use the Name [God] too, and so at once there is an end of Atheism' (Section XVIII).

The end of atheism has been achieved by the assertion of a God devoid of divine attributes. A new definition of God is produced such that everyone must be a theist; and a new definition of atheism is also devised such that nobody could count as an atheist. Thus Radicati argues. To be sure, his list of naturalistic alternatives to God is rather different. He mentions 'Nature, Eternal Being, Matter, universal Motion or Soul'; whereas Berkeley speaks of 'Fate, or Chaos or Plastic Nature'. But the result is the same: an axe has severed the root of religion; or as Berkeley puts it: if God's attributes are 'admitted in no particular Sense, ... nothing can be inferred from such an Account of God, about Conscience, or Worship, or Religion' (Section XVIII).

If Radicati's linguistic reform were accepted, the result would be not the elimination of atheism (as he and the dialogist in *Alciphron* ironically suggest) but the elimination of the pejorative word 'atheism'. By eliminating or suppressing 'atheism' Radicati is — like Gildon — protecting himself. For if rejecting the received conception of God is no longer tantamount to atheism, then Radicati — and those like him — need not suffer its odium.

IV. Hume's atheism

It is in this context that we must see Hume's two denials of atheism. Indeed, it is here that our historical efforts are likely to reap their richest reward, since Hume's statements are still the subject of lively discussion. One denial is to be found in his posthumous *Dialogues concerning natural religion* (1779), the other was orally delivered at the 'Synagogue' of Baron d'Holbach. In the *Dialogues* Hume writes: 'I next turn to the atheist, who, I assert, is only nominally so, and can never possibly be in earnest'.[12] The story of Hume's oral denial is told by Denis Diderot, who was present:

> The first time that M. Hume found himself at the table of the Baron [d'Holbach] he was seated beside him. I do not know for what purpose the English philosopher took it into his head to remark to the Baron that he did not believe in atheists, that he had never seen any. The Baron said to him: 'Count how many we are here.' We are eighteen. The Baron added: 'It is not too bad a showing to be able to point out to you fifteen at once: the three others have not made up their minds.'[13]

How are we to understand Hume's two denials of the existence of atheists? Some commentators have taken the second as evidence that he was not an atheist, apparently assuming that it was what it appears to be: a simple factual claim. Thus Ernest Mossner has recently written: 'From the biographical point of view, at least, it is certain that Hume did not regard himself as an atheist. Witness the confrontation in Paris with Baron d'Holbach and his atheistical club.'[14] But this interpretation is implausible , first because Hume's denial was in a long tradition of which he himself was aware. Secondly, if we take the denial in the *Dialogues* as expressing Hume's own opinion, then it conflicts with the oral denial. Most commentators would allow that the published denial does express Hume's opinion; for one thing it is spoken by Philo, who is generally allowed to be his spokesman. Now Hume added the passage which contains the denial some months prior to his death in 1776; whereas the conversation with d'Holbach and his friends had taken place in 1763. But then Hume *did* meet 15 convinced atheists some 13 years before his death; and one of these — d'Holbach — published, six years before Hume's death, a most formidable defence of speculative atheism. Thus the oral denial, rather than confirming the published one, is in conflict with it. So it seems unlikely that Hume was issuing a simple factual denial of atheists in the *Dialogues*. This conclusion is supported by an interesting passage in the Introduction to *The natural history of religion*, which appeared in 1757, six years before the conversation with d'Holbach. Hume first states that 'The belief of invisible, intelligent power has been very generally diffused over the human race, in all places and in all ages.' He then adds the qualification 'but it has neither perhaps been so universal as to admit no exception ... Some nations have been discovered, who entertained no sentiments of Religion, if Travellers and historians may be credited.'[15] Like Bayle and Locke, Hume is here contesting (although more cautiously) the anthropological denials that there are atheists. By implication he is admitting, albeit guardedly, the existence of atheists.

If there is any lingering doubt that Hume believed in the existence of real, and not merely nominal, atheists, it should be dispelled by his remark as reported by Boswell: 'One of the men ... of the greatest honour that I ever knew is my Lord Marischal, who is a downright atheist. I remember [Hume continues] I once hinted something as if I believed in the being of a God, and he would not speak to me for a week.'[16] No doubt there is an element of drollery in Hume's remark; and Boswell does indeed add that Hume 'said this with his usual grunting pleasantry'; yet it is clear evidence that Hume knew at least one downright atheist.

Thus far I have been arguing that Hume's denial in the *Dialogues* should not be read as expressing a simple disbelief in the existence of atheists. But the oral denial seems to be, if anything, even less straightforward. Why, for instance, should Hume declare, with no apparent external motivation, that he did not believe in atheists? And why should he weaken this first statement by saying that he had never *seen* any? I think Hume was being intentionally provocative. He believed that he was in the company of atheists and wished to provoke them to an avowal. This would help to explain his second, weaker, assertion about not having seen any atheists: it called for d'Holbach's triumphant retort. (It is a pity that we do not have Hume's reply.) I should like to go further, however, and suggest that Hume's opening gambit was rather like a Masonic handshake: an attempt to elicit a response from, and communicate with, someone whose secret identity he guesses. Uncoded, Hume's message — like that of Gildon and Radicati — amounted to a repudiation of the word 'atheism' and an affirmation of something close to atheism.

This suppression of 'atheism' is to be found in a complex form in the *Dialogues,* where Hume gradually but devastatingly strips the concept of God of religious meaning. It is because he has succeeded in eliminating God's essential qualities that he can conclude that there can be only nominal atheists. What atheist would deny that it is 'probable, that the principle which first arranged, and still maintains, order in the universe, bears ... some remote inconceivable analogy to the other operations of nature, and among the rest to the economy of human mind and thought'.[17] But if no atheist would deny this attenuated conception of God, which Hume presents towards the end of the *Dialogues,* then only 'atheism' has been eliminated. Hume's characterisation of God would not exclude Radicati's naturalistic surrogates or those mentioned by Berkeley. The conception of God is so vague and dilute that no past or present atheist would bother to attack it. Atheism is defeated and God is rescued: but both victories are only verbal.

Hume and Radicati can be seen as making use of what Charles Stevenson has called a persuasive definition.[18] They retain the emotive meanings of the words 'God' and 'atheism', but they alter their cognitive meanings. 'God' continues to have a positive emotive meaning, and 'atheism' a negative one. But fortunately on account of the new diluted and extended meaning of 'God', and the consequent restricted meaning of 'atheism', everyone now believes in the first and no one believes in the second.

I have described the denials of Radicati, Hume and Gildon as instances of the suppression of 'atheism'; but I do not mean to imply that this class is entirely clear-cut and homogenous. It is possible that Hume was concerned more to diffuse the conflict between theism and atheism than he was in exploding theism. He may have been trying to bury the debate by arguing that it was really a verbal one; yet within an eighteenth-century context this would still amount to an encouragement of atheism. For to impose a truce on two belligerents of vastly different strengths is tantamount to assisting the weaker party. After asserting that there were only nominal atheists he might with justice have added that there were only nominal theists.

I think that Radicati and Gildon were less interested in burying the debate than in burying theism; for their writings — especially Radicati's — are less agnostic than Hume's. Radicati's denial, like many of his other statements, is very indiscreet and all too transparent. This becomes especially clear if we compare it with the following passage from Richard Bentley's well-known Boyle lectures:

> I must beg to leave to think, both that the *Fool in the Text* [who said in his heart, there is no God] was a thorough confirmed *Atheist;* and that the modern disguised *Deists* do only call themselves so to decline the publick *Odium,* and resentment of the Magistrate, and that they cover the most arrant Atheism under the mask and shadow of a Deity; by which they understand no more than some eternal inanimate Matter, some universal Nature, and Soul of the World.[19]

For Bentley the disguised atheists *say*: 'God exists,' but 'understand no more than Matter ... Nature, and Soul.' Writing some 40 years later, Radicati removes much of atheism's deistic disguise. Now one need only 'admit a first cause under the name ... Nature ... Matter ... or Soul' in order to be considered a deist.

The denial of atheism was, I suspect, part of a strategy widely known to British free-thinkers. Another writer who doubts the existence of atheists is Lord Hervey. In *Some remarks on the minute philosopher* (London, 1732) he declares that 'there is not one atheist in a million free-thinkers, and perhaps not one atheist among them all' (pp. 34–5). Now as *Some remarks* is written — despite its apparent Christian fideism — from a free-thinking point of view, and as Lord Hervey had a reputation for being an unbeliever, we can be reasonably sure that his denial is an instance of the suppression of 'atheism'. But as we do not know very much about Lord Hervey's views on God and atheism, it is difficult to say whether he wished to encourage atheism or merely to bury the whole debate. I suspect the latter. A similar judgement seems appropriate in the case of Thomas Gordon, free-thinker and friend of Anthony Collins. In his imaginary 'Dialogue between Monsieur Jurieu and a Burgomaster of Rotterdam', Gordon has his spokesman, the Burgomaster, say: 'I never saw an Atheist,' and 'No Man who owns the Being of a God, is an Atheist; and I never knew any man that denied his Being: And till any Man does, it is false wicked, and barbarous, to call him an Atheist. As to the Idea of God ... I am sure, no Man can ascertain it.'[20] It will be noticed that the second of these denials has much in common with that of Radicati, and that the first is almost identical with the oral denial of Gordon's fellow Scotsman, Hume. That Gordon was aware of the emotive force of the word 'atheism', and wished to eliminate it, comes out most clearly in an essay he published on 21 October 1721. Here he speaks of 'the Odium of that Name' — 'atheist' — and then goes on to declare: 'For my own particular, I cannot think that there are any such Men; but if there were, I cannot think that Truth and Sobriety in an *Atheist* are worse than in another Man.'[21]

In Section XII of the *Enquiry concerning human understanding*, Hume points to a contradiction amongst 'the most religious philosophers': they dispute the existence of speculative atheists while, none the less, arguing against them. Yet, as he coyly observes, 'The knights errant, who wandered about to clear the world of dragons and giants, never entertained the least doubt with regard to the existence of these monsters.' In this chapter I have examined a related anomaly amongst the most irreligious philosophers, the putative 'dragons and giants'. They, too, dispute that there are atheistic monsters, and they do so, I suggest, to disarm the knights errant and to protect themselves.

V. Concluding remarks

Before passing on to Chapter 5 and the history of avowed atheism, it may be useful to make a few brief retrospective comments and also some further observations on the esoteric/exoteric distinction. In this and the previous chapters I have tried to bring to light two largely hidden movements of thought: the tendency to repress atheism and the esoteric expressions of unavowed atheism. To some the idea of a secret history may appear intrinsically suspect. But for this writer the revealing of an interesting secret is one of the best reasons for writing a book. I have examined the repressive denials and the esoteric strategy separately, but it seems natural to enquire whether there are any pertinent comparisons to be drawn between them. To begin with, they can both be described as movements of thought, of which the public mind was unaware. There was, to be sure, a difference in extent of unawareness. Not only was the repressive aim not a part of the public consciousness but it was also not a part of the individual consciousness. Whereas with the esoteric strategy it was only the public consciousness which was unaware of its actual meaning; for those individuals who employed the strategy were well aware of what they were insinuating. Both were faced, however, with the same fundamental problem: how to influence the public mind without allowing it to become aware that it was being influenced. In the case of those employing the repressive denials of atheism the problem was to prevent or inhibit atheism without appearing to take atheism seriously; for taking it seriously would confer strength and logical respectability on atheism. For the esoteric strategists, too, there was the (conscious) wish to influence, but probably also the need to give vent to their ideas and to communicate with others of a like mind. This could not be done openly without risk of legal persecution.

Some of the ways in which the two movements of thought went about solving their problems are also similar. The most striking similarity we have found is that they both use the same formula: there are no atheists. Another suggestive similarity between them is the presence of internal conflicts. The crucial clash revealed repression to us; and we were advised by Toland to suspect the existence of the esoteric when we found a writer contradicting himself. From conflicting verbal statements we inferred a hidden movement of thought. We inferred an esoteric atheistic strategy in Gildon and Collins, because their bare theistic avowals were belied by weighty argumentation that pointed to atheism. Similarly, where we found denials of the existence of atheism followed by strenuous argumentation against atheism, we reinterpreted the denials as having a repressive purpose. And where we found denials associated with argumentation in support of atheism — as in Radicati and Hume — we reinterpreted the denials as being suppressive of 'atheism'. Where the weight of argumentation (or emotion) is, there, all things being equal, we have placed conscious or unconscious purpose. We also proceeded in Chapter 1 in accordance with the maxim that one should judge the deeply unconscious by that which is less so; and a similar maxim can be employed in the case of the esoteric.

Some instances of the esoteric strategy are very transparent, as for example Collins's attack on the Messianic prophecies. All commentators agree that Collins's real purpose was to attack Christianity. But *why* are his pro-Christian avowals dismissed? The answer is that such avowals are slight and feeble in comparison with the destructive weight of his anti-Christian argumentation.

This is, if anything, even clearer in the case of a pamphlet entitled *A summary account of the deists religion* (London, 1745). The editor of this free-thinking anthology wastes no time in letting slip his esoteric disguise; for he notes on his title-page: 'N.B. This last PIECE [Essay on natural religion] contains the strongest arguments against the necessity and advantages of a DIVINE REVELATION, ever yet published.' And if the reader missed this message, the editor drives it home in his Preface. It is worth quoting some of his statements, because they provide an almost perfect concentrated illustration of the thinly disguised esoteric strategy in action:

> My great Desire ... of having the *Necessity* and *Advantage* of a Revelation *still more fully* prov'd, prevail'd on me thus *publickly* to invite some *Able* and *Masterly* Hand to the confutation of the seeming solid and indisputable *truths* of the *Essay on natural religion* [supposedly by Dryden. This essay, which is here reprinted, is] the most *formidable* Piece that *ever yet* appeared against the usefullness of the *Christian* Religion ... and, what is still more surprising, no one has hitherto endeavor'd to demonstrate those Arguments [to be false which have caused] more real hurt to Christianity ... than all the modern writers of infidelity put together ... I must confess myself *incapable* of answering the *forcible* arguments of Mr *Dryden's* Essay, yet I am not a jot *shaken* by it in my *Christian* Principles.[22]

This strategy clearly recalls Collins's statement of the atheistic argument from the eternity of matter, which I have examined in Chapter 3, Section V. Like the editor, Collins professes his good intentions: 'out of inclination I have to see the foundation of all religion established on demonstration ... I shall conclude this debate with an essay, showing a way how to demonstrate *the existence of God'*. Of course what we actually received in both cases is a powerful argument *against* the very thing they profess such concern to support. They then underline the strength of their destructive arguments, calling attention to the fact that the anti-religious arguments have not been answered. Finally they apologise for being unable themselves to answer the arguments, but they express the pious hope that some future champion of religion will be able to do so.

Admittedly the texts that I am taking for my model are aimed against revealed religion. Neither Collins's *Grounds* nor the *Summary* is atheistic. But this should hardly surprise us. The more subversive the attack the more disguise one should expect. And even the *Summary* is not lacking in disguise. Take for example this sentence from page 28: ' 'Tis want of proper *Application,* and not the *Insufficiency* of the Gospel *Evidence,* which is the Occasion of so many *Unbelievers*'; and in the Preface the editor earnestly recommends his readers to study such anti-deistical writers as Bishops Gibson, Conybeare, Sherlock, Butler and Synge. But then he writes: 'N.B. I have heard it *objected* by the Adversaries of *Christianity*, that few of their writings are fairly answer'd, but that many of their material objections are artfully evaded, or passed over with disdainful Assurance of their being too evident to require a confutation.' This is a particularly poignant observation from someone who is reprinting what he takes to be the 'most formidable piece ever yet appeared against Christianity' and one that has never been adequately answered.

Radicati's *Philosophical dissertation* is a noteworthy exception to this rule. Not only does Radicati cast the thinnest veil over his pantheistic materialism, but he openly advocates suicide and free love. His attitude to crime must also have been shocking to his contemporaries: 'I have proved [he writes, that men] are not blamable for the crimes they commit, since they are always forced either by education or habit to commit them' (p. 80).

Notes

1. *Twelve discourses*, p. 2 note; see above, Chapter 3.

2. *Philosophical dissertation*, p. 5. The pamphlet is said to be 'By a friend of truth'. Like the *Twelve discourses*, it was published in London. For an account of Radicati, see Margaret C. Jacob, *The radical enlightenment* (London, 1981), pp. 172–6.

3. The *Philosophical dissertion* was abusively criticised in the free-thinking periodical the *London Journal* (November 25 1732). The writer signs himself 'Socrates', and speaks of Radicati as a 'pretended free-thinker' and says: 'The worse superstition is better than this immoral philosophy.' On 16th December 1732 'Socrates' returned to a defence of free-thinking.

4. In his scarce edition of Langbain's *Lives and characters of the English dramatic poets,* 2nd edn (1698), Gildon records his lapse from Catholicism: 'In him [Gildon] there was an Example how difficult a thing it is, to overcome the Prejudice of Education; for I am assured that it cost him about Seven Years Study and Contest, before he could entirely shake off all Opinions that had grown up with him from a Child [i.e. his Catholicism] ... I have heard him say, that the first Book that gave him the greatest conviction was, the *Discourse* of the late pious and ingenious *Dr Tillotson,* ... against *Transubstantiation,* lent him by a Lawyer, that at the same time cheated him of about Four Hundred Pounds, tho he made way for the Peace of Mind that this Book first opened the Door to' (pp. 174–5).

5. See *Oracles of reason* (1693), p. 178. In *Essay* I.iv.8, Locke had asserted the existence of atheists on the basis of reports in travel books.

6. *The oracles of reason*, p. 182. The text in Blount's *Miscellaneous works* is the same.

7. *The Deist's manual,* pp. 40–1. The work is in the form of a dialogue.

8. Blount's letter is entitled: 'To his Friend Mr Gildon, concerning the World's Age, beginning and end'; the first half contains a translation of Ocellus Lucanus' *De univers natura.*

9. See pp. ix–xi. Joseph Trapp calls attention to a similar strategy in his *Thoughts upon the four last things,* 2nd edn (London, 1745), p. 97.

10. 'To R.B.', p. 180.

11. See above, Chapter 3, Section II.

12. See Hume's *Dialogues concerning natural religion* (Oxford, 1935), edited and introduced by Norman Kemp Smith, p. 269. According to Kemp Smith the passage in which the denial occurs was added by Hume in his 1776 revision of the *Dialogues*, pp. 119–21. In two other places in Part XII Hume comes close to denying the existence of atheists: 'A purpose, an intention, a design strikes everywhere the most careless, the most stupid thinker; and no man can be so hardened in absurd systems, as at all times to reject it' (p. 264). Here Hume invokes the constancy criterion; in the next quotation he refers to those who 'doubt of a Supreme Intelligence', and says: 'Could I meet with one of this species (who, I thank God, are very rare) I would ask him' (p. 266). These remarks are spoken by Philo, and were written in 1751 or 1761.

13. Quoted in E. Mossner's *Life of David Hume* (Oxford, 1970), p. 483. For a searching examination of the story, see A.C. Kors, *D'Holbach coterie* (Princeton, 1976), Ch. 2.

14. 'Hume and the Legacy of the Dialogues', in *David Hume: bicentenary papers*, G.P. Morice (Edinburgh, 1977), p. 22; also see R. Wollheim, *Hume on religion* (2nd impression, 1966), p. 28; Terence Penelhum, *Hume* (London, 1975), p. 166; Kemp Smith in his edition of Hume's *Dialogues*, p. 48; and T.E. Jessop, 'Hume's Limited Scepticism', in *Revue Internationale de Philosophie* (1976), pp. 25–6.

15. See *Essays and treatises* (1777), vol. 2, pp. 401–2.

16. See *Boswell in extremes: 1776–1778* (London, 1971), edited by C.M. Weis and F.A. Pottle; p. 14. In his *Treatise of Human Nature* (1739), Hume speaks of 'the atheism of *Spinoza*' (Book I, part iv, section v).

17. See Hume's *Dialogues*, ed. Kemp Smith, pp. 269–70.

18. Stevenson, *Facts and Values* (New Haven, 1963), Ch. 3.

19. *Eight sermons preach'd at Robert Boyle's lecture*, 6th edn (1735), p. 9.

20. The 'Dialogue' is printed by Gordon in vol. iii of the *Independent Whig*, 3rd edn (1752); the two denials are on pp. 27 and 45.

21. *Cato's letters: or, essays on liberty*, 5th edn (1748), vol. 2, p. 114.

22. Preface; on this essay, see my 'A disputed Deistic classic', *The Library* (6th series, vol. 8, no. 1, March 1984), pp. 58–9.

5

The Birth of Avowed Atheism: 1782–1797

I. The first declaration

In the foregoing three chapters I have tried to uncover covert atheism — either as it was disguised by esoteric presentation, confined (as Richard Bentley put it) to 'the private study and select conversation', or condemned retrospectively by apostate free-thinkers. I now turn to the history of overt atheism in Britain, and to the first avowedly atheistic book which was the *Answer to Dr. Priestley's letters to a philosophical unbeliever* (London, 1782).[1] My aim here is to rescue this pioneer book from its undeserved obscurity; and one reason why its obscurity is undeserved is that it highlights how extraordinarily recent the birth of avowed atheism is. This pregnant but unnoticed fact should be of considerable interest to atheists and non-atheists alike. Atheists should be stimulated by the realisation that their position has had comparatively little time to prove itself or even show itself; while non-atheists may take comfort in knowing that, though atheism now seems entrenched, its power of survival has by no means been demonstrated.

Various factors have tended to obscure the comparative infancy of avowed atheism. Thus it is hard for us to believe that a position which is now so influential and powerful has had such a slight history. We may have been swayed by the frequently expressed opinion that all really interesting theories have an extensive history. In our specific case, this feeling has probably been reinforced by historians who have tended to confuse *accusations* of atheism with *professions* of atheism. Historians seemed to have assumed that with so much polemical smoke there must have been some atheistic fire. There is another way in which the smoke of religious apologists has tended to *create* a history of atheism. Theological writers in the seventeenth and eighteenth centuries frequently attempted to belittle their opponents by casting doubts on their originality.[2] This has created the impression that even the most novel attacks on religion had been made long ago, and were already old-fashioned. We find something of this tendency in the early review of the *Answer to Priestley* in the *Monthly Review* of 1783:

> We shall not trouble ourselves or the reader with a detail of this writer's arguments [asserts the reviewer]. He goes over the ground of the French atheist *Mirabeau*. To the learned they are already well known: as are also their confutation. There is no end of idle cavilling.[3]

The reviewer is undoubtedly referring to the *System of nature,* which was then thought to be by Mirabeau. The author of the *Answer* is quite explicit about his debt to this first work of avowed atheism; but the reviewer has little justification in giving the impression that the *Answer* is a trite repetition of the *System*.

Before examining the *Answer* and its claims to fame, I should emphasise the following terminological proviso. I am not claiming that the *Answer* was the first atheistic book, but that it was the first *avowedly* atheistic book. For, as I have argued, there were a number of crypto-atheistic works, of which Hobbes's *Leviathan* (1651) may be the earliest.

There may also have been authors who sincerely believed that they were *not* atheists but who, all the same, wrote atheistic books. Spinoza's *Ethics* is, in my opinion, an example of one such atheistic book. I would argue that the pantheism of the *Ethics* amounts to atheism, even though Spinoza himself would have denied this. Spinoza seems to have believed that he was not rejecting the theist's conception of God but only correcting it. But since by 'God' he meant the whole universe rigidly determined, one might well regard such pantheism as a species of atheism. Just as there are various kinds of theism, for example Judaism and Islam, so there are different species of atheism; it may be materialistic, pantheistic or idealistic.

But it is not such vexed questions that I shall be concerned with here. For it is far easier to say that a writer is an *avowed* atheist. All that is required is that he should claim to disbelieve in the existence of God and/or apply to himself the label 'atheist'. This is what we find in the case of the *Answer*. In the Prefatory Address the writer states: 'as to the question whether there is such an existent Being as an atheist, to put that out of all manner of doubt, I do declare upon my honour that I am one' (p. xvii).

I would not wish to claim that I have provided an uncontroversial criterion for identifying avowed atheism. There will, I expect, always be exceptions, borderline cases, and so on. Indeed, one early critic of the *Answer* even doubted whether the above avowal was sufficient evidence of avowed atheism. In Chapter 1, Section XII, I suggested that this critic's doubts were part of the tendency to repress atheism, and that the almost histrionic manner of our author's avowal of atheism indicates his awareness of the repressive tendency and his wish to overcome it once and for all. He seems to recognise that no previous British writer has hitherto proclaimed himself an atheist. This is made even clearer in a letter he had sent to Priestley prior to the publication of the *Answer*. In this letter, printed in his Postscript with the date 23 October 1781, he solicits Priestley's protection against possible persecution resulting from the publication of his atheistic book:

> Of you I may certainly expect, that you will promise to use your influence, as well with lawyers as ecclesiastics, not to stir up a persecution against a poor atheist *in case there should be one found in the kingdom, which people in general will not admit to be possible.* (p. 61, my italics)

And in his reply to the *Answer* Priestley takes himself to be dealing with the first atheist to proclaim his atheism in print. He writes: 'For my own part, I rejoice that a *professed atheist* has thought proper to stand forth in defence of his principles.'[4]

My thesis that the *Answer* contains the first published avowal of atheism in Britain is further supported by the fact that standard histories of atheism and free-thought mention no earlier book.[5] Finally the present writer has claimed, in papers published in 1975 and 1978, this distinction for the *Answer*; and this claim has not been challenged.[6]

II. Hammon and Turner

But who, exactly, has the distinction of being the first to publish his atheism? The *Answer* was initially thought to be the work of a William Hammon, the signatory of the prefatory address and of the letter to Priestley in the Postscript. Priestley in his reply to the *Answer* casts doubt on Hammon's authorship: 'Your Prefatory Address [Priestley writes] is dated Oxford-street, no. 418, but at that place no such person [called Hammon] could be heard of' (p. 243). Priestley had noticed that Hammon's letter had a Liverpool postmark. However, 'No person of your name could be found in Liverpool, though several persons, some of them my particular friends, and at my request, made diligent enquiry concerning you' (p. 242). Priestley seems to have persisted in thinking that Hammon was probably a pseudonym; for in his *Memoirs* he writes: 'The first part [of the *Letters to a philosophical unbeliever, 1780*] being replied to by a person who *called* himself Mr Hammon, I wrote a reply to his piece, which has hitherto remained unanswered.'[7]

The earliest direct denial of Hammon's authorship, and the first alternative attribution of the *Answer*, was made in a long note to the American edition of the *Memoirs of Priestley* (1805). This note was penned by Priestley's friend, Thomas Cooper, then President Judge of the fourth district of Pennsylvania, who named Matthew Turner as the author. Since Turner is generally credited with the authorship of the *Answer*, and as Cooper's note contains the fullest single account of him — I shall quote it in its entirety:

Dr Turner was a physician at Liverpool: among his friends a professed Atheist. It was Dr Turner who wrote the reply to Dr Priestley's Letters to a Philosophical Unbeliever, under the feigned name of Hammon. He was in his day a good practical chemist. I believe it was Dr Turner who first invented, or at least brought to tolerable perfection, the art of copying upon glass, by striking impressions with a coloured solution of silver, and fixing them on the glass by baking on an iron plate in a heat sufficient to incorporate the solution with the glass. Some of them are very neatly performed, producing transparent copies in a bright yellow upon the clear glass. Dr Turner was not merely a Whig, but a republican. In a friendly debating society at Liverpool, about the close of the American war, he observed, in a reply to a speaker who had been descanting on the honour Great Britain had gained during the reign of his present Majesty, that it was true we had lost the *terra firma* of the thirteen colonies in America, but we ought to be satisfied with having gained in return, by the generalship of Dr Herschel, a *terra incognita* of a much greater extent *in nubibus*.[8]

Cooper was himself a chemist, republican and free-thinker, as well as a former resident of Manchester; hence he may have been acquainted with Turner. He does not, however, offer any support for his attribution, which is, I think, the basis for all subsequent attributions of the *Answer* to Turner. It is likely to have been behind Richard Carlile's statement in his (second) edition of the *Answer*, published in London in 1826. In his 'Note by the Publisher', he writes: 'Though the Author has put forth Hammon as his real name, it has been questioned; and the authorship attributed to the late Mr Turner, a Surgeon of Liverpool.'[9]

While I do not wish to impugn entirely the confident testimony of Cooper and Carlile, I must point out certain difficulties in their attribution, the most important of which is that despite their suggestion to the contrary, Hammon never claimed to have written the body of the *Answer*. He calls himself the 'editor' of the work, and speaks of a friend as its author. Hammon tells us that he had sent Priestley's *Letters to a philosophical unbeliever* to this friend, and that it was his answer to it which turned Hammon into a convinced atheist (p. x). Neither Cooper nor Carlile appears to be aware of the fact that, at least prima facie, the *Answer* was the work of two writers. The book can be divided into four parts, as follows:

(1) Advertisement, pp. vi–vii. Unsigned but almost certainly by the editor, i.e. Hammon.
(2) Prefatory Address, pp. viii–xxxiv. Signed by Hammon, who calls himself the editor.
(3) Body of the work, pp. 1–59. Unsigned, but probably the work of Turner.
(4) Postscript, pp. 60–1. Containing a letter to Priestley signed by Hammon.

On the basis of internal evidence, such as style, I am inclined to the view that there actually were two authors; e.g. the writer of (2), unlike that of (3), had a fondness for Latin quotation. I am even more inclined to accept that Turner was the author of the body of the *Answer*. For, apart from Cooper's confident assertion, Hammon's description of his friend corresponds with what we know of Turner. Of himself and his friend Hammon writes: 'we are so proud in our singularity of being atheists that we hardly open our lips in company, when the question is started for fear of making converts' (p. xvi); but his friend is 'neither ashamed nor afraid of that [title] of an Unbeliever' (p. viii). This may be compared with Cooper's assertion that 'among his friends [Turner] was a professed atheist'.

There is another even more interesting link between Turner and Hammon's friend. In his *Memoirs* Priestley informs us that in 1765 he 'knew little of *Chemistry*, and had in a manner no idea on the subject before he attended a course of lectures, delivered in the academy of Warrington, by Dr Turner, of Liverpool'.[10] Turner and Priestley were probably acquainted by 1762 or 1763; for in a letter of 16 March 1762, in which Turner agrees to give a course of lectures at the Warrington Academy, he says:

> It would give me much pleasure to have your [John Seddon's, Secretary of the Academy] Company during the Courses, as all the Gentlemen there are strangers to me, except Mr Priestley and yourself. I greatly admire Mr Priestley, and am certain any school must flourish that has such teachers in it.[11]

This evidence of a personal connection between Priestley and Turner fits in with an equally intriguing bit of information Hammon offers about his friend. His friend, according to Hammon, believed that 'he was the person whom Priestley meant to address, if [he] had a particular person in view' as the philosophical unbeliever (p. viii). Finally, as I noted above, the letter Priestley received from Hammon (and which was printed in the Postscript) was sent from Turner's home town of Liverpool.

I suggest, therefore, that we accept the attribution of Cooper and Carlile, and regard Turner as the author of the body of the *Answer*. It is more difficult to know exactly what to do with the rest of the work, and with the shadowy William Hammon. For convenience I shall regard Hammon as the author of the remaining three parts of the *Answer*.

Our knowledge of Turner, though extremely limited, suggests that he was an extraordinary man. He was a founder-member of the Liverpool Academy, in which he lectured on 'anatomy and the theory of forms'.[12] Even more interesting is his connection with Josiah Wedgwood. According to Eliza Meteyard, Turner rendered a number of important services to Wedgwood, and hence to English pottery. Not only was he a valued physician to Wedgwood, but he also 'supplied Wedgwood with several receipts for varnishes and other appliances of great utility in his manufacture' (p. 301). But his greatest service was to introduce Wedgwood to the designer Thomas Bentley, since it was their collaboration which won for Wedgwood pottery its extraordinary success and unique reputation. Turner was also a pioneer in medical research. In his *An account of the extraordinary medicinal fluid, called aether* (1743) — his only other known publication — he played an important part in establishing the place of ether in medical treatment.[13] These facts seem to constitute our hard knowledge of Turner. We do not, for example, know exactly either when he was born or when he died. He is characterised as 'a man of unusual attainments. A good surgeon, a skillful anatomist, a practiced chemist, a draughtsman, a classical scholar, and a ready wit'.[14] To this list of accomplishments we can now add: an author of the first professedly atheistic book published in Britain. It is this book which I shall now examine.

III. The *Answer's* atheism

It may seem surprising that the *Answer* was written in opposition to Priestley's *Letters*; for Priestley himself was regarded as a free-thinker, and he certainly suffered for his unorthodoxy. One explanation is that the authors of the *Answer* were opposed to Priestley's brand of rationalism in religion precisely because they had so much in common with it. Perhaps even more curious is the claim in the Advertisement to the *Answer* that 'Revealed knowledge is not descanted upon; therefore Christians at least need take no offence' (p. iv). But how, one might ask, could a defence of atheism *not* give offence to Christians? In fact, as was pointed out by Priestley and an early reviewer, this disclaimer was insincere. Priestley described it as 'manifestly disingenuous',[15] and the reviewer, more bitterly, as 'This low subterfuge in base equivocation'.[16] But what, one might still wonder, could be gained by such equivocation? The answer is: evasion of legal prosecution for blasphemy. To those who framed the blasphemy laws it had seemed that natural religion did not require protection: for who (they must have thought) would seriously assert atheism?[17] Hence, doubting the existence of God was legally less dangerous than doubting the miracles of Jesus or the Athanasian doctrine of the Trinity.[18] As Priestley nicely puts it: 'at this day a *heretic* is, I should think, in more danger than an *unbeliever*' (p. 240). It is this loophole which Hammon is trying to slip through when he remarks: 'The religion established in this country is not the religion of Nature, but the religion of Moses and Jesus, with whom the writer has nothing to do' (p. vi). In exploiting this loophole Hammon was following in the footsteps of Collins and Hume; and he in turn would be followed by others, including Shelley in the *Refutation of deism* (1814) and Grote and Bentham in the *Analysis of the influence of natural religion* (1822). The formula was this: in order with impunity to deny God one must appear to be affirming Christianity — and Christianity of an extremely fideistic or fundamentalist variety.[19]

The Prefatory Address — dated 1 January 1782 — is less an answer to Priestley than a general discussion of problems connected with atheism. Hammon makes a number of acute observations; for example: 'If upon sick beds or in dying moments men revert to their old weaknesses and superstitions, their fall off may afford triumph to religionists; for my part I care not so much for the opinion of sick and dying men, as of those who at the time are strong and healthy' (p. xxv). As might be expected from this, Hammon is a militant rationalist. 'My faith is in reasoning,' he writes. And he even regards his rationalism as having primacy over the peace of society: 'I have a right to truth, and to publish truth, let society suffer or not suffer by it. That society which suffers by truth should be otherwise constituted' (pp. xix–xx). This radical assertion may suggest revolution, but unlike most British radicals following the French Revolution, Hammon makes his appeal to the learned and not to the masses (p. xxxiv).

Turner's answer to Priestley can be divided into three parts: introductory remarks, quotations from Priestley, and critical observations. In the first part he considers, among other things, whether any theist would say that he would *not* behave morally were he to become convinced that God did not exist. If the theist would not give up acting morally, then why should he maintain — as theists generally do — that morality requires a belief in God (p. 2)? In the second part of his answer Turner prints some 65 quotations from Priestley's *Letters to a philosophical unbeliever* arranged under the following headings: 'Truisms', 'False Assertions', 'Absurdities', and 'Inadmissible or Inconclusive'. The quotations fill eleven pages (from page 3 to page 14) and are followed by a section entitled 'Observations' which begins: 'Dr Priestley will hardly doubt, after this collection [of quotations] from his work that it has at least been read before it is attempted to be answered' (p. 14).

Turner then goes on to criticise Priestley's defence of the existence of God. He argues (pp. 15-18 and 34) that Priestley's proof depends on the unsupported and unjustifiable premise that the universe is an effect. But once the universe is viewed as eternal and absolute, there is no need to regard it as a dependent effect which requires a divine cause. Turner then contrasts the intelligibility of reasoning upon the universe with Priestley's own admission that 'we cannot properly speak' of an 'uncaused Being' (p. 16). 'Is not', Turner asks, this admission by Priestley 'alone an argument of there being no such thing? [For] this discovered Deity is allowed to be that of which we can have no idea. So far at least it is allied to the impossible.'[20]

Turner draws attention to many of the traditionally-recognised weak points of theism. He dwells (pp. 20–3) on the problem of evil, e.g. 'That lesser evils exist instead of greater is indeed but a poor proof in the favour of the benevolence of an all-powerful Being' (p. 20). He accuses religion of being not only unnecessary but also dangerous to morality (pp. 25–7 and 43–4). Theism may be able to engender practical theism in the sense of religious rites, but not practical theism in the sense of moral behaviour. It is primarily human laws that promote morality. 'But it will be said', he writes, that 'those who commit crimes are atheists at the time at least they do so'. He responds to this curious dogma in a typically empiricistic spirit: 'To support still the efficacy of religion in making men virtuous is to oppose metaphysical reasoning to the truth of fact: it is like the philosopher denying motion, and being refuted by one of his scholars walking across the room.'[21]

Turner also calls attention to the 'wish' aspect of religion (see pages 20, 25, 47, and quotation 27 on page 14). A good specimen of his critical skill can be seen in the following encounter with Priestley on the problem of pain. According to Priestley, pain does not qualify God's goodness because 'pain is necessary for happiness'. To this Turner replies:

> But if pain is, as he says, in this world necessary for happiness, why will it not still be necessary hereafter? He answers, because by that time we shall have experienced pain enough for a future supply of happiness. If it is objected why have we not pain enough by the time each of us are twenty or thirty years of age, instead of waiting 'till our deaths at so many different ages? He can only finish his argument by allowing that the ways of God are inscrutable to man.[22]

Among Turner's other specific criticisms of Priestley's theism is an *ad hominem* argument against the omnipresence of God (p. 29) and the following *reductio ad absurdum* against Priestley which is similar to one we found (Chapter 3, Section V) Collins using against Clarke:

> If nothing can begin to exist of itself or by the energy of material nature, it is more consistent to allow a plurality of Deities, than one immediate Deity. An equality in a plurality

of Deities might be objectionable. But that is not at all
necessary, rather the contrary; and so was the Pagan theory,
which is not so absurd as the modern one. This universe or
mundane system may be the work of one hand, another of
another, and so on. (p. 35)

Why, in short, stop at a *deus ex machina*; why not suppose *dei ex
machinis?*

One of Turner's criticisms of the idea of a first cause, as against
an infinite regress of causes, is reminiscent of Kant's discussion of
this subject in the *Critique of pure reason* (1781). 'What is there more
[asks Turner] which hinders a series of finite causes to be carried
back *ad infinitum*, than that the reasoner or contemplator of the course
of nature is tired?'[23] But it is most unlikely that Turner would have
read Kant's *Critique*. The works he clearly did read, and which
greatly influenced his atheistic position, were Hume's *Dialogues
concerning natural religion* (1779) and essay 'Of miracles', and
d'Holbach's *System of nature*, which Turner mistakenly believes to be
the work of Helvetius. From the *System* Turner quotes long passages
in translation (pp. 53–9) and one untranslated sentence (p. 49). [24]
He praises Hume's cheerful death (p. 27); endorses his views on
motion and matter (pp. 32–3), and theological analogy (p. 34); and
quotes the essential argument from the 'Of miracles' (p. 52).

Turner's positive atheistic metaphysics may also have been influenced by these two heroes of the Enlightenment. In general,
however, he is guarded in his positive account. He emphasises the
role of experience. He is even prepared to allow the possibility of a
future life within his atheistic system (pp. 10, 24–5).[25] He thinks
that there is design in the universe and that the atheist has no difficulty in accounting for it (p. 28). His view of the world tends to
be materialistic and pantheistic. He provides an interesting
naturalistic account (pp. 41–2) of the origin of species, an account
clearly influenced by the *System of nature* (vol. I, Chapter 6) and,
perhaps, by Hume's *Dialogues*, Section VIII.

For all its inauguration of overt atheism, the *Answer* had a relatively
undistinguished reception. It was criticised at some length by
Priestley, and reviewed in three contemporary journals. It was (as I
have mentioned) reprinted by Carlile in 1826. It was also reprinted
in 1833 by John Brooks, 421 Oxford Street (London); and extracts
from it were published in an obscure free-thinking anthology entitled *The law of reason, embracing the subjects of utility of discussion*
(London, 1831), pp. 113–19. Priestley's reply is restrained and often

perceptive; the review in the *European Magazine* (of August 1782, pp. 122–3) is polite. The notices in the *New Annual Register* of 1782 and the *Monthly Review* of 1783 are abusive.

This relatively slight reaction to the *Answer* calls for some explanation or, at least, wonder. For it is surely odd that a doctrine that was so long dreaded, and whose very possibility was often doubted, should create so little stir on its first being pronounced. One possible explanation is that, whether consciously or unconsciously, the believers felt that the best way to damn such a book was by silence or faint abuse. They bared their teeth not in an angry cry but in a more effective yawn.

IV. *Watson refuted*

In the fourth and final edition of his *History of freethought*, J.M. Robertson calls attention to 'the *Watson refuted* (1796) of Samuel Francis, M.D., who makes the first explicit avowal of atheism in English controversy' (p. 797). As we have seen, Robertson is mistaken: the first such avowal was made 14 years earlier in the *Answer*. Robertson's statement is also misleading, for *Watson refuted* does not contain an 'explicit avowal' of atheism; there is nothing in it as explicit as that in the *Answer*. There is no denial of God's existence; nor does Francis avow himself an atheist. The closest he comes to an atheistic avowal is in the following passages:

> I differ in my philosophical opinions from Mr. Paine; my principles extend so much further than his, that I suspect I come under the class which you [Watson] are pleased to call madmen...[26]

> The remainder of your [Watson's] first letter contains observations to which I perfectly accede. Your conclusion against Thomas Paine is perfectly fair. Any apparent deviation from moral justice in the world must prove as much against the goodness of God, as a similar inconsistency in his immediate actions and commands proves against revealed religion. My Lord, we are in the abyss of error; your question with Thomas Paine is about the comparative absurdity of the two opinions. The deistical notions of your adversary do not agree with his reasonable tenets; but I readily grant, that, to a religious person, nothing is incredible; and that the greater the incon-

sistencies, the more sublime the system. But let me ask your Lordship, what you conclude against one, who, like myself, is not a Deist?[27]

In the first passage Francis states that his position is far more extreme than Paine's deism; and he suggests that it would be regarded as atheism, as atheists were often said to be madmen.[28] The second passage is also important because it gives us some idea of the particular form his atheism may have taken. Here Francis is commenting upon an argument for revealed religion which is generally associated with Bishop Butler.[29] Deists, such as Tindal and, later, Paine, had denied that the Bible could be the word of God because some of the actions and commands of the biblical God violate our ideas of moral justice, for example, God's commanding the Jews to massacre the innocent Canaanite children. But against this Bishop Watson argued that we find comparable violations of moral justice in nature, which, according to Paine, is the only true word of God. In his *Apology for the Bible*, Watson asks Paine:

Why do you not maintain it to be repugnant to His moral justice, that He should suffer crying or smiling infants to be swallowed up by an earthquake, drowned by an inundation, consumed by fire, starved by famine, or destroyed by a pestilence? The word of God is in perfect harmony with His work; crying or smiling infants are subjected to death in both [the Bible and nature].[30]

Of course, adds Watson:

I am far from being guilty of the impiety of questioning the existence of the moral justice of God, as proved either by natural or revealed religion. What I contend for is shortly this — that you have no right, in fairness of reasoning, to urge any apparent deviation from moral justice as an argument against revealed religion, because you do not urge an equally apparent deviation from it, as an argument against natural religion: you reject the former, and admit the latter, without considering that, as to you your objection, they must stand or fall together.[31]

Francis accepts this argument from parity of reasoning, but he rejects Watson's conclusion. In his view natural and revealed religion *fall together*. He believes that the cause or causes of the world 'neither possess benevolence, nor any other passion' (p. 13). But in saying this Francis does not say that *all* meaningful conceptions of God must be rejected. A God that was not good or loving might still count as God, for He might still possess various intellectual and natural attributes. However, the drift of Francis's argument is that there is no tenable conception of God; and his specific remarks on atheism lend support to the supposition that he was an atheist:

> I am glad you have no recourse to the silly causes of atheism, as given by that illustrious dreamer, Plato. The world has too long been imposed upon by ridiculous attempts to vilify atheists and show their non-existence. That name has been a cant word, like Jacobin in France, and the Whig and Tory in England (pp. 13–14).

Here we can easily detect a certain sympathy for atheists. Even more noteworthy is Francis's resistance to the (repressive) denial of atheists, which he associates with their vilification. Of interest also is his criticism of those who magnify what I have called unthinking atheism. As we have seen in Chapter 1, the repressive denial was often effected by assimilating theoretical atheism to unthinking atheism.

Most of Francis's book is taken up with defending Paine's criticism of the Bible against Watson's apology for it. Robertson refers to Francis as 'A much more learned man than Paine, he grants that several of Mr Paine's objections are not valid and often trifling [and that] the chief proofs against the genuineness of the Pentateuch have been overlooked by Mr Paine. [Francis] makes short work of most of Watson's apologetic, but does not add very considerably to Paine's case' (Ibid). Because *Watson refuted* is a work on revealed rather than natural religion, our understanding of Francis's atheism is confined to the passages I have quoted. His primary contribution to the development of atheism is that he is the first to call Butler's bluff, so to speak, and reject both natural and revealed religion. The deists had been unwilling to do this.

We know virtually nothing about Francis, apart from the fact that he was, like Turner, a physician. Of course, it is not out of the question that 'Samuel Francis, M.D.' was a pseudonym. If it was not, Francis must have been a daring man to sign his name to such a radical work, even granting that he never explicitly professes himself an atheist. A question can also be raised about the date of publication of *Watson refuted*. Robertson gives the date as 1796, but this is probably because Francis signs his Advertisement 'London 15 Aug. 1796'. I have not been able to find a copy of the first edition of the pamphlet. I have seen only the Carlile reprint of 1819 — which does not mention the publication date; and it is to this reprint that Robertson also refers. The pamphlet may have been published in the following year, 1797. There appears to be no other work either signed by Francis or attributed to him; although he tells us in the Advertisement that he had to interrupt work on another book in order to write *Watson refuted*.

V. Metaphysical atheism

It is possible, though unlikely, that the pamphlet upon which Francis had been working was *An investigation of the essence of the Deity*, which was published in London late in 1797. Like *Watson refuted*, this pamphlet is by someone who is theologically more extreme than a deist. This is evident from the subtitle, which runs: *'with a word or two by way of postscript, to the professors of deism in refutation of their doctrine that the Bible is not the word of God.'* Like Francis, he never openly avows himself an atheist, but his atheism is at least as explicit — and I think more so — than that of Francis. The *Investigation* is far more important in the development of atheism than Francis's book, partly because it contains the first direct and self-contained defence of atheism. It is not, like the *Answer* and *Watson refuted*, a polemical work directed against a person or book. In the *Investigation* few names are even mentioned. One reason for believing that Francis was *not* the author of the *Investigation* is that it is a short work — a mere 46 pages — whereas *Watson refuted* is over 100 pages in the 1819 edition; hence it is unlikely that a writer would interrupt work on a 46 page pamphlet in order to begin work on a book of more than twice that size. The *Investigation* is signed 'Scepticus Britannicus', and as there seems to be no information concerning the actual identity of the writer, I shall refer to him as 'Scepticus'. Scepticus signs his pamphlet from 'Greenwich Dec. 10, 1797'; it was printed for T.S. Billopp. The *Investigation* seems virtually unknown. It is not noticed by Robertson. Nor was it ever reprinted by Carlile or any other free-thought publisher. This may have been on account of Scepticus's highly critical attitude to the deists. He is far more critical of the deists than Francis; and although Paine is not mentioned by name in the *Investigation*, there are clear allusions to him.

Scepticus has implicit faith in the utility of truth: 'the more we examine it, the more we shall be convinced of its authenticity, and the greater will be our admiration of it' (p. 7). On the other hand, he regards tradition as a danger. As he wittily observes:

> Man receives as little comfort from a persuasion that he has followed a like system of opinions with his forefathers, as the unfortunate culprit, who under the gallows is told, that many others have suffered the same fate before him. (p. 10)

The traditional belief which he is primarily concerned to explode is belief in the existence of God. This is not to say that he flatly denies the existence of God, or all conceptions of God. Indeed, he affirms the existence of a material God equivalent to the whole world: *'The Deity is material* ... In fine, ... the *universe, or the whole material world, is God'* (p. 42). His arguments are directed against the God of Christianity and deism, whom he calls (perhaps following d'Holbach) the 'theological Deity' (p. 25).

Scepticus would seem to be the first explicit pantheistic materialist. Spinoza's pantheism, although it was frequently misunderstood and condemned as materialistic, was neither materialistic nor immaterialistic. For Spinoza, God or nature is both an extended and thinking being; indeed, God has all possible attributes. I know of at least one instance in the eighteenth century of an openly immaterialistic version of pantheism; this was elaborated by a Scottish free-thinker, William Dudgeon, in a series of published letters to John Jackson. [32] In Chapters 3 and 4 I have argued that Collins and Radicati, were pantheistic materialists, but this was not a position that they openly professed. However, whether it is esoterically adhered to, as I have argued it was with Collins and Radicati, or exoterically as we find with Scepticus, pantheistic materialism is even more plainly atheistic than Spinoza's pantheism.

Scepticus's atheism clearly manifests itself in his critique of the theological deity, who is supposed to be 'omnipotent, incomprehensible, immaterial, invisible and immutable ' (p. 19). According to Scepticus the conception of such a deity is 'contradictory and inconsistent' (p. 26), a conclusion he attempts to demonstrate in his fourth chapter. God is said to be omnipotent, but this is in conflict with His apparent inability to prevent, among other things, Adam from sinning (pp. 19–20). God is supposed to be omnipresent, but he is also said to be distinct from the material world He is alleged to have created (pp. 20–1). God is supposed to be incomprehensible, and yet believers say, and wish to say, a great deal about Him (pp. 21–2). God is also supposed to be immaterial; and as Scepticus's critical comments on this attribute are especially instructive I shall quote his own words:

> If the Deity possesses this attribute, how are we to believe that he created this material world? It is an indubitable axiom that cause and effect are analogous; that they bear relation the one to the other. Now, what relation can a spirit (for such the theological Christian God is) bear to matter? or how can it act upon matter? In doing this, would it not cease to be immaterial? (p. 22)

Scepticus also tries to show that there is similar internal conflict in the attribute of immutability; for God is frequently said to change His mind (p. 25). Moreover, 'If the God of the Christians is immutable, how truly ridiculous it is in them to pray to him to alter his intentions' (p. 25).

Scepticus's concentrated attempt to show that the theological God is 'contradictory and inconsistent' represents an important achievement in British atheism. For the first time we find a non-empiricistic *a priori* approach to the non-existence of God. Unlike Hammon, Turner and (as we shall see) Shelley, Scepticus is essentially an intellectualist: his method is conceptual rather than empirical. He is concerned to point out inconsistencies and contradictions in the theist's conception of God, rather than pointing out weaknesses in the argument from design. His argument against the immateriality of God (quoted above) is of particular interest for it reveals the influence of Spinoza. The 'indubitable axiom' at the basis of Scepticus's argument is surely a conflation of axioms iv and v of Spinoza's *Ethics*, Part 1:

> (iv) The knowledge of an effect depends on and involves the knowledge of its cause.
> (v) Things that have nothing in common with one another also cannot be understood through one another; or the concept of the one does not involve the concept of the other.[33]

These axioms are also implicitly used by Scepticus against the theory that matter was originally (or is by nature) inert, and that God communicated motion to it. Against this generally accepted theistic theory Scepticus contends that if God could communicate motion to matter then God must himself have, or have been in, motion. This conclusion, which would hardly be accepted by theists, depends on the Spinozistic assumption that causality can take place only between things that have common natures.

Like Spinoza, Scepticus denies that there was a creation of the world by God. But neither does he believe, as atheists were supposed according to tradition to believe, that the world arose from chance:

> we do not attribute the creation of the world to chance; on the contrary, we are of the opinion that it was not created, that it never had a beginning, and that it will never have an end, but that it exists necessarily (p. 18).

Against the creation of matter he also argues, by parity of reasoning, that since it is generally conceded that matter cannot be annihilated, we should conclude that it cannot have been created (p. 23).

We find throughout the *Investigation* a number of perceptive comments on, for example, the Mosaic account of God and the soul (pp. 27f), and on the nature of the soul. Scepticus suggests that man 'was necessitated to invent a power superior to nature, in order to account for the creation of his soul' (p. 17). Thus the belief, or wish to believe, in the immortality of the soul, is a cause rather than an effect of belief in God. The hypothesis that desire for immortality generated our belief in God was later to be developed by Schopenhauer.[34] Scepticus holds a surprisingly modern and naturalistic (but also Aristotelian) view of the mind: for him *'the soul of man* instead of being a distinct being from the body, is merely the body considered relatively to some of its functions' (p. 34). In Chapter VII he argues, predictably enough, that the moral effects of belief in the theological God have been bad. Although he does not explicitly commit himself to atheism, his specific remarks on atheism are sympathetic: 'if the definition of this word ['atheism'] given by a late French writer [Mirabeau, i.e. d'Holbach] is just and applicable, it appears the greatest philosophical honor man can have bestowed on him'. 'An atheist', he says 'is a man, who destroyeth chimeras prejudicial to the human species'.[35]

VI. Atheism against deism

In his Postscript, Scepticus's target shifts from theism to deism. He asks the 'Professors of Deism', the following searching questions:

> If you admit, Sirs, the omnipotency of the theological God,
> with what propriety can you deny that the Bible is his work?
> Is it impossible for an omnipotent Being to have caused a work
> of this kind to be written? Could he not have inspired (i.e.
> prompted and urged) the various men to whom its separate
> parts are ascribed to write it? (p. 45)

This interrogation has two goals: firstly, the writer wishes to uncover
an inconsistency in the deist position; but secondly, he also wishes
to give the impression that he has some sympathy with the Bible.
Scepticus, like Hammon, insinuates that revealed religion is not his
enemy. With Hammon it took the form of a direct caveat: Scepticus
is more subtle. The blow he strikes against deism (and hence against
a minimally meaningful conception of God) could also be taken as
a defence of narrow biblical religion. The use of this ingenious
two-edged sword is somewhat anticipated in his remarks on the
Mosaic God, who, according to him, is 'material, visible, comprehensible and mutable' (p. 27). These features are in direct conflict
with the deistic God, and they seem, prima facie, to be consistent
with Scepticus's own materialistic conception of God. But, of course,
the resemblance is only superficial; for him God is not the sort of
being who could come down from heaven and confer with some
latter-day Moses. His God is nothing less than the *whole* material
world.

Scepticus continues his attack on the deists, and here his use of the
two-edged sword raises some problems:

> The arguments used by you, Sirs, against this point (if we are
> not misinformed) are, that if the Bible was the word of God,
> all its parts would agree. But Sirs, assigning as you do to the
> Deity those negative attributes which (as hath been shown in
> chapter iv) necessarily counteract each other, and which, were
> it possible they could be united, would make him a heap of in-
> consistencies, what right have you to expect that his works
> should be either consistent or uncontradictory? If they were so,
> they would bear no semblance of their author. (p. 46)

In this passage Scepticus implies that his critique of the theological
God of Christianity was also a critique of the God of deism; whereas
in Chapter IV he seems to consider his criticisms as directed exclusively against the Christian God (see pp. 22 and 25–6). I think
that most of his criticisms can be, and were intended to be, applied

to the deistic God. But, we must ask, of whose deistic God was he thinking? At which deist or deists was he aiming his criticisms? The answer, I think, is Thomas Paine. On purely external grounds he is the obvious candidate, since his *Age of reason* was published in 1793 (Part 1) and 1795 (Part 2); and it was unquestionably the most famous and influential deistic work of that time, and probably of the whole English Enlightenment. But there are less circumstantial reasons for regarding Paine and *The age of reason* as Scepticus's unnamed targets. Like the unnamed deists alluded to by Scepticus, Paine does deny that the Bible is the word of God because all its parts do not agree.[36] We find Paine making this charge in a number of places in *The age of reason*, especially in Part 2. He speaks of the 'contradictions in time, place and circumstance, that abound in the books ascribed to Moses' (p. 15); and though he does not find as many inconsistencies in the New Testament — as 'there is not room for very numerous violation of the unities' — 'These are, however, some glaring contradictions'. He then goes on to state the following methodological rule which Scepticus may have had specifically in mind:

> I lay it down as a position which cannot be controverted, first, that the *agreement* of all the parts of a story does not prove that story to be true, because the parts may agree, and the whole may be false; secondly, that the *disagreement* of the parts of a story proves *the whole cannot be true.* The agreement does not prove truth, but the disagreement proves falsehood. (p. 56; see also pp. 19 and 51 of Part 1 and p. 22 of Part 2)

It seems likely, therefore, that Paine was Scepticus's principal deistic target. But this still leaves us with the question of whether Scepticus's criticisms of the theological deity in Chapter IV can also be validly levelled against Paine's deistic conception of God. Let us consider the attributes *seriatim*, beginning with incomprehensibility. One might expect a deist to reject this attribute, but Paine does not. In Part 1 of *The age of reason* he asks: 'Canst thou find out the Almighty to *perfection*?' To this he answers:

> No. Not only because the power and wisdom he has manifested in the structure of the creation that I behold, is to me incomprehensible; but because even this manifestation, great as it is, is probably but a small display of that immensity of power and wisdom. (p. 25)

I am not sure whether Paine believed that God was omnipresent. If he did, then Scepticus's attempt to show an incoherency would be successful, for deists as well as theists believe that God is different from the material world he created. God, writes Paine, is 'of a nature totally different to any material existence we know of' (Part 1, p. 23). Because Paine accepts God's immateriality Scepticus can properly argue — with the help of his Spinozistic axioms — that such a God could not have created the world; and this is a damaging criticism of Paine, since he makes much of God's being the creator of the world.

Paine also accepts God's omnipotence (see Part 1, pp. 5 and 43), but he would not allow that God was thwarted by Adam's eating the apple, as he utterly rejects the biblical story. Scepticus might argue that the deistic God's omnipotence is thwarted by the evil actions of certain men. But the argument that he actually uses, as we have seen above, is that the deists themselves deny God's omnipotence when they say that He could not have caused the Bible. Now, in two places in *The age of reason* Paine does allow that God might have caused the Bible. In Part 1 he states: 'No one will deny or dispute the power of the Almighty to make use of a communication, if he pleases' (p. 5, also see Part 2, p. 81). But elsewhere Paine argues that it is impossible for God to have caused the Bible. This is so, essentially, because language is mutable whereas God's creation is immutable. Because

of [the] unchangeableness, [and] of the utter impossibility of any change taking place, by any means or accident whatever, in that which we would honour with the name of the word of God: and therefore the word of God cannot exist in any written human language.
The continually progressive change to which the meaning of words is subject, the want of a universal language ... the errors to which translations are again subject ... evidences that human language ... cannot be the vehicles of the word of God. (Part 1, p. 16)

Thus Scepticus has identified a striking contradiction in *The age of reason*. Paine says that God is omnipotent and might have caused the Bible; but he also declares that the 'word of God cannot exist in any written language' such as that in which the Bible is written.

For Paine the word of God is manifest in the created world: 'It is only in the CREATION that all our ideas and conceptions of a *word of God* can unite. The creation speaketh an universal language.' This is a central theme for Paine; in Part 2 he calls 'the creation the true and only word of God' (p. 78). It is also the subject of Scepticus's final thrust at the deists and their conception of God:

> In declaring that the creation or the whole material world which we inhabit is the word of God, have you not, Sirs, made the difficulty of proving your assertion to be true, more insuperable? Have you not run into an enormous error in order to avoid one of less magnitude? For until the mystery is fully explained and cleared up how an *immaterial* Being could *create* (i.e. form out of nothing) matter, so that the human mind shall not have the least scruple of cause to doubt its possibility, this point of your doctrine will always remain unsubstantiated. (p. 46)

This is followed by the concluding paragraph of the *Investigation*, in which Scepticus makes a last disingenuous show of regard for the Bible at the expense of the deists: 'Thus, Sirs, we flatter ourselves we have refuted the aspersion thrown by you upon that most venerable of all Books, the Bible' (p. 46).

In his final criticism of the deistic God Scepticus makes use of an argument similar to that used by Collins (see Chapter 3, Section V). In accordance with his method Scepticus develops his argument metaphysically in the manner of Spinoza, whereas Collins develops his epistemologically in the manner of Locke. But both are using essentially the same argument: creation of matter *ex nihilo* by an immaterial God is impossible. Here we have a clear meeting between Collins, the disguised pantheistic materialist, and Scepticus, the less disguised pantheistic materialist. Scepticus's atheistic criticism forms a counterpart to that of Francis. Where Francis directs his attack against the moral attributes of the deistic God, Scepticus concentrates on the natural attributes. Both agree in seeing deism as falling foul of difficulties similar to those which undermine revealed religion. Francis's method, or what we are able to see of it, is more *a posteriori* than that of Scepticus, who is anxious to show internal conflicts in God's supposedly essential attributes. They both, however, argue by parity of reason against the deists. Francis accepted the parity from Watson, whereas Scepticus himself developed his particular parity of reasoning, namely, that if conflicts in the Bible show that it is false, then the conflicts in the deistic conception of God show that it, too, is false. Whether some sceptical fideist of the Butlerian school actually argued in this way, I am not sure. Some writers come quite close to it, as, for example, John Ellis, the author of *Knowledge of divine things from revelation and not from reason* (London, 1743), and Bishop Watson, not only in the early part of his *Apology for the Bible* (which I have quoted above, Section IV) but also towards the end (pp. 367–9), where his brief arguments are more in the metaphysical manner of Scepticus. But the most perfect representative of this theological type was — as we shall see — created by Shelley in the character Eusebes in the *Refutation of deism.*

Notes

1. I shall refer to it as the *Answer.* All page references, unless otherwise stated, will be to the 1782 edition of the *Answer.* The title page does not contain the name of a printer or publisher; it does describe the pamphlet as 'Part I'. Part II, which did not appear, was almost certainly meant to be an answer to Priestley's projected defence of revealed religion, which was published as the second part of his *Letters to a philosophical unbeliever* 2nd edn (1787); see *Answer,* pp. xiv–xv.

2. This point is nicely made in *The Creation*, where Blackmore accuses Hobbes of having borrowed all his doctrines from Epicurus (see p. 80). Blackmore asks (p. 151):

    Can he one Flower in all his garden show
    which in his *Grecian* master's did not grow?

3. *Monthly Review* February (1783); art. viii, p. 131.

4. Priestley's *Letters to a philosophical unbeliever,* Part I, 2nd edn (Birmingham, 1787), pp. 229-230. To this edition Priestley added 'Additional letters to a Philosophical Unbeliever. In answer to Mr William Hammon' (which were first published in 1782), pp. 229–304; I shall be using this edition and referring to it as *Letters.*

5. See J.M. Robertson, *A History of freethought* (p. 784), who merely mentions the *Answer*; James Thrower, *A short history of western atheism* (1972); and Robert Flint, *Anti-theistic theories* (1899), p. 457. I have found only one writer who refers to Turner as the first avowed atheist in Britain; this is Percy Vaughan, who says: 'only one English author [i.e. Turner], as far as I can discover, had ventured [before Shelley] to adopt [atheism] as expressing his opinion'; *Early Shelley pamphlets* (London, 1905), p. 17.

6. See my 'Anthony Collins and the question of atheism in the early part of the eighteenth century', in *Proceedings of the Royal Irish Academy,* vol. 75, Section C, no. 5, note 21, and 'The genesis of avowed atheism in Britain', in *Question* 11 (1978).

7. See *Memoirs of Priestley,* in the *Theological and miscellaneous works of Joseph Priestley,* edited with notes by J.T. Rutt, vol. 1 (1817), p. 199; my italics.

8. *Memoirs of Priestley,* p. 76.

9. *An answer to Priestley,* (London, 1826), p. iv.

10. *Memoirs of Priestley,* p. 76. Priestley also lectured at the Warrington Academy.

11. This letter is in the Manchester College Library. I am grateful to Mr John Stephens for calling my attention to it.

12. See Eliza Meteyard, *Life of Josiah Wedgwood* (London, 1865), vol. 1, pp. 300–1. Also see *Historical society of Lancashire and Cheshire, proceedings and papers;* Session V (1853), p. 147.

13. See M.H.A. Davison, *The evolution of anaesthesia* (1965), p. 111. Turner recommended a few teaspoons of ether in wine as a cure for headaches and other complaints.

14. Meteyard, *Life of Josiah Wedgwood*, p. 300.

15. *Letters*, p. 247.

16. *Monthly Review*, p. 129.

17. See above, Chapter 1, Section X and below, Chapter 7, Section III; also *Letters*, p. 244.

18. Hume seems to be alluding to this anomaly in a letter of 8 June 1776 to Strahan, whom he wished to persuade to publish the *Dialogues concerning natural religion:* 'I know of no reason why you should have the least scruple with regard to these Dialogues. They will be much less obnoxious to the Law', i.e. than the 'Essay on Miracles', which, unlike the *Dialogues*, was directed against revealed rather than natural religion.

19. See above Chapter 4; for instances of Hume's fideistic subterfuge see the last two paragraphs of *Dialogues concerning natural religion* and his 'Essay on miracles'. I do not wish to claim that it is evident in all cases when this formula is being used. It is still not certain, for example, whether men such as Thomas Woolston and Henry Dodwell (the younger) were sincere in their Christian professions or whether such professions cloaked — as is more likely — irreligious aims.

20. Ibid., p. 16; compare *Letters,* pp. 256f.

21. Ibid., p. 45; compare *Letters,* pp. 291f. Also see below, Chapters 7 and 8.

22. Ibid., pp. 21–2; compare *Letters,* pp. 284f.

23. See page 37; compare *Critique of pure reason*, trans. Kemp Smith, 'Antinomy of pure reason', Section 3, A 467.

24. He quotes from *The system of nature*, Part II, Chapters III and VII; compare *Letters*, pp. 286–9. Priestley had devoted Letter XI to a refutation of the *System*.

25. Priestley had suggested that a belief in an afterlife was not incompatible with disbelief in God; *Letters,* p. 119. Hammon takes up this suggestion in a Kantian manner: 'For my part [he writes] I firmly wish for such a future state, and though I cannot firmly believe it, I am resolved to live as if such a state were to ensue.' (p. xxx). Compare Kant's *Critique of practical reason*, trans. T.K. Abbott, Book II, Chapter 2, Section IV.

26. *Watson refuted* was reprinted by Richard Carlile in *The Deist* (London, 1819), second tract, and it is to this edition that I refer; see p. 7.

27. *Ibid.*, pp. 12–13.

28. In his *Academic questions* (London, 1805), William Drummond speaks of the 'insanity of atheism' (p. 217). I have not, however, found any passage in which Bishop Watson calls atheists madmen.

29. See, for example, J.S. Mill's *Three essays on religion,* 2nd edn (London, 1874), p. 214.

30. *Apology for the Bible* (see 6th edn, London, 1796), p. 15.

31. *Ibid.*, pp. 17–18.

32. See *Several letters to the Rev Mr Jackson from William Dudgeon ... concerning the immensity and unity of God; the existence of material and spiritual substance ...* (London, 1737), and *Some additional letters* (London, 1737).

33. See *The Collected Works of Spinoza* (Princeton, 1985) edited and translated by Edwin Curley, p. 410. My quotations from Spinoza are from Curley's edition.

34. See Schopenhauer's essay 'On man's need for metaphysics', in vol. 2 of the *World as will and representation* (trans. Payne, 1966), especially pp. 161–2.

35. See p. 40; the definition is from the *System*, vol. 2, Chapter IX. It is mentioned with approval by a writer in the *Theological inquirer* (1815), p. 201. Scepticus also quotes from the *System* on p. 18.

36. Paine's main objection to the Bible is that it inculcates a base morality; see *The age of reason* — reprinted in the *Theological works of Thomas Paine* (London, 1818) — Part One, pp. 4, 32–3, 44, Part Two, pp. 2, 7, 9, 12–15, 21–3, 55, and 82–3. I shall be using this (Carlile) reprint of *The age of reason*, unless otherwise stated.

6

Shelley's Deicide

I. The fourth act

In Chapter 5 I examined the first three indigenous atheistic works published in Britain. They do not, of course, agree in all significant respects; the *Watson refuted* and the *Investigation* are much less openly atheistic than the *Answer*; and the atheism developed in *Watson refuted* is extremely slight compared with its two companions. Clearly, we cannot be sure whether these were the *only* eighteenth-century atheistic works published in Britain. That there were other British atheists flourishing between 1782 and 1797 seems fairly certain. According to A. Benn: 'Erasmus Darwin, Bentham, Godwin and Charles Fox were atheists.'[1] But as they did not publish their atheism, our evidence for ascribing atheism to them is, with the exception of Godwin and Bentham, far from certain.[2] That J.M. Robertson, despite his wide and conscientious research, was unable to find an earlier atheistic work than *Watson refuted* strongly suggests that, apart from the three works I have examined, there are few other atheistic works to be found.

It is striking that there should be such a large gap between the *Answer* in 1782 and *Watson refuted* in 1796. Part of the explanation for this latency period, so to speak, is probably to be found in the French Revolution. The resurgence of atheism in 1796/7 is possibly connected with the publication in 1795/6 of the first English translation of the *System of nature*.[3] But this is not to say that after 1797 we find a gradual and steady emergence of atheistic works. We must again wait some 14 years for another atheistic publication. But then, for the first time, we are face to face with a great name — Percy Bysshe Shelley. In 1811 appeared his brief but daring *Necessity of atheism*, in which he was probably assisted by his friend T. J. Hogg, and for which they were sent down from Oxford. Two other atheistic works were published by Shelley in the next few years — *Queen Mab* in 1813 and the brilliant *Refutation of deism* in 1814.

In the *Refutation* Shelley brings to even greater artistic perfection the protective artifice which we found employed by Hammon and Scepticus. The *Refutation* is cast in the form of a dialogue between a deist (Theosophus) and a fideistic Christian (Eusebes). Apart from some preliminary and transitional exchanges, the dialogue can be divided into two parts. In the first part Theosophus explodes Christianity, largely in the manner of Paine; in the second part deism is exploded by Eusebes in the manner of Hume and d'Holbach. Before launching into his eloquent atheising, Shelley sets the stage for his protective artifice by having Eusebes address Theosophus as follows: 'I require you to declare, O Theosophus, whether you would embrace Christianity or Atheism, if no other systems of belief shall be found to stand the touchstone of enquiry.'[4] To which Theosophus replies: 'I do not hesitate to prefer the Christian system, or indeed any system, however rude and gross, to atheism ... The atheist is a monster among men.' Thus the *apparent* result of the debate is the victory of Christianity; the *actual* result is that both Christianity and deism have been exploded. The substantial atheistic conclusion is masked by an apparent victory for fundamentalist Christianity.

Shelley's philosophical method is closer to that of Hammon, Turner and Collins than it is to Scepticus's. It is epistemological rather than metaphysical. Shelley is more interested in the nature of our knowledge and belief in God than in the nature of God *per se*. Particularly in the *Necessity* and the note to 'There is no God' in *Queen Mab* — a note which is largely a redaction of the *Necessity* — Shelley develops an empiricist critique of belief in God. He derives all knowledge from three sources or degrees of sense experience, and argues that none of these provides credible knowledge of God. Thus, because belief for him is not something in which we are active, 'the mind *cannot* believe the existence of God'[5] The necessity of atheism is the necessity to believe in atheism. As Shelley puts it in the advertisement to the *Necessity*: he is 'Thro' deficiency of proof, AN ATHEIST'.

Shelley's most cogent and sustained defence of atheism is to be found in the *Refutation*. Eusebes's final speech comprises an atheistic tract, impressive by nearly any standards. Based firmly on an empiricist epistemology, it subjects versions of the cosmological, teleological and universal consent arguments to damaging criticisms.

Nor is this atheistic tract purely negative; for interspersed between his criticism Shelley offers various naturalistic alternatives to theism.

II. Denials of Shelley's atheism

From the brief sketch in the previous section it should be clear that Shelley's claim to be considered a pioneer atheist is unassailable. But, in fact, the claim has been assailed by nearly all Shelley scholars. For various reasons they resist the conclusion that Shelley was an atheist, a denier or disbeliever in God's existence. Consider the following statement from Carlos Baker's *Shelley's major poetry* (Princeton, 1948):

> The title of his college pamphlet should have been *The Necessity of Agnosticism* rather than *The Necessity of Atheism*, for the argument developed there is not that God does not exist, but rather that no proofs of his existence thus far adduced will stand up under rational scrutiny. Moreover, Shelley's use of the term *atheism* is always rather narrow; he means that he does not believe in the Old Testament God of wrath. (p. 29)

Baker makes two claims here; the first is interesting but, as I hope to show, mistaken; the second is obviously false. It should be obvious to anyone who has read the *Necessity* and *Refutation* that Shelley uses the term 'atheism' with reference primarily to the God of deism. The arguments in Eusebes' last speech, and the second type of argument in the *Necessity*, are in no way directed against the Old Testament God. The deistic arguments of Theosophus, and the first and second types of arguments in the *Necessity*, have disposed of the Old Testament God of wrath and, for that matter, the New Testament God of love. It is worth pointing this out, because the same mistake is made by Carl Grabo in his *A Newton among the poets* (Chapel Hill, 1930). Referring to Shelley's note 'There is no God' in *Queen Mab*, Grabo writes: 'Apparently what Shelley wishes to deny is the God of the Christians, the God of the Book of Genesis' (p. 18).

Baker's more interesting claim is that Shelley's position in the *Necessity* is really agnostic rather than atheistic; this is so because, although Shelley believes that the proofs *thus far* adduced will not stand up to rational scrutiny, he also realises that there may be other proofs for His existence in addition to the ones that he opposes. Yet in the *Necessity* he states that 'Every [!] proof may be referred to one of these three divisions' (that is, the three sources of belief, which are all ultimately derived from some kind of sense experience). Thus Shelley, like Kant in the 'Transcendental dialectic', apparently thinks that he has examined and refuted *all* the possible *types* of arguments for God's existence, even if he has not dealt with all the specific variations. However, this is not the most serious objection to Baker's claim; for Shelley probably did allow the bare possibility that other proofs might be offered of which he was unaware. What is more objectionable in Baker's claim is that by the criteria he produces it becomes extremely difficult for anyone to deny or disbelieve in the existence of anything. Denials will tend to collapse into agnosticism and doubt. For example, could we deny the actual existence of Cerberus, Aphrodite and the three-mile-long snake (mentioned in Shelley's letter of 6 February 1811); and might we not have to say that Berkeley does not *deny* the existence of matter, but only says 'that no proofs of (matter's) existence thus far adduced will stand up under rational scrutiny'? Certainly Berkeley claims the latter, but he also *denies* the existence of matter. Similar things can be said about other classic denials — such as Locke on innate principles. But few would say that Berkeley and Locke are merely agnostic about matter and innate ideas. The fact that no proofs for the existence of something have thus far been adduced, or that all of them have been shown to be fallacious, is a good ground for denying that thing, particularly if one thinks (as Shelley did) that he has examined all the types of proofs that could be adduced. For the onus of proof is with those who assert the existence of God.

A critic might, however, try to defend Baker in the following way. In addition to denying that there are proofs for matter and innate ideas, Berkeley and Locke also attempt to explode their respective targets by showing that they involve a contradiction. In this way they show that no proof can be given, and thus their line of attack may be distinguished from Shelley's more agnostic approach. Although plausible, I do not think that this defence will prove effective, either in general or specifically in Shelley's case. One may concede that the denials of Berkeley and Locke are stronger than that of Shelley without conceding that Shelley's is agnostic. I can justifiably deny the existence of Cerberus and the three-mile-long snake, without being able to show that such things involve a contradiction. If some-one can show not only that there are no reasons for such things, but they also involve a contradiction, this only means that he has stronger grounds for his denial than I have; it does not mean that I have not justifiably denied these things. I do not wish to suggest that this question is uncontroversial. It is still being debated. Some atheists believe that most agnosticism amounts to atheism, and vice versa. But if we allow that it is debatable, we must then ask whether a commentator should impose on his author his debatable opinion? Should he, in other words, be allowed to assimilate his author's *professed* atheism to agnosticism?

There are, however, ever more powerful reasons for regarding Shelley as an atheist. These hinge on his fundamental principle that belief is passive and involuntary. Shelley assigned the utmost importance to this principle, and it appears repeatedly in his writings between 1811 and 1814. In the short *Necessity* it occurs no less than three times. In the second paragraph Shelley states his principle generally, and adduces from it a defence of toleration in matters of belief. Because belief is involuntary, no merit or demerit should attach to any belief or unbelief. He next uses it as a premise in an argument against believing the existence of God. According to Christian theologians, God will reward belief in certain religious dogmas and punish disbelief. But since belief is involuntary and hence not culpable, and since God is supposed to be perfectly wise and good, the testimonies of these theologians cannot be trusted. The theologians show by their contradictory and irrational description of God that we cannot believe in God on their testimony. Now this argument could also be converted into an *ad hominem* argument against the theologians' God. Their conception of God involves a contradiction in that they claim God is perfect and also that He (irrationally) blames unbelief. But a God who shows such a basic ignorance of human psychology cannot be perfect; and a being who is both perfect and imperfect cannot exist.

Therefore Shelley could have presented at least one of his arguments in such a way as to demonstrate the impossibility of the theologians' God. He did not, because he was concerned with belief rather than being. But it amounts to the same thing. Because of the passivity of belief Shelley could not believe in the existence of God; his inability was as great as if he were to observe a plain contradiction in the conception of God. In signing himself 'Thro' deficiency of proof, AN ATHEIST', Shelley is saying that he cannot believe otherwise: as he clearly puts it in the penultimate paragraph: 'the mind *cannot* believe in the existence of a God'. The necessity of atheism is as strong for him as the more logical necessity of immaterialism was for Berkeley. Expressing the necessity in terms of belief had obvious advantages for Shelley. Because no blame could (or should) attach to belief, he felt that no blame should attach to his atheism: 'it is ... evident that as belief is a passion of the mind, no degree of criminality can attach to unbelief.' But someone who cannot believe in God can hardly be an agnostic. An agnostic must have some doubt or uncertainty; but Shelley had not. A believer in the activity or voluntariness of belief — like Descartes, for example — could hold that although all reason and evidence are against God's existence, he still is not sure. He might even suspend his judgement altogether. But this is not in Shelley's power, any more than it is in the power of metal filings to resist being drawn to a nearby magnet.

I have argued against Baker at length because his agnostic interpretation is shared, in one way or another, by many Shelley scholars. Thus Neville Rogers ascribes agnosticism to Shelley in his editorial commentary on Shelley's notes to *Queen Mab*:

> His much publicised Oxford pamphlet, *The Necessity of Atheism*, asks questions rather than assumes their answers, an attitude for which there was no name in 1810 — not till 1870 did T.H. Huxley coin the word 'agnostic'[6] ... Alike in Shelley's day, among the Victorians, and in our own time, atheists and Christians have combined in isolating the words [from *Queen Mab*] 'There is no God' from the general context of Shelley's thought and treating them as the mature conclusion of a mature thinker.[7]

Now the first thing one must point out is that in the *Necessity* and the relevant note in *Queen Mab* Shelley does not ask questions. Nor does he 'assume' answers. He gives answers. He cannot believe in God because none of the three sources which might provide evidence for God's existence do provide it. The phrase 'assumes their answers' is tendentious; nor is the last part of Rogers's statement much better. He suggests that various unnamed readers of Shelley have misunderstood him by treating the words 'There is no God' 'as the mature conclusion of a mature thinker'. But this is beside the point. We are not concerned with whether they coincided with the views he held ten years later, but with whether they represented his considered view at the time he wrote and printed *Queen Mab*.

The agnostic interpretation is also at the basis of David Lee Clark's statements. In his otherwise helpful editorial commentary on Shelley's prose works, Clark asserts that Shelley 'does not here [in the *Necessity*] nor did he ever, flatly deny the existence of God. He merely asserts that with existing data and the known laws of logic, the existence of God cannot be proved.'[8] Here again we must ask whether the conditions laid down by Clark for the non-denial of God do not amount to sufficient conditions for denial. There can be few better reasons for denying *x* than that given the existing data and the known laws of logic, the existence of *x* cannot be proved. Certainly neither Hobbes on immaterial substance, Locke on innate ideas, nor Berkeley on matter had much stronger grounds for their denials. Consider also firstly, an infinite fly, secondly a patch of colour with no extension or shape, and thirdly a four-sided triangle. These absurdities *only* defy the existing data and the known laws of logic, but they are none the less impossibilites. It may also be questioned whether Shelley ever made the curiously qualified assertion that Clark attributes to him. But Shelley did flatly deny the existence of God. He did so in the words to which, Rogers thinks, certain readers have unfairly drawn attention, namely, 'There is no God.' Nothing, I think, could be a flatter denial of the existence of God than this series of four monosyllables. And these words occur not just once in *Queen Mab*, but three times: twice in the poem itself, and again as the title to the note. But it must, of course, be immediately pointed out that the note opens with the following qualification: 'This negation [Shelley says] must be understood solely to affect a *creative* Deity. The hypothesis of a pervading Spirit co-eternal with the universe remains unshaken.' But what, we must ask, is this qualifier — 'creative' — actually meant to do? In my view, it does not represent a substantive qualification but a harmless and possibly useful elucidation of the term 'deity'. It may also have been designed to protect Shelley against possible prosecution. A creative deity is for him no different from just plain deity.

There is much in Shelley's essays and letters which can be brought to support this interpretation, but one piece of evidence should be sufficient. In an early incomplete draft of the *Refutation*, no doubt written around the same time as *Queen Mab,* Shelley states: 'The word *God* signifies an intelligent Creator' (Ibid., p. 138) and in the same work this definition is repeated: 'God may be defined to be the intelligent Creator and Preserver of the Universe' (p. 134). By the 'hypothesis of a pervading Spirit co-eternal with the universe' Shelley seems to have meant the mass of finite minds — a naturalistic notion with virtually no theological implications.[9] That Shelley was aware of the temptation to supernaturalise the natural, but was determined to resist it, is reasonably clear from the second note to *Queen Mab* in which he says: 'He who rightly feels its [i.e. the plurality of worlds] mystery and grandeur is in no danger of seduction from falsehoods of religious systems, *or of deifying the principle of the universe'* (my italics). Thus the denial of a creative God, and the affirmation of a pervading Spirit, does not qualify Shelley's atheism. An illustration of the weakness of Clark's interpretation can be gathered from one of his editorial notes to the *Refutation*. Towards the end of the dialogue we read: 'I have proved that on the principles of that philosophy to which Epicurus, Lord Bacon, Newton, Locke, and Hume were addicted, the existence of God is a chimera.' Here we have something approaching a flat denial; but in his note it is Clark who brings in various qualifications. He comments: 'This statement is true in the sense in which Shelley uses the word *God*, as an anthropomorphic creativity deity' (p. 137).

III. Shelley and the repressive tendency

The unwillingness of some to accept Shelley's straightforward professions of atheism and his denial of God's existence goes back very far, at least to the year 1812. We know this from Shelley's revealing letter of 2 January 1812 to Elizabeth Hitchener, in which he says: 'I have lately had some conversation with Southey which has elicited my true opinions of God — he says I ought not to call myself an Atheist, since in reality I believe that the Universe is God.' But although Southey tries to deny Shelley's atheism, Shelley resists the denial. His response to Southey is: 'I tell him I believe that God is another signification for the universe.' So for Southey the universe (in Shelley's thought) is another name for God; whereas for Shelley God is another name for the universe. The distinction is not un-important, particularly in the light of our examination (in Chapter 1) of the repressive tendency to deny the existence of atheists. I believe that Southey was in the grips of this tendency, and that Shelley was resisting it. I am tempted also to interpret the denials by some Shelley scholars in a similar way. Just as Southey tried to convince Shelley that, despite his own remarks to the contrary, he was not an atheist, so Baker, Grabo, Rogers and Clark wish to persuade us that, despite Shelley's statements to the contrary, he was not an atheist. And the techniques which they use to deny Shelley's atheism are similar to those we have seen (in Chapter 1) used to deny all atheism: the conditions for atheism are made so unrealistic that no potential atheist could satisfy them. As the denials of atheism are more glaringly unrealistic and groundless, the more they seem to require some such genetic explanation. At the least, a reader must be cautioned against blandly accepting such confident statements as this one from

Ellsworth Barnard's *Shelley's religion* (Minnesota, 1937): 'It is not *true* that he was ever consistently an atheist or even a pantheist' (p. 18). Nor is the question of Shelley's atheism merely a matter of literary interpretation. The agnostic interpretation of Baker, Rogers and Clark can also be read as a concealed argument against atheism. Under their scrutiny, apparent and feasible atheism dissolves into some form of agnosticism. But if Shelley was not an atheist, then who could be one?

Even the most careful commentator might benefit from the warning against inadvertently slipping into the repressive tendency. In his scholarly *Shelley and his circle* (New York, 1961) Kenneth Cameron asserts: 'At the time of the composition of the pamphlet [the *Necessity*] he was still a deist; and the request in its Advertisement for further illumination was seriously intended.'[10] There is nothing in the Advertisement, however, which suggests that Shelley was a deist. Here is the whole Advertisement:

> As a love of truth is the only motive which actuates the Author
> of this little tract, he earnestly entreats that those of his readers
> who may discover any deficiency in his reasoning, or may be
> in possession of proofs which his mind could never obtain,
> would offer them, together with their objections to the Public,
> as briefly, as methodically, as plainly as he has taken the liberty
> of doing. Thro' deficiency of proof, AN ATHEIST.

Part of Cameron's misunderstanding arises from his failure to see the vital connection between the Advertisement and Shelley's passivity of belief principle. Because belief is passive, and because he has no evidence for God, he cannot be other than an atheist: again, 'the mind *cannot* believe the existence of God'. But while he cannot change his understanding, he may volitionally seek criticism of his belief. As a rational and responsible man he wishes to put himself in the position of having his beliefs changed if they are weak. 'They only are reprehensible [Shelley urges in the *Necessity*] who willingly neglect to remove the false medium thro' which their minds view the subject.' That much is in his power, and that is what he is asking for in the Advertisement. But he is by no means affirming deism, nor is he even expressing his wish to be convinced of the truth of deism. And even if the latter were true — which it is not — we would still not be right to call him a deist. He would be an atheist who wished that he were a deist. Similarly, the fact that Leslie Stephen in his *Agnostic's apology* expressed a wish to be a theist rather than an agnostic does not tempt us to withold the latter title from him.[11] (Shelley's awareness of this complex sort of mental conflict is apparent from his letter of 11 June 1811 to Elizabeth Hitchener.) Of course, if all, or most, of Shelley's statements and behaviour were expressive of belief in deism, then we might wonder whether to take his bare assertion of atheism very seriously. But this is not the case. Hence Shelley's wish to entertain opinions and arguments contrary to his own does not indicate any uncertainty of his own opinions. Perhaps at a deeper level there *may* be an incoherence in Shelley's philosophical position. If I *cannot* now believe in God, then can I sensibly wish to entertain new arguments for His existence? Thus I would be unwilling to consider arguments which might be brought to support the probability of four-sided triangles. But here we have gone well beyond interpretation. We are now asking whether Shelley's bifurcation of belief and volition is tenable or true.

My conclusion is that in the period 1811–1814 Shelley was an atheist. He was so because, firstly, he called himself an atheist, not merely in the *Necessity*, but also in letters written at that time. Secondly, he also denies the existence of God in both published works and private letters.[12] And, thirdly, far from having an idiosyncratic understanding of the words 'atheist' and 'God', he has an unusually firm grasp of their ordinary meanings. Fourthly, he also presents a reasoned case against the existence of God, perhaps as powerful a case as has ever been presented in such a short work. He is, therefore, not just an atheist but a speculative atheist.

There is also evidence that Shelley was consciously resisting the repressive tendency. Like Hammon and Francis, he seems to have realised that atheism was being inhibited by its inability to pronounce openly its own name. Covert and ironic atheism suffered from being unable to take itself seriously. The formulas 'I am an atheist' and 'There is no God' are more than mere words or dispensible formulas. Shelley realised this, I think, in his discussion with Southey, and this realisation is also behind his audacious thrice-repeated statement in *Queen Mab*: 'There is no God.' I am also inclined to interpret in the same light Shelley's remark about atheism to Trelawny: 'I used it [atheism] to express my abhorrence of superstition; *I took up the word, as a knight took up a gauntlet*, in defiance of injustice' (my italics).[13] Of course, this spirited assertion of the older Shelley can be interpreted in other ways; one way is given by Neville Rogers in his *Shelley at work* (Oxford, 1956): 'It is to be doubted [writes Rogers] if he was ever naturally a denier of religion although like many young men he was liable to deny anything, and to do so with ever increasing vehemence once somebody else had denied his right to question it' (p. 276). As in Rogers's statement which I quoted above, there is an element of truth here, but also a *suggestio falsi*. Although Shelley's atheism was youthful, vehement and rebellious, it was also sustained, self-conscious and rationally formidable. (Nor should it surprise us to find vehemence in the second avowal of atheism.) The condescending attitude adopted by Rogers is just not appropriate; nor is his curious qualification 'naturally'. What does it mean to say that someone is not 'naturally a denier of religion'? I cannot think it has any distinct meaning. All that it seems to allow is the expression of a certain attitude without risk of criticism; but the danger of criticism is averted at the expense of triviality. So someone can say without serious risk of criticism that Shelley was not a natural denier of religion, but so can he say that Hitler was not a natural hater of Jews. Lastly among Shelley commentators I should like to quote Richard Holmes, who in his recent *Shelley, the pursuit* (London, 1976) tells us that if Shelley had admitted having written the *Necessity* 'He could not have been accused of actual atheism; he could only have been convicted of debating unpalatable arguments in public' (pp. 54–5). But what more could Shelley have done to have been accused of 'actual atheism'? Can one do more than (1) call oneself an atheist, and (2) produce arguments against the existence of God? It is difficult to imagine how Holmes could conceive *actual* atheism. If a man asserts the existence of God and the divinity of Jesus, and offers arguments to justify these assertions, would this mean that he could only be 'convicted of debating (un)palatable arguments in public'?

I have suggested that the repressive tendency is the best way of accounting for such puzzling denials of Shelley's atheism by (otherwise helpful) writers on Shelley. But there is a more generous interpretation which I should like briefly to mention. It may be said that although Shelley was an avowed atheist, and although he may have believed himself to be an atheist, he was none the less not *really* an atheist, or as Holmes has it, he was not an 'actual' atheist. Now this might mean that, because of the nature of God, or of the nature of belief, no one could be an atheist. Of course on this sort of interpretation, an atheist can retort that there have never been any theists. There is a variation of this rather crude interpretation, however, which may be more relevant to our study. Some Shelley scholars may think that they understand more clearly than Shelley what he did and did not believe; for they have a better definition of God than he had. But this again seems to be bringing substantive questions into a field where the interpreter should keep his opinions to himself. Now, admittedly, if a writer uses a certain word in a highly idiosyncratic way, then the interpreter must step in. (For example, a man might say that he does not believe in colours, and by colours he means moral qualities.) But this is not Shelley's case.

What seems clear is that we have moved out of the realm of interpretation. We are now engaged, at the very least, in theory-laden interpretation. We are not merely examining Shelley's testimony but we are cross-examining it and finding fault with it. We are, in effect, changing Shelley's beliefs. Even more important, we are altering the beliefs of a major cultural hero, whose authority has a wide and potent influence on the beliefs of that culture.

IV. Shelley's system

The significance of Shelley's atheism does not derive merely from the fact that Shelley was and perhaps still is the most famous British atheist. Perhaps the chief merit of his atheistic writings is that they present a most formidable systematic defence of atheism from the empiricist standpoint. Shelley's atheism can be regarded as the irreligious culmination of British empiricism. If Hume is Locke made consistent, then Shelley is Hume made explicit. To see this one must use the *Necessity* as a key or 'syllabus', as Shelley called it, to the *Refutation*. The *Refutation* should then be regarded as the detailed expansion of the *Necessity*. These two primary sources of Shelley's atheism, although published three years apart, show a considerable degree of unity and coherency, as I hope to show.

In the *Necessity* Shelley maintains that there are only three ways of knowing that something exists. The first way, or 'division', is sense experience, which is the basis for the two others. The second way is by reasoning on sense experience. The third, and least reliable, division is testimony. The first way is little more than a straw man, with regard to the existence of God; and as the third way is based on the first, it is not any better. By 1813 Shelley had come to see this, for in revising the *Necessity* for the note 'There is no God' in *Queen Mab* he added the sentence: 'But the God of theologians is incapable of local visibility'. However, the first and the second divisions are by no means useless. They can accommodate, if slightly modified, a type of evidence which Shelley examines in the *Refutation*, namely, evidence for the Christian God derived from miracles. Thus someone who saw a miracle — for example, Jesus raising Lazarus from the dead — could have strong evidence for believing in the Christian God, and the testimony of such a witness might also convince others. Thus Theosophus' long speech against belief in the Christian God can be usefully accommodated by the first and third divisions. Not, of course, that witnessing and testifying to miracles is exclusively a matter for these divisions. There would have to be an element of the second division involved. For someone who observes a strange event must infer that it was caused by such and such a God before he could call it a miracle. In any case, it is the second division that is relevant to Shelley's arguments for atheism and against a deistic God. These arguments are, with one exception, contained in Eusebes's long concluding speech.

I shall consider the exception first, for it is somewhat subdued and apt to be overlooked. Between Theosophus' forty-one-paragraph refutation of Christianity and Eusebes' forty-two paragraph refutation of deism, there is some transitional interchange in which Eusebes employs the Butlerian parity of reasoning against Theosophus in a manner highly reminiscent of Watson's critique of Paine. Eusebes concedes:

> I will not dissemble, O Theosophus, the difficulty of solving your general objections to Christianity on the grounds of human reason ... But this is a difficulty which attends Christianity in common with the belief in the being and attributes of God. This whole scheme of things might have been, according to our partial conceptions, infinitely more admirable and perfect. Poisons, earthquakes, disease, war, famine, venomous serpents, slavery, and persecution are the consequences of certain causes, which according to human judgement, might well have been dispensed with in arranging the economy of the globe.

Like Francis, Shelley points to atheism as the only *reasonable* way to resolve the dilemma posed by the Butlerian parity of reasoning; although Shelley's point is somewhat dulled by irony. Will the deist, asks Eusebes,

> place his God between the horns of a logical dilemma which shall restrict the fulness either of his power or his bounty? ... Certainly he will prefer to resign his objections to Christianity than pursue the reasoning upon which they are found [bound?] to the dreadful conclusions of cold and dreary atheism.

In the first 37 paragraphs of Eusebes' speech, Shelley does not permit his irony to obscure the force of his atheism. It is this crucial speech which I shall now examine *seriatim*. Paragraphs 1 and 2 can be seen as referring back to the first division in the *Necessity*. Shelley draws attention to what is *not* given in sense experience: we do not directly perceive design in nature, nor do we see that nature is inert. Since these things are not given in experience, the theist or deist must argue for them if he is not to commit the fallacy of *petitio principii*. In paragraphs 3 and 4 Shelley considers the question: How do we know that something is designed? We know that a human artefact, such as a book, is designed because we know beforehand what humans can do; but we know nothing of God 'beforehand'. We have no experience of His contriving; thus we cannot infer that the natural world is His contrivance.

Having concentrated on experience (division one) in paragraphs 1 to 4, Shelley moves to pure reason in 5–8. He points out internal difficulties in the design argument. If the admirable fitness of the universe for producing certain effects implies that the universe needs a cause, then the admirable fitness of God to produce the universe implies that He has a cause, and so on. Thus, as in Collins's similar argument, there will be a plurality of deities.

In paragraphs 9 and 10 Shelley presents an alternative hypothesis to theism: the universe is not contingent but eternal. This hypothesis, he urges, is less incomprehensible, obscure and question-begging than the hypothesis of an eternal God who creates the universe. (We have found this thesis in Turner and Scepticus, and also in Collins.) Shelley confesses his ignorance of the 'generative power' of nature — what Turner called 'the energy of nature' — but he thinks that to identify this power with God is to gain nothing but additional obscurity. Shelley took these two paragraphs, nearly verbatim, from the *Necessity*, where they comprise the only arguments of the second division, i.e. arguments for God based on reason and experience.

In paragraph 11, Shelley further explores possible reasoning to God based on experience. Following Hume, he affirms that any causes which we postulate must be strictly proportioned to the observable effects. Hence, since the observable natural effects are in conflict — the cause of the 'blight by which the harvest is destroyed, and the sunshine by which it is matured' cannot be the same — we should infer a number of rival and hostile deities, some good others bad. This point is elaborated in paragraph 21; it is also made by Shelley in *Queen Mab*, in the note 'Necessity, thou mother of the world', where Shelley is prepared to accept the concept of *a* God who is both good and bad, and thus responsible for blights as well as plentiful harvests.

In paragraphs 12–20, Shelley argues that the world can be satisfactorily explained in a non-theistic naturalistic way. He proposes a materialistic explanation; but most of his arguments against God are independent of this explanation. Thus his later repudiation of materialism for immaterialism is not in essential conflict with his earlier atheism. An immaterialist can be an atheist. (Indeed, a number of prominent British atheists — for instance, George Grote and John McTaggart — were immaterialists; see Chapters 9 and 10.) In paragraph 17, Shelley rejects the conception of pure inert matter without qualities, a conception which Berkeley also opposed. But unlike Berkeley he claims that we observe active physical bodies. (A Berkeleian might justifiably retort, however, that it is no more evident that we immediately see activity in nature than that we see design in nature.) Shelley's account, in paragraph 18, of the adaptation of living things to their environment recalls that of d'Holbach and Turner. In paragraphs 22 to 26 he warns against anthropomorphic understanding of nature.

Paragraphs 26 to 31 contain a critique of the argument from universal consent — an argument which had recently been used by Paine — together with a genetic account of religious belief. The consensus argument would fall under the second and third divisions in the *Necessity*, as it employs elements from both reason and testimony. Shelley shows that conceptions of God vary, depending upon the human passions of the particular community of believers: 'The word "God" cannot mean at the same time an ape, a snake, a bone, a calabash, a trinity, a unity' (paragraph 31). Thus belief in God is not universal; and its being widespread does not indicate that it is true, for many falsehoods are widely held.

Paragraphs 32 to 37 contain miscellaneous criticisms, drawn from various sources. Paragraph 32 uses Hume's doctrine — that our idea of causality is derived from constant conjunction — to preclude any inference to God based on the existence of this world. Not only have we not observed any constant conjunction between God's various creative activities and the coming into being of various worlds, but we have not observed even one conjunction of this kind. In 33, Shelley tries to show that power is essential to the world, and hence the world does not require God to activate it.

Having shown that the world does need God, Shelley now attempts in 34 to prove that, if God did exist, He would need a body.

Because intelligence requires sensation, and since sensation can only exist in an organised body, it follows that if God is intelligent He must also have an organised body. Shelley associates this argument with Locke, but it is used even more explicitly by Collins (see above, Chapter 3).

The next paragraph, 35, also has a Collins as well as a Berkeley association. Collins, as we have seen, challenged theists to make sense of God's creation of the world *ex nihilo*, an atheistic challenge to which Berkeley saw his Immaterialism as providing an answer.[14] Because there is no matter, the creation of the world must be the continual creation by God of vivid (sensible) ideas; thus we can gain some conception of this creative activity, Berkeley holds, by reflecting on our own ability to produce weak (imaginative) ideas. Now for one critic of Berkeley's philosophy, Charles Lloyd, a friend of Robert Southey, this will not do. When Shelley was visiting Southey in 1811/12 he found in Lloyd's copy of Berkeley's *Works* the striking annotation: 'Mind cannot create, it can only perceive,' which he used as the first sentence in 35. For Shelley, and also apparently for Lloyd, Berkeley had *not* succeeded in answering the atheistic challenge. Our mind does not create its imaginative ideas; it merely builds and arranges these ideas from the vivid sensible ideas. In Lockean terms, we cannot create simple ideas. Therefore, as our minds are unable to create weak imaginative ideas, we found no reason to suppose that the divine mind is able to create vivid sensible ideas. The incapacity of the mind to create ideas was a central doctrine of Shelley's atheism; it was a doctrine, he wrote in 1819, 'on which I had founded much of my persuasion regarding the imagined cause of the Universe'.[15] The doctrine is closely connected with his principle concerning passivity of belief.

In paragraph 37 we find a succinct statement of Spinoza's rejection of theism's creative God. Since the universe is absolutely infinite and inclusive, nothing can exist beyond it; but then no transcendent creator of the universe can exist.

Paragraphs 38 to 41 conclude Eusebes' speech. After some recapitulation in 38–40, he proceeds to mask his atheism in 41 and 42. The final paragraph, number 42, looks back to the Preface, where Shelley had informed his readers of his purpose, namely 'to show that there is no alternative between Atheism and Christianity'. Eusebes now calls upon Theosophus to 'decide between' the two. For Shelley there should, however, be no choice; there should be a necessity of atheism.

One thing at least should be clear from this sketch: Shelley was a strong minded speculative atheist. This is not to say that there are no difficulties or weaknesses in his atheism. Certain arguments in the *Refutation* — particularly those in paragraphs 32 to 37 — are so compressed as to be barely more than abstracts or titles of arguments. Some of Shelley's assumptions can also be questioned. I have pointed out one in my comment on paragraph 36; Shelley also uncritically assumes the truth of Hume's theory of causality in 32. Even more serious is his underlying assumption of the truth of empiricism. It is probably because of this assumption that Shelley does not even mention the ontological argument for God's existence. Nor does he examine the Cartesian argument that we have an innate idea of God which could only have been implanted in us by God. It is perhaps more surprising that Shelley does not discuss the proof for God based on mystical experience; for this argument might, *prima facie*, seem to come within the scope of his empiricist assumptions. The closest he comes to examining the two latter proofs is in a letter of 11 June 1811 to Elizabeth Hitchener. Elizabeth had said that her belief in God was founded on a feeling. Shelley responded by appealing to Locke's demonstration that there are no innate ideas or principles. According to Shelley, this demonstration overturns

> all appeals of *feeling* in favour of *Deity*, since that feeling must be referable to some origin; there must have been a time when it did not exist, in consequence a time when it began to exist, since all ideas are derived from the senses this *feeling* must have originated from some sensual excitation, consequently the possessor of it may be aware of the time, of the circumstances attending its commencement. Locke proves this, by induction too clear to admit of *rational* objection.

This criticism by Shelley raises a few questions. Why, we might wonder, did he not publish it in some form in the *Refutation*? The most probable answer, I think, is that he regarded the feeling-argument as so weak as to be undeserving of serious rebuttal. A question also arises as to the precise nature of Shelley's target. I have described it as the 'feeling-argument', but there are also features taken from the Cartesian innate-idea proof. Shelley seems to be opposing an argument in which the feeling of God is supposed to carry conviction because only God could have implanted, or could account for, such a sublime feeling. By showing that the feeling is not innate but has a naturalistic origin in sensation, Shelley hopes to sever the connection between the feeling and the conviction that God exists. Shelley probably had in mind here believers such as Lord Kaimes, who maintained that there is in man an innate 'sense of Deity'.[16] Now Lord Kaimes's case for this non-empirical sense of Deity depends, as he himself allows, on the universality of belief in God.[17] Hence Shelley may have felt that there was no need in the *Refutation* to waste words on the Kaimesian thesis because it had been undermined by his critique of universality in paragraphs 26–31.

Notes

1. *History of rationalism in the 19th century*, vol. 1, p. 210. According to John Quincy Adams — *Memoirs* (Philadelphia, 1874) vol. 3, p. 563 — Jeremy Bentham told him in 1817 that Francis Place was an atheist.

2. In a MS note (in the uncatalogued Abinger collection, Bodleian Library) Godwin says that 'I became ... in my 36th year [i.e. 1792] an atheist'. I am grateful to Don Locke for this reference. Also see below, Chapter 9, Section I.

3. This was done by William Hodgson, while imprisoned in Newgate for sedition.

4. *Shelley's prose, or the trumpet of prophecy* (Albuquerque, 1966), edited by David Lee Clark, p. 128. All quotations from the *Necessity* (and its redaction in *Queen Mab*), the *Refutation* (and the early fragment of a draft of the *Refutation*) are taken from this edition.

5. *Necessity, Shelley's prose*, p. 39.

6. According to the *Oxford English Dictionary* (Oxford, 1933), Huxley coined the word 'agnostic' in 1869.

7. *Complete poetical works of Shelley* (Oxford, 1972), edited by N. Rogers, vol. 1, p. 387.

8. *Shelley's prose*, p. 37; see also p. 6.

9. Compare Shelley's letter to Elizabeth Hitchener, 2 January, 1812; in Frederick L. Jones (ed.), *The Letters of Percy Bysshe Shelley* (Oxford, 1964), vol. 1, pp. 214–16. All quotations from Shelley's letters are taken from this collection.

10. Vol. ii, p. 712. I should point out that in his excellent studies, *The young Shelley: a genesis of a radical* (London, 1951) and *Shelley, the golden years* (Cambridge, Mass. 1974), Cameron clearly ascribes atheism to Shelley; see the latter work, p. 157.

11. See *An Agnostic's apology and other essays* (London, 1931), p. 2.

12. Shelley's correspondence with Elizabeth Hitchener is most revealing; in his letter of 11 June 1811, he writes: 'To a belief in Deity I have no objection on the score of feeling, I would as gladly perhaps with greater pleasure admit than doubt his existence. I now do neither, I have not the shadow of a doubt. My wish to convince you of his nonexistence...', and on 8 October 1811 he says: 'You will enquire how *I* an *Atheist* chose to subject myself to the ceremony of *marriage*.' Also see *Letters*, p. 70.

13. See his *Records of Shelley, Byron, and the author* (London, 1887), p. 62. Trelawny's own comment on Shelley's atheism is worth quoting: 'The principal fault I have to find is that the Shelleyan writers, being Christians themselves, seem to think that a man of genius cannot be an Atheist, and so they strain their faculties to disprove what Shelley asserted from the earliest stage of his career to the last day of his life.' *Records*, Appendix, p. 312.

14. See 'Anthony Collins, his thought and writings', *Hermathena* cxix (1977), pp. 55–6.

15. See *Letters*, vol. 2, pp. 122–3.

16. See his *Sketches of the history of man* (Dublin, 1775), vol. 2, p. 100.

17. Ibid., pp. 95–6. Shelley mentions Kaimes in his letters of 6 February 1811 and 11 November 1811.

7

The Struggle of Theoretical Atheism over Practical Atheism

I. Atheism and the theoretical/practical distinction

Why did atheism emerge so late? and why did it emerge when it did? In Chapter 1 I have suggested that part of the explanation is to be found in the repressive tendency. But, clearly, that could provide only part of the answer; for it still leaves us with the question: Why was there a repressive tendency? Nor will it do to answer that atheism was a fearful menace which had to be repressed. For we will again ask: Why was it fearful and menacing? and why did it begin to be particularly fearful towards the end of the eighteenth century? In this and the following chapter I shall try to answer these questions. And I shall do so by means of the theoretical/practical distinction — which I shall sometimes call 'the distinction' — and its application to the question of God's existence — which I shall often call 'the question'.

Our distinction as applied to the question has traditionally allowed this sort of thing to be said: 'Although X believes, or says that he believes, in the existence of God, he does not behave as though God did actually exist. For example, X breaks his promises.' Here, according to our theological distinction, we are saying that X is a theoretical (or speculative) theist but a practical atheist. On the other hand, one might be a theoretical atheist but a practical theist. That is, one might not believe in the existence of God, but one might act as though one did. So the theoretical embraces beliefs, whereas the practical is seen as a translation of beliefs into action or behaviour.

A typical way of presenting the distinction can be seen in Archbishop Tillotson's 'Sermon on the wisdom of being religious':

Now all that are irreligious are so upon one of these two accounts: either, *first*, because they do not believe the foundations and principles of Religion, as *the existence of God* ... or else, secondly, because tho' they do in some sort believe these things, yet they live contrary to this their belief ... The *first* sort are guilty of that which we call *speculative*, the *other* of *practical Atheism*. [1]

It may be noted at the outset that just as theologians generally divided (theoretical) theism into a natural and revealed side — i.e. the belief in God as derived from reason or nature on the one hand and from Scripture and tradition on the other — so there is a corresponding division made in the case of practical theism. In general, natural religion was thought to provide a basis for moral behaviour, whereas revealed religion grounded religious behaviour, such as prayers, fasting, burial practices and so on. Although the religious side of practical theism was of considerable importance in the seventeenth century, and earlier, it became less dominant in the eighteenth century as a result of pressure from the liberal Christians and deists. [2] At any rate, in the movement of thought which I shall be surveying, it is the natural side of theoretical theism, and the moral side of practical theism, which will appear in the foreground.

Now clearly there is much even in this that is problematic. For example, when are we entitled to say that X does, or does not, believe in the existence of God? And what sort of conception must one have of God? It is also clear that our decision to call someone a theoretical atheist, for example, will depend on our beliefs or theological allegiances. So Spinoza was regarded by most seventeenth-century and early eighteenth-century writers as a theoretical atheist. But late eighteenth-century German writers, like Lessing and Novalis, hardly agreed; nor would Spinoza himself have agreed. Again, a deist, such as Paine, was regarded by most contemporary churchmen as a practical atheist (for alleged blasphemy, among other things), yet Paine not only repudiated the charge of practical atheism but vigorously returned it. [3] Qualifications, additions and modifications will, as we shall see, be necessary; but my aim has been to let these things develop and work themselves out historically.

II. The orthodox position: Locke and Berkeley

In his *Letter concerning toleration* (1689) Locke refuses toleration to those 'who deny the being of God'. [4] One reason he gives for this intolerance is that: 'Promises, covenants, and oaths, which are bonds of human society, can have no hold upon an atheist. The taking away of God, though even in thought, dissolves all.' Although Locke does not use the term 'theoretical atheism' here, the 'taking away of God in thought' is a fairly good characterisation of it. This is even clearer in the case of the partner conception. For breaking promises seems to have been regarded as a prominent way in which practical atheism was exhibited. Moreover, in the *Essay concerning human understanding* (I.iv.8) Locke provides an even better characterisation of practical atheism; he speaks of some 'wretched profligates', whose lives 'proclaim their atheism'. This he distinguishes from the atheism which is verbally proclaimed.

But we must still ask why, in Locke's view, theoretical atheism must lead to moral chaos, i.e. to the dissolving of promises and oaths. Part of his answer is to be found in *Essay*, II. xxviii, where we learn that it is God who both produces and enforces moral laws. Hence, if we did not believe in God we would, presumably, be removing the basis of morality. Without a moral-law-giver and enforcer there could be no moral laws. If God did not exist we might still take delight in keeping our promises, but such behaviour would not be good, according to Locke, since it would be neither co-ordinated with, nor would it conform to, any moral law (as such things could not exist). It is, therefore, not suprising that Locke should wish to deny toleration to theoretical atheists, for their 'practical opinion' — as he calls it in the *Letter* and by which he appears to mean a sort of performative belief — would seem to undermine morality itself.

Let us now turn from Locke to the second man in the eighteenth century British triumvirate, namely Berkeley. As we shall see, Locke and Berkeley are in fundamental agreement concerning the distinction as applied to the question. For Berkeley (as for Locke) it is God who determines what is right and wrong: 'nothing is a [moral] law merely because it conduceth to the public good, but because it is decreed by the will of God, which alone can give the sanction of a law of nature to any precept' (*Passive obedience*, Section 31). As Berkeley succinctly puts it in one of his sermon notes: 'no solid morality without religion.'[5] However, where Locke is interested in the practical consequences which might follow from theoretical atheism, Berkeley is also concerned — especially in the *Principles of human knowledge* (1710) — with theoretical theism and the practices which will (or should) flow from it. For him belief in theoretical theism is not only a necessary but also a sufficient condition for practical theism. In the penultimate section of the *Principles*, namely 155, he states that 'it is downright impossible, that a soul pierced and enlightened with a thorough sense of omnipresence, holiness and justice of that *Almighty Spirit*, should persist in a remorseful violation of his laws'. In our terminology, Berkeley is saying that if one is really a theoretical theist then it is not possible that one should also be a practical atheist, i.e. one who violates God's moral laws.

Berkeley's God, as an essentially and eminently percipient God, is admirably suited to preclude, or, at any rate, combat practical atheism. The secret crime can be no secret to an omnipercipient God. Hence the morally sensitive area that is not perceived by finite spirits *is* perceived by God (see *Alciphron*, I. 7).

But an obvious doubt naturally arises: How is it that there *are* many, or any, crimes in theistic countries? That is, how is this possible if there is a firm connection — as Berkeley maintains — between theoretical and practical theism? Berkeley's answer is that those who commit crimes (and are therefore practical atheists) just cannot really be theoretical theists. While it is true that 'They can't say there is not a God ... neither are they convinced that there is. For what else can it be [Berkeley asks] but some lurking infidelity, some secret misgivings of mind, with regard to the existence and attributes of God, which permits sinners to grow and harden in their impiety? (*Principles*, Section 155.) These people *say*, and perhaps even think that, they believe in God; but they cannot really believe it; for if they did they would not act impiously. Berkeley calls such people 'demy-atheists'. But we might call them, following our terminology, un-thinking theists. As with the class of unthinking atheists, this new class allows us, among other things, to distinguish between theism which is the result of some non-reasonable cause (e.g. custom or fashion) and theism that is the result of reason and reflection.

Without some such new class it would be harder to resist the con-clusion that theoretical theism need not lead to practical theism.[6] But then it would be harder to deny toleration to theoretical atheists — and Berkeley, like Locke, wishes to deny toleration to theoretical atheists. For example, in *An essay towards preventing the ruin of Great Britain* (1721) he says: 'the public safety requireth that the avowed contemners of all religion should be severely chastised'.[7]

III. Prevalence of the orthodox position

The position supported by Locke and Berkeley — that theoretical atheism issues in practical atheism and theoretical theism issues in practical theism — was the orthodox view. The orthodox view or position (as I shall call it) seems to have been held, or assumed, by the great majority of theological writers of the seventeenth and early part of the eighteenth century.[8] This is not to say that all or most theologians upheld the orthodox position in the extreme manner of Locke and Berkeley. Some did not believe that God both (1) created moral laws and (2) enforced them by other-worldly rewards and punishments. Some held that practical theism required (2) but not (1). (It is also possible that some theologians held (1) without (2), although I have not encountered any who do so.) Again, not all adherents of the orthodox position regarded belief in theoretical theism as a necessary and sufficient condition of practical theism. Berkeley did; but his allegiance to the orthodox position seems to have been more extreme than the majority of theologians. Most supporters of the orthodox position held that belief in a divine rewarder and punisher was essential to theoretical theism, and that this belief was *either* a necessary *or* a sufficient condition for practical theism. Francis Atterbury held the former, necessary condition. In the Preface to the second volume of his *Sermons and discourses* (5th edn, London, 1740) he writes:

> Thus to cry up Virtue, to the weakening our Belief and Hope of the Immortality of the Soul, however at first blush it may seem plausible, is in effect no better than a subtle Invention to ruin Virtue by itself, since it cannot possibly subsist but by the Belief and Support of another Life. (p. 71)

Bishop John Brown, however, in his *Essays on the Characteristics* (London, 1751) asserted the latter; for him belief in a divine rewarder and punisher is a sufficient condition of practical theism:

> where the Mind is convinced of the Being of a GOD; that he *is*, and is a *Rewarder* of them that diligently seek him; where the *Imagination* hath gained a Habit of connecting this great Truth with every Thought, Word, and Action; there it may be justly affirmed, that Piety and Virtue cannot but *prevail*. To say, in a Case of this Nature, that Man will not act according to his Principle, is to contradict the full Evidence of known Facts. (p. 226)

John Milton, on the other hand, embraced the more extreme view: that practical theism required a belief in a God who *created* our moral distinctions. For 'If there were no God', Milton writes in the second chapter of *The Christian doctrine,*

> there would be no distinction between right and wrong; the
> estimate of virtue and vice would entirely depend on the blind
> opinion of men; none would follow virtue, none would be
> restrained from vice by any sense of shame, or fear of laws,
> unless conscience or right reason did from time to time con-
> vince every one, however unwilling, of the existence of God.[9]

Not uncommonly we find the orthodox position expressed figura-
tively, as in Archbishop Bramhall's: 'Without religion, societies are
like but soapy bubbles, quickly dissolved.'[10] Bramhall's opponent,
Thomas Hobbes, states the orthodox view more literally and
threateningly: 'if words spoken in a passion signify a denial of a
God, no punishment preordained by law can be too great for such
insolence; because there is no living in a commonwealth with men
to whose oaths we cannot reasonably give credit.' (See Chapter 2,
Section V.)

The general position to which most prominent exponents of
Puritanism, Royalism and Hobbism assent, is held also by the irasci-
ble John Edwards, who flatly declares that 'no man can be ... virtuous unless he believes there is a God'. The orthodox position cut
across party and ideological lines. Although Bentley regards Hobbes
as his chief enemy, his own defence of the orthodox position is none
the less along Hobbist (and Lockean) lines:

> No Community ever was or can be begun or maintained, but
> upon the Basis of Religion. What Government can be
> imagined without judicial Proceedings? And what methods of
> Judicature without a religious Oath? which implies and sup-
> poses an Omniscient Being, as conscious to its falshood or
> truth, and revenger of Perjury. So that the very nature of an
> Oath (and therefore of Society also) is subverted by the Atheist;
> who professeth to acknowledge nothing superior to himself, no
> omnipresent Observer of the actions of Men.[11]

Nor does this statement by the belligerent champion of the established church differ much from a passage contained in the most
notorious anticlerical work of the period — *The rights of the Christian
Church* (London, 1706); and the similarity even extends to the choice
of such key words as 'subverts' and 'acknowledge'. According to
Matthew Tindal, author of *The rights*, an atheist

may justly be reackon'd an Enemy to the whole Race of Mankind, as subverting that Foundation on which their Preservation and Happiness is mainly built ... In a word, Religion is so very necessary for the Support of human Societys that 'tis impossible ... they can subsist without acknowledging some invisible power that concerns himself with human Affairs. (pp. 12–13)

Atheism was perceived as a fatal threat to morality and civil society not only by philosophers but by the leading judges and lawyers. As Lord Justice Hale expressed it in 1676: 'to say religion is a cheat is to dissolve all those obligations whereby civil societies are preserved; and Christianity being part and parcel of the laws of England, therefore, to reproach the Christian religion is to speak in subversion of the law.'[12] In his celebrated *Commentaries on the laws of England* (Oxford, 1769), vol. 4, Chapter 4, William Blackstone goes through seven species of irreligious offence, the fourth of which is *'blasphemy'* against the Almighty, by denying his being or providence', an offence which is 'punishable at common law by fine and imprisonment, or other infamous corporeal punishment' (p. 59). For, as Blackstone observes 'all moral evidence [judicial oaths] therefore, all confidence in human veracity, must be weakened by irreligion, and overthrown by infidelity' (p. 44), a claim which he supports by the etymology of the word 'miscreants'; for *'mescroyantz* in our antient law books is the name of unbelievers' (p. 44).

When the emergence of overt atheism is seen within this social context, its lateness becomes less surprising. One would expect avowed atheism to appear only when the orthodox position had lost its hold. I shall want to argue this more specifically in connection with the *Answer*; but it will first be necessary to trace the main lines of the opposition to the orthodox view, since Hammon and Turner drew heavily on previous opposition.

IV. The anti-orthodox position: Bayle and Shaftesbury

Roughly between Locke and Berkeley there emerged two notable challengers of the orthodox position: Pierre Bayle and Lord Shaftesbury. Both sought to weaken the link between the theoretical and practical; they certainly denied that the latter followed from the former in the inevitable way suggested by the orthodox position. Bayle, especially, casts considerable doubt on the efficacy of all theory, but particularly theological theory. His general scepticism brings into question whether any theoretical belief is certain and intelligible enough to justify assent, to say nothing of its being put into practice. Furthermore, he took delight in pointing out that most alleged theoretical atheists, like Spinoza and Epicurus, seemed to be, to all intents and purposes, practical theists; whereas many theoretical theists often acted like practical atheists.[13] One famous example here is King David, the man after God's own heart.

Bayle's biographical assault on the orthodox position reaches its climax with the following rather curious *ad hominem* argument. The most evil and depraved being is the most complete practical atheist. But if such a being believes firmly in the existence of God (and probably also has an adequate understanding of God) then there can hardly be a necessary connection, or any firm link, between theoretical and practical atheism. And these conditions are indeed fulfilled, since Satan is the most complete practical atheist, but he is also a convinced believer in God.[14]

Apart from such rare conceptual, or *a priori*, sallies, Bayle's attempt to break down the connection between theoretical beliefs and practical consequences is derived from an essentially empiricist source. It is experience or history which shows us that people do not translate their religious theory into practice. As he succinctly expresses it in his *Miscellaneous reflexions occasioned by a comet:* 'Experience overthrows all reasonings tending to prove that the sense of God corrects the vicious inclinations of men' (p. 271). If we consider the matter conceptually, i.e. apart from experience, then, Bayle allows, we will be inclined to accept the orthodox position. But, unfortunately, that is not the way it is in real life. 'I own [says Bayle] if people of another world were left to guess at the manners of Christians, and merely informed that they are creatures endued with reason and good sense, thirsting after happiness, persuaded that there is happiness for those who obey the Divine Law, and hell for such as transgress it' the people from another world would, Bayle concedes, suppose that Christians were virtuous in their behaviour. But experience, or seeing one 'fortnight's way of the world' would soon dispel this favourable judgement based on definition and deduction. And because experience clearly shows us that there is no strong connection between theory and practice, it follows that people should not be persecuted for their theoretical beliefs, including those concerning God. Why should they be persecuted if their theory (or lack of it) will not lead to practice?

Now whereas Bayle's argument for tolerance is based on his

empiricism, Locke and Berkeley defend their intolerance of theoretical atheism on a rationalist basis. They appear to hold that, given a particular theoretical belief, we can, independently of any experience, be sure that a certain practice will result. As Berkeley says, it is 'downright impossible' that a theoretical theist should not be virtuous. Similarly with Locke: thinking the non-existence of God dissolves the bonds of society. Hence we find, in this instance, two of the (supposedly) classic empiricists holding a strong rationalist position.

Bayle contends that theoretical beliefs are not the springs or incentives to action; rather we act from our dominant passions and the bias of our constitution.[15] So there are at least two sides to Bayle's empiricist attack against the orthodox rationalist position. Bayle argues that, firstly, we do not, in fact, act from theories, principles, or reasons; and, secondly, we cannot know how people will behave by considering their principles alone. Rather, people act from passions, and in order to know how they will act we must wait and observe their behaviour. While theory, in Bayle's opinion, is unlikely to result in practice, practice may sometimes lead to theory. And this is so, Bayle contends, in the case of our distinction and question. Practical atheism may lead to theoretical atheism. That is to say, the resolved sinner will realise, or feel, that it is in his 'interest that there should be no God'; hence he will endeavour to persuade himself that there is none.[16] In short, he will rationalise his practical atheism.

Bayle's ingenious attempt to play down theory, and especially its causal efficacy, is not free from difficulties. For example, if theory does not really influence behaviour, then how can Bayle's reasoned case influence *our* behaviour? That is, how could it make us more tolerant of rival religious theories, if, by hypothesis, theories and reasons cannot, or do not, motivate or cause? Why, then, did he bother? Presumably, Bayle bothered to compose and publish his *Reflexions on a comet*, say, because he thought that he was expressing important truths. If so, his belief that a certain theory was true *did* translate itself into the appropriate behaviour or practice.

The second great challenger to the orthodox position was Locke's pupil, Shaftesbury, the author of *An inquiry concerning virtue and merit* (1699). Shaftesbury (who was also on friendly terms with Bayle) continues the process of detaching theoretical from practical theism. The practical, in this case doing what is virtuous, does not require a theoretical belief in God: acting virtuously is a more intuitive matter, according to Shaftesbury, not unlike appreciating that a painting is beautiful. Shaftesbury specifically denies the two things that his teacher, Locke, held to be essential to morality. The first is that rightness and wrongness are determined by God. Quite the contrary: if anything, true religion follows from (or is based on) morality. 'The belief in justice must, as he urges, precede a belief in a just God.'[17] Again, 'if the mere will, decree, or law of God be said absolutely to constitute right and wrong, then are these latter words of no significancy. For [argues Shaftesbury] if each part of a contradiction were affirmed for truth [or as right] by the Supreme Power, they would consequently become true [or right]'; but this is absurd; hence rightness must be independent of God's will.[18] The second thing which Shaftesbury denies is that divine rewards or punishment should enter into our practical or moral behaviour. To do what is right because we will be rewarded subverts morality. We should do what is right because it is right. 'The man who obeys the law under threats is no better than the man who breaks it when at liberty. There is no more of rectitude, piety, or sanctity in a creature thus reformed than there is of meekness or gentleness in a tiger strongly chained.'[19] So an atheist may be virtuous, since virtue does not depend on God.

In subtracting these two features from (theoretical) theism, Shaftesbury is, in my opinion, rejecting (theoretical) theism. This is not to say, however, that he is accepting (theoretical) atheism. Rather, I suggest, he is accepting a theoretical deism that tends towards pantheism. So, for Shaftesbury, God's immanence is emphasised, while His transcendence is played down. Natural religion is allowed, revealed religion is rejected. While his God is identified with what is right, He neither creates nor enforces it. God does not interfere with men: the supernatural elements in religion are excised. God can do nothing for us; we can do nothing for Him. 'True affection for God [Shaftesbury insists] must be disinterested, having no other object than the excellency of that being itself.'[20] All this, or at least most of it, I submit, is central to the deistic conception of God. God is retained, but at a price: and that price (in effect) is religion.[21]

Supposing that Shaftesbury's position is aptly described as a theoretical deism, then the problem naturally arises as to the nature of practical deism. Berkeley felt that the practical translation of Shaftesbury's theoretical deism would be practical atheism. He compares Shaftesbury's removal of divine rewards and punishments to a king that would 'give out that there was neither jail nor executioner in his kingdom to enforce the laws, but that it would be beautiful to observe them, and that in so doing men would taste the pure delight which results from order and *decorum*'.[22] Such a pronouncement by a king would give rise to mass criminality, and if a parallel situation pertained in the moral world, there would be mass immorality.

Shaftesbury himself would, no doubt, have objected that it is practical (and not theoretical) deism which has primacy; and it encompasses the admirable part of practical theism, e.g., keeping promises, while excluding such undesirable behaviour as entreating God's special favour by prayer. Practical deism would retain the moral part of practical theism, and it would explicitly dismiss the religious part. We might call this morally practical theism, or, even better, moral theism.[23]

V. Variations and transitions in the early eighteenth century

Obviously, not all thinkers were as decided as Locke and Berkeley on the one side and Bayle and Shaftesbury on the other. Samuel Clarke, for example, seems to steer a middle course. He holds (with Shaftesbury) that God wills what is right, and that it is not right because God wills it: *x* is good independent of God's will, *but God does will x*; doing *x* would be a duty even if God did not reward *x*; *but God does reward x*. For Clarke these additional factors (which I have italicised) are not necessary for morality, but they follow necessarily from God's goodness.[24] This is also the position of the deist, Thomas Chubb, who minimises, even more than Clarke does, the role of other-worldly rewards and punishments.[25] If Chubb may be described as a left-wing Clarkean, then Philip Doddridge can be described as a member of the right wing. With Clarke and Chubb he insists that moral laws are prior to God's will, but he is reluctant to free morality altogether from its dependence on divine rewards and punishments. Doddridge's uncertainty is evident in the following passage from his *Lectures on pneumatology* (no. xci): '...the support and comfort of a good man in his troubles, *greatly depends* on the expectation of a future state; and this expectation [is] his greatest encouragement to persevere in virtue under its greatest disadvantages'.[26] The transitional state of the debate can also be seen in the popular literature. In an enlightened essay in the *London Magazine* of 1749, the anonymous writer states: 'To conclude: there is nothing in atheism to correct evil passions and inclinations ... But superstitions implanteth and animateth inhuman dispositions' (vol. 18, p. 553). So theoretical atheism is not able to prevent practical atheism, but it does not (unlike false religion) lead to practical atheism.

The conflict between the two positions can also be seen in the case of Shaftesbury's follower, Francis Hutcheson, who in 1738 was brought before the Glasgow Presbytery and charged with maintaining that 'we could have a knowledge of good and evil without and prior to a knowledge of God'. It is indicative of the growing strength of the anti-orthodox movement that the prosecution had no effect, except to intensify the devotion of Hutcheson's students.[27]

Another indication of the same tendency can be seen in the works of Anthony Collins, a friend of both Locke and Shaftesbury. In some essays published in a periodical called the *Independent Whig* (1720) Collins develops a persuasive definition — which nicely relates to our question.[28] Collins accepts that atheism is a bad thing, i.e. he endorses its negative emotive meaning. But he attempts to change, or, at least, shift the cognitive meaning of the term 'atheism'; and he tries to do this by means of the theoretical/practical distinction.

He begins his essay of 2 November 1720, by reassuring his readers that there is no real danger from theoretical atheism — this is so because men naturally and inevitably believe in some sort of God.[29] But in any case, theoretical atheism is really only objectionable because it *may* lead to practical atheism. It is this possible link between the two which makes us dislike theoretical atheism; for it is practical atheism which is 'to be dreaded and feared' (pp. 261–263). Hence, in the next essay, practical atheism becomes 'true atheism'. And this 'true atheism' — the phrase is used three times — is what the High-Church party indulge in, for example, by false swearing.[30]

Collins then goes on to show, mostly by a series of rhetorical questions, that the cognitive difference between atheism and the position of the High-Church party is of 'small moment'; for the two are pragmatically so much alike. He asks: 'What is this difference to their neighbours, while they [those of the High-Church] act like atheists, that they believe in God and religion?' (p. 267). So Collins retains the negative emotive force of the term 'atheist', but he shifts the meaning from theoretical atheism to practical atheism, and attempts to fasten the label on the High-Church party, a party that is normally identified with (theoretical) theism.

In his essay of 30 November 1720, Collins continues this line of argument with the claim that immorality or practical atheism tends to produce theoretical atheism. His point (although it is not singular) is not the same as Bayle's, i.e. it is not that the immoral man rationalises his practical atheism, thereby convincing himself that his practical atheism is based on a theoretical atheism. Collins's point is that the widespread practical atheism of many professed theoretical theists, and especially of clergymen, disposes the moral onlooker to link and reject practical atheism with theoretical theism, thereby becoming a theoretical atheist. It is for this reason, suggests Collins, 'that there are more people of no religion in Italy, than in the world besides' (p. 281).

VI. Hume's anti-orthodoxy

Hume has a prominent position in this anti-orthodox movement: like Bayle and Shaftesbury, he magnifies the practical and belittles the theoretical. Again like Bayle, Shaftesbury and Collins, Hume sceptically attacks theoretical theism. Although in his attack on theoretical deism he probably parts company with Shaftesbury. But like Shaftesbury he tries to develop an autonomous secular morality. What I should like to concentrate on here is Hume's thesis that those who believe in theoretical theism are inclined to practical atheism.

According to Boswell, Hume 'said flatly that the morality of every religion was bad, and [continues Boswell], I really thought, was not jocular when he said that when he heard a man was religious, he concluded he was a rascal, though he had known some instances of very good men being religious. This was an extravagant reverse of the common remark as to infidels.'[31]

Hume's most concentrated attack on the orthodox position is in Part XII of the *Dialogues*, where he examines among other things the central question of oaths. For Hume, the authority of oaths does not arise from religion:

> It is the solemnity and importance of the occasion, the regard to reputation, and the reflecting on the general interests of society, which are chief restraints upon mankind. Customhouse oaths and political oaths are but little regarded even by some who pretend to principles of honesty and religion: and a Quaker's asserveration is with us justly put upon the same footing with the oath of any other person. (p. 277)

This may be Hume's answer to such adherents of the orthodox position as Locke and Bentley. Hume also suggests that theoretical theism tends to misdirect attention to the revealed side of practical theism: 'the very diverting of the attention, the raising up a new and frivolous species of merit ... must have the pernicious consequences, and weaken extremely men's attachment to the natural motives of justice and humanity' (p. 274). Again: 'where the interests of religion are concerned, no morality can be forcible enough to bind the enthusiastic zealot. The sacredness of the cause sanctifies every measure, which can be made use of to promote it' (p. 275).

It is appropriate that one way in which Hume justifies the thesis that belief in God leads to immorality is by combining his philosophical work with his historical writing. For, as he states in the *Treatise of human nature* (1740) III.ii.10: 'the study of history confirms the reasonings of true philosophy'. And 'If the religious spirit be ever mentioned in any historical narration, we are sure to meet afterwards with a detail of miseries which attend it.' A particularly striking 'historical narration' in which we meet with abundant 'detail of miseries' is Hume's account of the October 1641 massacre in Ireland: 'an event', he tells us, 'memorable in the annals of human kind, and worthy to be held in perpetual detestation and abhorrence'.[32] Hume's picture of the alleged massacre of the Protestants by the Catholic rebels is — there can be little doubt — exaggerated and emotional, even by the standards of his own time; and such an account was especially surprising from the pen of a philosopher known for his religious neutrality. How are we to explain this? I suggest that Hume's design was to show concretely and dramatically how theism leads to practical atheism. So in his account of the massacre he is vividly describing an historical event, which, in his view, confirms the reasonings of true philosophy.

But what exactly are the reasonings of true philosophy in this case? For the answer we must go to Hume's *Natural history of religion* (1757), Section XIV — aptly entitled 'Bad influence of popular religions on morality' — where he argues that 'the greatest crimes have been found, in many instances, compatible with superstitious piety and devotion'.[33] His justification for claiming that popular religions are likely to encourage acts of exceptional immorality is, briefly, as follows. If a man does something because he believes that it is moral, then he is *not* doing it for God's sake alone; he is doing it, at least in part, because he thinks it right. When, on the other hand, something is done which 'either [1] serves to no purpose in life, or [2] offers the strongest violence to his natural inclinations' (Ibid.), then we have something which might have been done for God's sake alone. Certainly it is not, in Hume's view, for the sake of morality or what is right. Now both of these conditions are fulfilled, or exemplified, in Hume's account of the 1641 massacre. Thus one contra-utilitarian act which the Irish rebels are supposed to have performed is described by Hume as follows: 'Such was their frenzy that the cattle, which they had seized, and by rapine made their own, yet, because they bore the name English, were wantonly slaughtered, or, when covered with wounds, turned into the woods and deserts.'[34] Hume also mentions that the rebels wasted the 'cultivated fields' of the Protestants (p. 375). And turning to the second condition — that of sympathy — one can cite a number of pertinent passages from Hume's *History*. Thus after recounting a number of bloody deeds, supposedly committed by the rebels, he writes: 'Amidst all these enormities, the sacred name of RELIGION [sic] resounded on every side; not to stop the hands of these savages, but to endorse their blows, and to steel their hearts against every movement of human or social sympathy' (p. 374). The use of religion to 'steel their hearts against every movement of human or social sympathy' is clearly very close to offering 'the strongest violence to ... natural inclinations'.

So we see here how theism can and (in Hume's view) did lead to an exceptionally horrible variety of practical atheism. (We see the 'how' in the *History* and the 'why' in the *Natural history of religion*.) In order to do something for God's sake alone, a religious person or group may go directly against what they feel to be right. The strong link which Hume tries to forge between practical atheism and zealous theoretical theism may remind us of Bayle's Satan argument. It may also be noticed that Hume's approach is partly empiricistic and partly rationalistic. The theoretical beliefs of the rebels (e.g. that God exists and wishes them to do certain things) do affect their practice. Moreover, we can understand conceptually why theoretical theism (in certain situations) should lead to practical atheism — and of an extremely blameworthy variety. On the other hand, our only source for knowing that all this has, in fact, happened is experience or history.

Would Hume's attack also apply to theoretical deism, such as that held by Shaftesbury, as well as theoretical theism? I tend to think not, since it would hardly make sense for a theoretical deist to act in the same way towards his God as the rebels, in Hume's account, acted towards their God. One cannot do anything for a deist God, nor can He (nor does He) want us to do anything for Him. This becomes even clearer as the deistic conception tends towards pantheism — and, in my opinion, this tendency is logically difficult to resist.

On the other hand, it is more than barely conceivable that the theistic God might wish us to do things for His sake (and reward us for doing them) although they are immoral. Nor can I see that this situation would be essentially altered if we imagine a theistic God who produces moral laws (as in Locke), or a theistic God who is subservient to them (as in Clarke). In either case, we seem to have the *possibility* that God might want us to do *x*, even though He knows that *x* is wrong. This option must be open to the theist's God. If not, then we have already moved towards a more deistic (or pantheistic) conception of God, in which choice is eliminated (as implying imperfection). Such a God *cannot* do what is wrong: He is necessarily and not contingently perfect.

It seems even more likely that the theist might convince himself that he should perform some action for God, even though he thought that the action was wrong. (One naturally thinks here of Abraham sacrificing Isaac.) And in such a distressing situation, the conscientious theist might support and comfort himself — while he was doing what he thought to be wrong — with the reflexion 'great is the mystery of Godliness,' or 'His ways are higher than our ways.'[35] Furthermore, it can be argued that implied in the problem of evil — or in taking the problem seriously — there is the possibility, at least, that God might (for unknown reasons) be responsible for some evils.

VII. Late eighteenth-century compromises and vacillation

The movement of thought which I have been exploring may be seen to reach a culmination in Kant. Practical deism or moral theism has become primary; and it no longer needs the help or support of theoretical theism. (Indeed, in some cases, it repudiates theoretical theism as a danger.) In the 'Transcendental dialectic' of the first *Critique* Kant had argued that all the theoretical attempts to prove the existence of God — whether through the ontological, cosmological, or teleogical argument — are doomed to failure. In arguing thus, Kant is following in the well-worn tracks of, among others, Bayle and Hume.

But this is not to say that moral theism is not firmly grounded. It is; but not in the manner of the orthodox position, where it stands on theoretical theism. Now, it does not have to: for now moral theism has acquired enough strength and independence to stand on its own. (Formerly a dependent, it has now reached maturity and gained independence: *morality has come of age.*) Indeed, it may be able, Kant suggests, to support theoretical theism (or deism). For in understanding our moral actions we come to realise that they require (or will be assisted by) the existence of a God. Because 'we ought to promote the highest good' we should postulate that which would support this.[36] And since the existence of a God — who could proportion happiness and morality — would support this, we should postulate His existence. The former dependent — we might say — is now able to support its infirm parent. Whereas in the orthodox position theoretical theism justifies practical theism, for Kant practical theism (or deism) justifies theoretical theism (or deism).

In describing this reversal of the orthodox position on the distinction as applied to the question, we may well be tempted to say — following the well-known image of Marx — that Kant sets Locke and theism back on their feet, in that practice now supports theory. Thus it would not be correct to see Kant as a destroyer of the orthodox view; he is as much its preserver and reviser. The old relationship can no longer be sustained. But there is to be no divorce. The marriage has now been put on a sounder basis. This tendency to reconcile the partners is implicit in other deistic thinkers such as Voltaire and Paine.[37] Although they wish to protect morality from the wrong sort of liaison with religion, they are by no means utterly opposed to religion or to a suitable relationship between it and morality. Deism may represent a logical move towards atheism and the complete breakdown of the orthodox position; but it would be wrong to suppose that the deists themselves saw their efforts in that light.

Following a visit to England in 1765, d'Holbach reported to Diderot that, although 'the Christian religion is nearly extinct in England [and] the deists are innumerable; there are almost no atheists; those who are conceal it. An atheist and a scoundrel are almost synonymous terms for them' (see above, Chapter 2, Section I). Clearly, then, the success of deism did not lead to the destruction of the orthodox position. As in many a tumultuous marriage, neither partner could face the decision to divorce. (They had after all been married a very long time.) And deism had no intention of bringing about such an unnecessary divorce. In the second part of *The age of reason* (1795) we find Paine adhering to a modified version of the orthodox view reminiscent of that held by Berkeley:

> Were a man impressed as fully and as strongly as he ought to be, with the belief of a God, his moral life would be regulated by the force of that belief; he would stand in awe of God, and of himself, and would not do the thing that could not be concealed from either. (p. 87)

The more upper-class deists also regarded the belief in God as a necessary way of keeping the lower orders orderly. Religion and morality are to remain married, even though it is a marriage of convenience: truth is to be sacrificed to expediency. Voltaire presents this cynical version of the orthodox position in his well-known epigram: 'If God did not exist we should have to invent Him.' And in his *Treatise on religious toleration* (London, 1764) he argues in a similar vein:

> Such is the weakness and perversity of mankind, that it would doubtless be better for them to be subjected to all possible superstition, provided they were not destructive, than for them to live without religion. Man has always stood in need of some restraint; and tho' it was certainly ridiculous to sacrifice to Fauns, Sylvans, and Naiades, it was more rational and more useful to adore those fantastic images of divinity, than to give themselves up to atheism. (p. 207)

It should not surprise us to find, as we find here and have found elsewhere, deists and atheists at war. Their very theoretical similarity or proximity (like the physical proximity of porcupines) undoubtedly encouraged antagonism. The closer they became, the more uncomfortable.

But despite the hostility of deism to atheism, the former's success meant at least a logical weakening of the orthodox position and, one would suppose, an encouragement to the rise of atheism. The largely non-personal deistic God could not be as effective in sanctioning morality as the theistic God of wrath; and some deists themselves had argued, in the interests of morality, that morality *could* function without a God of any sort. As the eighteenth century wore on, the deists and liberal Christians were still castigating atheism, but their attacks were becoming increasingly more vacillating if not more accommodating. For example, in an article in the *Gentleman's Magazine* of 1797, we find the epigram: 'an Atheist, by his principles, is a knave *per se*, and an honest man *per accidens*'. In his gloss on this epigram the writer, who signs himself 'Christianus Catholicus', says that he is 'not unacquainted with some avowed Atheists, whose apparent moral conduct, and occasional command of tempter, is seldom equalled by many who would be thought good Christians'. But having spoken in favour of the morality of atheists he adds: 'But habits of intimacy with such persons are neither desirous nor very safe' (pp. 279–80).

Notes

1. *The works of ... John Tillotson*, 9th edn (Dublin, 1726), p. 5.
2. The religious side of practical theism is emphasised by Archbishop Wake in his formulation of the distinction. The chief offence against the first Commandment, he maintains, is 'First, *atheism*, and *infidelity*, whether it be speculative, or practical; that is to say, whether men do really believe there is no God; or live so as if they did not; without any due *worship* of *Him*'; see *Principles of the Christian religion* (London, 1699), Section XXIII.
3. See Paine's *The age of reason*, Part III, Introduction (in Carlile's *Theological works of Paine*); according to Paine, Christianity 'unships the helm of ... morality', it tends to 'de-moralize man'.
4. *Works of John Locke*, 2nd edn (London, 1722) vol. ii, p. 251. In the Charter of Carolina — which Locke had a hand in drawing up — no man was to be permitted to be a freeman of Carolina unless he acknowledged a God' (Robertson, *Dynamics*, p. 111).
5. This note is in the Chapman manuscript, Trinity College Dublin Library, fol. 34. The same thought is also emphasised in Berkeley's *Discourse addressed to the magistrates* (1738); in *Works*, vol. vi (1953), pp. 208–12.
6. In *Alciphron* V, Berkeley tries to avoid the conclusion by means of a number of more or less question-begging distinctions; thus in Section 6 he states: 'If a Believer doth Evil, it is owing to the man, not his Belief. And if an infidel doth Good, it is owing to the man, and not to his Infidelity'; also see Sections 13 and 15. Another way of resisting the conclusion is recorded by John Evelyn in his *Diary*: 'a presumptuous sinner is at that instant of time, an *Atheist*; since it were impossible, he should believe any such thing as a sin-revenging God, and yet commit such a deliberate sinn against God' (*Diary of John Evelyn* Oxford, 1955), vol. iv, p. 43.
7. See *Works,* vol. vi, pp. 20–1. In *Alciphron* (1732), II.xxiv, Berkeley writes: 'Nothing leads to vice so surely as irreligion.'
8. It is also the view of Richard Blackmore (who defends it in his essay 'Of atheism' and in the Introduction to *The Creation*), Philip Skelton (see *Ophiomaches, or deism revealed* (London, 1749), pp. 301–3), and John Leland (*View of the deistical writers*, vol. iii [London, 1756] Letter One) and Daniel Waterland, as quoted in *Deism fairly stated* (London, 1746), p. 4.
9. See *The works of John Milton* (New York, 1933), edited by J. Hanford and W. Dunn, vol. 4, p. 29.
10. Quoted in Hobbes's *Answer to Bramhall, English works*, vol. iv, p. 287.
11. See Bentley's *Eight sermons preached at the Boyle lectures*, p. 34; see also above Chapter 1, Section V.
12. See Bradlaugh's *The laws relating to blasphemy*, pp. 13f, and the recent (17 March 1978) blasphemy judgement by Lord Justice Roskell; reprinted in the *New Humanist* (Spring 1978), especially p. 171.
13. See Bayle's *Dictionary*, vol. x (1741), 'Illustration upon atheists'.
14. *Miscellaneous reflexions occasioned by a comet;* the *Reflexions* were printed in 1682 and 1705; see 3rd edn (London, 1708), pp. 297–8. The devil, writes Bayle, is 'an evident proof ... that the most notoriously wicked don't cast off the belief in God.'
15. Ibid., p. 272; also see *Dictionary*, 'Illustration upon atheists'.
16. Ibid., pp. 364–5.

17. See Leslie Stephen's *History of English thought in the 18th century*, IX.26.

18. J.M. Robertson (ed.), *Characteristics of men, manners, opinions...* (Indianapolis, 1964) with an Introduction by S. Grean (1964), p. 264.

19. Stephen, *History* IX.30, and *Characteristics*, p. 267.

20. *Characteristics*, Introduction, p. xxii, and vol. 2, p. 54.

21. Perhaps the classic expression of the deistic conception (with less apparent tendency to pantheism) is in Tindal's *Christianity as old as the creation* (1730).

22. *Alciphron*, III.xiii.

23. In his 'Letter to Erskine', Paine speaks of 'moral religion'; see *Theological works*, p. 23.

24. See Clarke's *Discourse concerning the being and attributes of God* 6th edn (London, 1725), Part 2, pp. 3–6, and 68–71; see also H. Sidgwick's *History of ethics*, Chapter 4.

25. See his *Discourse concerning reason* (London, 1733), pp. 43–5.

26. See *Works of Doddridge* (Leeds, 1803), vol. 4, p. 515.

27. See Robertson's *History of freethought*, p. 763.

28. See my 'Anthony Collins' essays in the *Independent Whig'*, in *Journal of the History of Philosophy* (October, 1975), pp. 463–9.

29. *Independent Whig* 6th edn (London 1732), pp. 259–60.

30. Ibid., pp. 263–4; Atterbury, for example, had sworn the oath of allegiance to George I, but had also tried to bring over the Pretender.

31. See *Boswell in extremes* (London, 1971), p. 11. Also see Hume's *Essays and treatises* (London, 1777), especially the long irreligious note I, pp. 547–9.

32. *History of England* (London, 1763), vol. vi, p. 375 (Chapter 55). See my 'David Hume and the 1641 Rebellion in Ireland' for a fuller account; in *Studies, an Irish quarterly review* (Summer 1976), pp. 101–12.

33. *Essays and treatises*, vol. ii, p. 464.

34. *History*, vol. vi, p. 373.

35. A theological justification for ethical nihilism or antimonianism is nearly explicit in Pascal's *Pensées*, no. 233. Pascal writes: 'The finite is annihilated in the presence of the infinite, and becomes pure nothing. So our spirit before God, *so our justice before divine justice*' (my italics). Another sort of justification is to be found in D. Waterland's *Remarks upon ... Clarke's exposition of the Church-catechism* (London, 1730): 'there may be in some cases, greater Excellency, and more real virtue in obeying *positive* Precepts, than in any *Moral* virtue' (p. 87); and 'He is a proud and sawcy servant that will never obey his Master but where he sees the *reason* of the command' (Ibid.). See also below, Epilogue.

36. *Critique of practical reason* (1788), Chapter 2, Section v.

37. See the *Works of Thomas Paine* (1896), edited by M. Conway, vol. iv, pp. 19–20.

8

The Causes of Atheism

I. The triumph of theoretical over practical atheism: the *Answer*

The orthodox position, according to which morality required a religious basis, may have been the 'common remark', as Boswell put it in 1776, but it was fast becoming something of a cliché (see above, Chapter 7, Section VI). The accumulated arguments and authority of Bayle, Shaftesbury, Hume and others were having their effect. They were driving proponents of the orthodox position to accommodations and compromises, such as those of Clarke, Chubb, Kant, Voltaire and Paine. The uncertainty of Priestley is fairly typical. He holds that a theoretical atheist may in fact be virtuous, although he has little or no motive to be so.[1]

Priestley's criticism is taken up in the *Answer* (see above, Chapter 5). Hammon admits that atheism is morally negligible, but, he argues, so is theism: 'The believer and the unbeliever we often see equally base, equally moral' (xxxii). More specifically:

> If it is asked me, 'why am I honest and honourable?' I answer, because of the satisfaction I have in being so. 'Do all people receive that satisfaction?' No, many who are ill educated, ill-exampled and perverted, do not. I do, that is enough for me. In short, I am well constructed, and feel that I can therefore act an honest and honourable part without a religious motive. (xxxi)

Hammon may have taken this line of argument from Bayle, whose *Reflexions on a comet* he approvingly refers to on page xviii. His thoughts on morality also show signs of the influence of Shaftesbury:

'I would', [he writes] fix morality upon a better basis than belief in a Deity. If it has indeed at present no other basis, it is not morality, it is selfishness, it is timidity; it is the hope of reward, it is the dread of punishment. (xxxiii)

The subject is given more sustained treatment by Turner, who, significantly, opens his response to Priestley with a passage that links belief in God and belief in the orthodox position:

It is the general fashion to believe in a God, the maker of all things, or at least to pretend to such a belief, to define the nature of this existing Deity by the attributes which are given to him, to place the foundation of morality on this belief, and in idea at least, to connect the welfare of civil society with the acknowledgement of such a Being. (p. 1)

But although it is the 'general fashion',

Few however are those, who being questioned can give any tolerable grounds for their assertions upon this subject, and hardly any two among the learned agree in their manner of proving what each will separately hold to be indisputably clear.

Turner seems to be saying that the general assent to these dogmas is mere lip service: they have become hollow. In any case, he proceeds to apply the hammer to both dogmas:

As to morality, those very people who are moral will not deny, they would be so though there were not a God, and there never yet has been a civil lawgiver, who left crimes to be punished by the author of the universe; not even the profanation of oaths upon the sacredness of which so much is built in society, and which yet is said to be a more immediate offence against the Deity than any other that can be named. (p. 2)

After some pages taken up with defending atheism, Turner returns to the question of religion and morality. He ingeniously uses the orthodox view as a premise in an *ad hominem* argument against God's goodness:

It were better to seek another support for morality than a belief in God; for the moral purpose in believing a Deity (an invisible Being, maker of all, our moral governor, who will hereafter take cognizance of our conduct) is not a little checked by considering, that he leaves the proof of his existence so ambiguous, that even men with a habit of piety upon them cannot but have their doubts, whilst on this existence so much of the moral purpose depends. If this is not an argument against the morality of a Deity, it is at all events one against his *infinite* morality; though moral is an attribute to be given to him in the infinite degree as much as any other. (pp. 25–6)

This passage can also be read as an argument *reductio ad absurdum* against the orthodox view. Because assuming the orthodox view leads to the absurd conclusion that God is not entirely moral, the assumption must be false.

Turner twice denies that his advocacy of theoretical atheism is intended to be an encouragement to practical atheism: 'It is not the wish of the answerer by supporting atheism to give any encouragement to immorality' (p. 25) and 'If necessary let it again be repeated, that it is not at all meant in this answer to make atheism a plea or protection for immorality' (p. 43).

Turner's final treatment of the subject is on pp. 43–6. Here Hume's influence is especially apparent: 'The knowledge of a God and even the belief of a providence are found but too slight a barrier against human passions, which are apt to fly out as licentiously as they would otherwise have done' (p. 43). It is not religious beliefs, but 'human laws' and 'the natural inclination of man for pleasure, or a taste contracted for certain objects by prejudice and habit' that makes men orderly and moral. (p. 44). Religious belief exhausts itself in generating practical theism of a revealed nature: 'It may make men build temples, sacrifice victims, offer up prayers, or perform something of the like nature; but never breaks a criminal intrigue, restore ill-gotten wealth, or mortify the lust of man' (p. 43). Turner is very expansive on this Humean theme (pp. 43–5). Again like Hume he suggests that 'religion even encourages crimes, by the hopes it gives of pardon through the efficacy of prayer' (p. 45). He also accuses partisans of the orthodox position of defending themselves by ignoring fact and history and retreating into metaphysics.

I have dwelt upon Hammon's and Turner's critique of the orthodox position, because I believe that there is an important connection between it and the genesis of atheism. It is no mere coincidence that we find in the same book an extensive and extreme anti-orthodox diatribe and also the first avowal of theoretical atheism. The connection is deeper and more complex. Granting the ultimate importance of practical or moral theism, it is tempting to regard the overcoming of the orthodox position as a necessary precondition for the emergence of atheism. Unless atheism could demonstrate its capacity to coexist peacefully with moral theism it would be kept down as an intolerable danger. If we accept this construction, then we shall also be inclined to see the repressive tendency both as illustrating the power of the orthodox position and also as a weapon in its defence. Plainly there is a great deal in the *Answer* that supports this practice-then-theory construction. For example, time and again our authors stress that their atheism presents no danger to morality.

There is also a deeper level at which the defeat of the orthodox position may have been necessary if atheism was to emerge. According to the orthodox view a theoretical atheist could not be trusted to keep his oaths or promises: only belief in God could guarantee a person's trustworthiness and the truthfulness of his statements. But then the logic of the orthodox position is to deny, at least epistemologically, the existence of atheists. For how are we to identify an atheist? Surely by his verbal or written statements. But because these statements are made by a man suspected of atheism, they cannot, according to the orthodox position, be trusted. Moreover, the more we were convinced that someone is an atheist, then, paradoxically, the less reason we should have for accepting his statement that he is an atheist. Thus an atheist's claim to atheism cannot fit within the framework of the orthodox view. Indeed, if the putative atheist is unlucky enough himself to subscribe to the orthodox position, then he will be unable to trust his own self-ascription of atheism. So the orthodox position not only protected itself by means of the repressive tendency as expressed in the denials of atheism, but by its internal logic it could metamorphise itself into a similar instrument of repression; (cp. Chapter 1, Section XII).

There is then a special poignancy in Hammon's declaring upon his honour that he is an atheist (p. xvii); for in this declaration he is resisting both the repressive tendency and the orthodox position. Hammon may also have been alluding to the repressive nature of the orthodox position when he says about Turner and himself: 'Behold then, *if we are to be believed*, two atheists instead of one' (p. xvii, my italics). Having cleared away the weeds of the repressive tendency and orthodox position their atheism was able to emerge.

One can, however, take a different perspective. The growth of the anti-orthodox view may itself be explained by the increasing opposition to theoretical theism. According to this theory-then-practice view, the orthodox position had to be abandoned because belief in God — at least in the moral-law-giver and enforcer God — was becoming less and less convincing. As educated religious belief moved from theism to deism to pantheism, the perceptive adherents of moral theism saw the writing on the wall. Morality must be saved, even at the expense of its former parent and support. Because God has become doubtful, God cannot be at the basis of morality.

Of course in the *Answer* we find both a disbelief in God and a disbelief in the orthodox view. How are we to know that it was the first that actually encouraged the second, or, more generally, had primacy over the second? We can offer at least two principal reasons in support of this construction. First, if the atheism of Hammon and Turner really arose from a disbelief in the orthodox view — as the rival practice-then-theory construction supposes — we should expect them to be thoroughly and utterly convinced of the falsity of the orthodox position. But there is evidence that they were not so convinced. For example, why is Hammon anxious to stress that atheism will only be accepted by a select few (pp. xvi and xxiv) and that 'low minds' will always believe in some sort of religion (pp. xxxiii–iv)? I am inclined to think that he had not entirely shaken off the patronising deistic belief that religion was a useful fiction for keeping the lower orders in order. If there is really no danger that atheism is going to lead to immorality, then why is Hammon so pleased that it will be accepted by so few? It is difficult to accept his statement that he simply wishes to belong to a select group. It is also difficult to believe that Turner's twice-repeated statement, that his advocacy of atheism is not meant to be an incitement to immorality, does not express an underlying suspicion that it may very well have that effect.

My second reason for believing that their atheism did not primarily arise from the overcoming of the orthodox position is that, although they wish to protect moral theism, they are not prepared to protect it at all costs. There are some things that are more important than the safety of society. This comes out clearly in Hammon's consideration of the question: whether 'mischief may ensue to society by such freedom of discussion' in which God is 'boldly' denied. I have quoted Hammon's daring words in Chapter 5, but some of them are worth quoting again: 'I have a right to truth, and to publish truth, let society suffer or not suffer by it. That society which suffers by truth should be otherwise constituted' (p. xix). This stirring and important passage reveals a fierce rationalism, a belief in the value of reason. The writer is not someone whose theory meekly follows practice, or whose speculations are determined by expedience or utility. We find a similar commitment to rationalism expressed elsewhere, where Hammon writes: 'Truth is his [my] aim' (p. vi) and 'My faith is in reasoning' (p. xxvi).

Hence, although the overcoming of the orthodox position may have provided the necessary condition and fertile soil for the emergence of atheism, the actual genesis of atheism in the *Answer* owed a great deal to the writers' aggressive rationalism. Moreover, if the overcoming of the orthodox position was a sufficient condition for atheism, then we must wonder why atheism did not appear in previous anti-orthodox writers. What was missing in these other writers, I would maintain, was aggressive rationalism. In the *Answer* the dissembling practicality of free-thinkers such as Voltaire has been overcome by a belief in the overriding value of reason and truth and honesty. Hammon is prepared to accept the *harmful truth*.

But how are we to explain this fierce belief in the value of truth? It should first be observed that truth-telling, like honesty, is a part of moral theism. Now we have seen that the autonomy and strength of moral theism had been steadily growing in the eighteenth century, and that it had reached a culmination in Kant's writings of the 1780s. Thus with its liberation came increased power for moral theism. Perhaps religion *had*, as Shaftesbury and his followers maintained, been suffocating it. In any case it was this increased power which, in my opinion, invested truth-telling with greater strength and self-confidence. In the *Answer* we find this concretely manifesting itself: because they believe in the value of truth Hammon and Turner are prepared to avow a potentially harmful truth. Thus the breakdown of the orthodox position led to the increased vitality of moral theism, which in turn led to the enhancement of truth-telling, which led finally to the denial of the existence of God.

Hence it is difficult to separate the theoretical and practical. Atheism in the *Answer* seems to have been born of a number of complicated factors: conscious opposition to the repressive denial of atheism, disbelief in the orthodox position, a reasoned belief in theoretical atheism, and a fierce belief in the value of truthfulness as derived from practical theism.

II. The birth of Shelley's atheism

There is little point in considering how Francis and Scepticus arrived at their atheism, for although we find evidence of the resistance to the repressive tendency in the former, and expressions of rationalism in the latter, in neither case is the data sufficient to reconstruct the paths which brought them to their atheism. It is otherwise with the next apostle of British atheism. Probably because of Shelley's fame, there is a wealth of material which throws much light on the genesis of his atheism and on the genesis of atheism in general.

At a very early age Shelley rejected the liberal Christianity which he had inherited from his family background:

> The first doubts [he wrote in a letter of 11 June 1812] which arose in my boyish mind concerning the genuineness of the Christian religion, as a revelation from the divinity, were excited by the contemplation of the virtues and genius of Greece and Rome. Shall Socrates and Cicero perish, whilst the meanest hind of modern England inherits eternal life?

By the time Shelley entered Oxford in 1810 he was, like many cultured men of the time, a deist. No doubt some of the reasons that drew him away from Christianity are to be found in Theosophus' long speech againt Christianity in the *Refutation*. The more important question, however, is how Shelley moved from deism to that 'hideous perversion of the intellect', as he was ironically to describe atheism in the *Refutation*. Once it is clearly realised that Shelley was only the second open avower of speculative atheism in Britain, and the first well-known writer to persistently champion the cause of atheism (at least over the three years from 1811 to 1814), then an answer to this question becomes necessary and relevant, not only for a proper understanding of the rise of British atheism but also for a proper understanding of Shelley. To appreciate early atheism we must understand the early Shelley, and to understand the early Shelley we must appreciate early atheism.

How, then, did Shelley move from deism to atheism? I shall argue that central to this movement was Shelley's principle that belief is an involuntary passion. (For convenience I shall call this 'Shelley's principle' or 'the belief principle'.) We have already seen that the belief principle played a significant role in Shelley's *Necessity*. It provided him with a reason for atheism, and with an account of belief such that he could feel his atheism to be necessary and also non-culpable. This principle, probably more than any single argument or doctrine in Shelley's atheistic writings, is most distinctive of his atheological position. Between 1811 and 1814 he adverts to it no fewer than 15 times, as we can see from the following list:

(1) Letter to his father, 6 February 1811.
(2) Three times in the *Necessity*, 1811.
(3) Letter to Elizabeth Hitchener, 11 June 1811.
(4) *Letter to Lord Ellenborough*, 1812; twice.
(5) *Address to the Irish People*, 1812.
(6) *Declaration of Rights*, 1812.
(7) Note *'There is no God'* in *Queen Mab* 1813; three times.
(8) Note 'I will beget a son' in *Queen Mab*.
(9) *Refutation* (1814); twice.

In spite of its obvious importance for him, Shelley nowhere attempts to justify his principle. Nor does it undergo any theoretical modification or — with the possible exception of (3) — development. He seems to have regarded it as intuitively evident. This may be considered surprising because he seems also to think that there is widespread ignorance of it: 'the investigation [of ideas] being confused with the perception [of ideas] has induced many falsely to imagine that the mind is active in belief'.[2] Thus his confidence in the principle would not have arisen from its being generally received. Contrary to claims by some scholars, it is not to be found in Locke,[3] or in Godwin.[4] Nor is it entailed by Shelley's determinism — for according to him the 'mind is active in the investigation' of ideas. A version of the principle is to be seen in Hume and d'Holbach,[5] and, earlier, in Collins.[6] Shelley is more likely to have been influenced by the statements of Hume and d'Holbach; but Collins's influence cannot be ruled out, because the book in which Collins expressed the principle had been popularised by Priestley, who reissued the *Philosophical inquiry* in 1790. But neither Collins nor Hume nor d'Holbach takes the principle nearly as seriously as does Shelley.

The authority of Hume, d'Holbach and Collins would have supported Shelley's belief in the truth of his principle; but their authority would hardly have convinced him of its self-evidence, nor of its enormous importance or utility. His deeply felt commitment to this principle arose, I believe, from personal experience, and specifically from his unhappy experience with Harriet Grove. We know that Shelley had a strong emotional attachment to this cousin and that he wished to marry her, but because of his advanced religious views — that is on account of his deism — Shelley was rejected by Harriet and her family. He was regarded, to use Kenneth Cameron's phrase, as a 'moral criminal'. That Shelley was very deeply hurt and angered by this rejection is apparent from his letters to his friend Hogg. On

20 December 1810 he writes: 'Oh! I burn with impatience for the moment of Xtianity's dissolution, it has injured me; I swear on the altar of perjured love to revenge myself on the hated cause.' Bitter, too, is the end of his letter of 23 December 1810; and, in his letter of 3 January 1811, he declares: 'I swear that never will I forgive Christianity ... she [Harriet] is no longer mine, she abhors me as a Deist ... Oh! Christianity when I pardon this last this severest of thy persecutions may God (if there be a God) blast me!'

Thus Shelley's suffering led him to a vehement hatred of Christianity, and, as we can see from the parenthetical qualification in this last quotation, to a questioning of the existence of God. This questioning (not denying) of God arose as a result of the resentment he felt against the religious intolerance of the Groves; and the resentment and the questioning of God's existence was, according to my hypothesis, mediated by the belief principle. Support for this hypothesis is to be found in the first letter (20 December 1810) in which Shelley expresses his resentment at Christianity for the injury it had inflicted upon him. Referring to his correspondence on religious matters with certain liberal theologians, Shelley asks Hogg: 'How therefore would you suppose that one of these *liberal* gents. would listen to a scepticism on the subject even of St. Athanasius' sweeping anathema?' Now in his first recorded statement of the belief principle (in the letter to his father less than two months later) Shelley firmly connects the principle with Athanasius' anathema against disbelief. Thus in the compass of the 20 December letter we find together: resentment, scepticism and (very probably) the principle.

Having suffered from the effects of the orthodox position Shelley turned his attention to it. In the 1810/11 letters we see the orthodox position directly and indirectly contested and abused. But this was not merely a theoretical matter. Shelley felt extremely sensitive about being suspected of immorality — of practical atheism following from his theoretical atheism.[7] His defiance of the orthodox view was motivated partly by defence, against people like the Groves, and, at a deeper level, partly against any lingering doubts he himself may have entertained concerning the falseness of the orthodox view. And as his early reflection on the anomoly of virtuous pagans being damned encouraged his abandoning Christianity for deism, so his more radical opposition to the orthodox position encouraged his movement from deism to atheism. His letter of 6 February 1811, written shortly before the publication of the *Necessity*, contains at least seven objections to the orthodox position: (1) reasonable people do not require religious belief in order to behave morally; (2) Christian belief is unreasonable and incredible; (3) the most famous non-Christians were noted for the 'strictest morality'; (4) irreligious periods in history have been most peaceful; (5) no truths, and hence not the truth in (2) above, have been 'known to be prejudicial to the best interests of mankind'; (6) religion is likely to have a negative effect on reasonable men: 'Religion fetters a reasoning mind with the very bonds which restrain the unthinking one from mischief.' Shelley's final objection (7) is made by reference to his belief principle.

Clearly Shelley felt acutely the need to defend himself against the orthodox position. The belief principle was developed to serve in his defence, and it was the defensive technique in which he came to put the most trust. Because our beliefs are involuntary we should not be blamed for them. Whereas Bayle delivered a frontal attack on the orthodox position in order to defend toleration, Shelley outflanks the orthodox position for a similar and perhaps a more personal end. His attack has the advantage over Bayle's in that theoretical belief is not precluded from influencing actions. For although we are not active in the formation of beliefs, our beliefs may be active.

Having accepted the principle which enabled him to protect himself against being branded a moral criminal for his deistic beliefs, Shelley was led, in my view, to the realisation that one should not be afraid to believe anything, no matter how apparently absurd or awful. One need not feel guilty even about believing in the non-existence of God, for all belief is involuntary. Reacting against the narrow religiosity of the Groves, and freed from any guilt with regard to belief, it would be natural for Shelley to contemplate atheism. But not only did the principle liberate him from feeling guilty about unbelief, it also gave him a powerful *ad hominem* argument against the theological God. Thus belief in the principle led logically to a disbelief in the theological God. And the pressure to believe in the principle was considerable for Shelley; for it was his main defence against moral criminality. The movement can be illustrated in the following five stages:

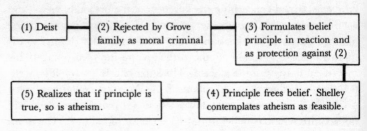

If I am right, Shelley's principle played a pivotal role in his movement towards atheism. This analysis also supposes a practice-then-theory construction. Before atheism could be reached, the orthodox position, or Shelley's lingering allegiance to it, had to be broken down. But that which broke down the intolerant orthodox position also became a reason for atheism.

This is, of course, a highly schematic picture of Shelley's movement to atheism. At the most, it offers a skeleton upon which we must build the additional flesh and blood of Shelley's thought: his reading of Pliny, Hume, d'Holbach and Spinoza; the liberation he obtained from the inhibitive orthodox position by his other objections to it; his reasoning concerning the non-existence of God; and, of course, his involuntary perception that God does not exist. Seeing Shelley's belief principle as central to the picture has various advantages: it helps to explain a number of odd facts, such as his frequent deployment of the principle and his extraordinary confidence in it. I suggest that the principle was to him what the *esse* is *percipi* principle was to Berkeley: 'an obvious tho Amazing truth'.[8] If we accept this construction it becomes easier to imagine how a youth of 19 years, even though precocious, could assert something so novel, so potent and so hedged around with stigma and taboos that throughout the whole of the British Enlightenment only a handful of writers had the courage to assert it.

Shelley's opposition to the orthodox position has features in common with that of Hammon and Turner, and he looks back, too, as one would expect, to the anti-orthodox objections of Shaftesbury and Hume. Although he does not mention Shaftesbury in the *Letter to Lord Ellenborough*, Shelley's arguments concerning the inability of God to alter the moral laws probably owe something to that aristocratic free-thinker. The *Letter to Lord Ellenborough* was directed at one of the most striking legal implementations of the orthodox position. Daniel Eaton had been sentenced to eighteen months imprisonment because he published the so-called third part of Paine's *The age of reason*, a work which 'must inevitably', according to the Attorney-General at the trial, destroy and subvert the morals of those who read it. In his speech, Attorney-General Gibbs affirmed: 'it seems to me most evident, that if men lose the reverence which they owe to ... the established religion, no effectual tie, no controlling check on their conduct remains.' Gibbs also gave expression (without realising it) to the paradox which we have discussed above: 'What reason have you [he asked the jury] to believe that the witnesses will speak the truth, except from the operation of those religious principles?'[9] (But if we cannot believe the assertions of unbelievers, then we cannot believe their self-ascription of deism or atheism: how are we to know that they *are* deists or atheists?) Shelley's primary defence of Eaton's right to hold and publish unpopular doctrines is based on the belief principle. Twice Shelley formulates his principle, once in roughly the same words as the *Necessity* and then in the following epigram: 'No man is accountable for his belief, because no man is capable of directing it.'

There is no indication that either Hammon or Turner holds the belief principle. Their justification for the toleration of beliefs is drawn, like Bayle's, from the practical impotence of beliefs, not from our inability to affect our beliefs. However, Shelley does hold in common with his two atheistic forerunners a commitment to reason and truth. He is an extreme rationalist. As he puts it in a letter of 5 June 1811: '*Truth* is my God.' This suggests the sort of overriding rationalism which we found in Hammon, who would prefer a dangerous truth to a useful lie. But when Shelley elaborates his militant rationalism we realise that it is not as radical as Hammon's. Truth is always to be preferred because there can never be a conflict between it and the good of society. 'Error', he writes in a letter of 28 April 1811, 'cannot in any of its shapes be good, I cannot conceive the possibility.' Writing on 6 February 1811 to his father, Shelley states this in a less conceptual and more descriptive way: '*Truth* whatever it may be has never been known to be prejudicial to the best interests of mankind.' There is, then, a sort of pre-ordained harmony between the truthful and the useful. As Shelley expresses it in the *Necessity*: Truth has always been found to promote the best interests of mankind.'

Thus Shelley's belief in the value of truth was more qualified than Hammon's; it is far closer to Scepticus's optimistic commitment to truth.[10] Hammon's lingering deistic belief in the utility of religion needed the impetus derived from the belief in the overriding value of truth, irrespective of its ill effects on society. Shelley also shares with Hammon a lingering allegiance to this condescending deistic attitude to social order. In his letter to his father he admits that most people need the restraining bonds of religion. He also takes this line when writing on 24 April 1811 to Hogg: 'let this horrid Galilean rule the Canaille'. So the lower orders do, it would appear, need religion. The orthodox position is, or ought to be, true for them. Now this qualified assent to the orthodox position is offset by one of Shelley's most interesting and original objections to that same position. As far as I am aware it is to be found in only the two letters from which

I have just quoted — the first to his father, the second to Hogg. In each case the same metaphor is employed. I have already quoted Shelley's statement to his father; the statement to Hogg runs: 'the reflecting part of the community, that part in whose happiness we have so strong an interest, certainly do not require his [Christ's] morality which when there is no *vice* fetters *virtue*.' It is not clear why Shelley did not publish this thought (a thought which may remind one of Blake's 'One law for the ox and the lion is oppression.')[11] He may have felt on reflection that it was in conflict with his egalitarianism. It is a pity that he never developed it, for it is an exciting speculation which recalls the evolutionary idea of values presented in the explosive writings of another atheist — Nietzsche.

I have now examined what I take to be the chief reasons for and causes of Shelley's atheism. These include his resentment at being rejected by the Groves, a resentment which suggested or enforced his anti-orthodox belief principle. Feeling deeply that his deistic beliefs did not make him a moral criminal, he came to realise that no beliefs are, or can be, criminal. Thus he could *consider* guiltlessly the possibility of atheism. And if atheism were true, then hated Christianity must be false. As he remarked in one of his letters, he had no moral objections to the belief in a (deistic) God; it was just false; deism was simply a 'heresy from Reason'.[12] But Christianity was morally objectionable. Thus atheism would, at one blow, destroy his hated enemy; and the contemplation of atheism and his belief principle led him to realise that the latter implied the former. Shelley would also have been pondering the formidable array of arguments of Hume and d'Holbach. And his belief in the value of reason would have enforced both his growing rationalism and also his rejection of the orthodox position — for truth cannot be hurtful. Having reached a position of speculative atheism he would not allow it to be called by any other name. Here no doubt many forces combined to resist the dilution or assimilation of atheism to other more acceptable titles.

There is a revealing parallel between Shelley's initial motivation to atheism and that of Richard Carlile. As social persecution encouraged Shelley, so legal persecution stimulated Carlile. [13] Had Shelley not been rejected by the Groves and had Carlile not been imprisoned, both men would probably have remained deists. The orthodox position proved to be counter-productive: it helped to produce rather than prevent atheism. Thus we can see from this alone that all was far from well with the orthodox position in the early part of the nineteenth century.

III. Hogg's role in the birth of atheism

There is, however, one major objection to my reconstruction of Shelley's path to atheism which I have intentionally deferred until now. That objection is Thomas Jefferson Hogg. For according to some Shelley scholars, Shelley came to his atheism through Hogg. How Hogg, in turn, came to his atheism no one seems to know or care. Hogg had no interest in publicly declaring his atheism. Indeed, he never even admitted having been partly responsible, as it is alleged, for the *Necessity*. Not only did he wish to prevent people from discovering that he was, as it is supposed, an atheist, but he attempted to play down Shelley's atheism. For example, when printing some of Shelley's letters in his biography he changed the word 'atheist' to 'philosopher'.[14] According to Hogg, the *Necessity* was simply the result of some idle speculations, the 'amusement of a rainy morning'[15]; it was a slight affair with a rather trivial genesis, to which the Oxford authorities over-reacted.

In this section I shall argue the following two points: (1) that Hogg was not an atheist before Shelly and (2) that his contribution to the *Necessity* was not consequential. I do not wish to argue that Hogg had *no* share in the *Necessity*; but I believe that his share has been exaggerated by Shelley scholars.[16]

The evidence from which we must reach a decision on these questions is contained in a handful of letters from Shelley to Hogg, and particularly in those that Shelley wrote prior to the publication of the *Necessity*. These letters were first printed by Hogg in his *Life of Shelley*, and are problematic partly because Hogg altered various readings, and also because Shelley wrote them in a period of intense mental fermentation. The first difficulty has now been largely overcome by scholarly transcriptions from the original manuscripts. I say 'largely' because Shelley scholars have, I suspect, over-reacted to Hogg's distortions. That is, whereas Hogg tried to give the impression that he was not implicated in Shelley's atheism, Shelley scholars have inferred that he was deeply implicated. In his valuable *The Young Shelley* (London, 1951), Cameron writes:

> The [Shelley/Hogg] correspondence reveals that Shelley was not an atheist but a deist at least as late as January 12 [1811], whereas Hogg was an atheist, denying not only Christian doctrine but 'the existence of an eternal and omnipresent spirit'. Nor is it probable that Shelley had become a convinced atheist between January 12 and February 9. Shelley, I suspect, found

himself sufficiently struck by the revelatory logic of Hogg's argument, and his own inability to answer it, to decide to put it in along with some of his own. And this procedure is implicit in the 'through deficiency of proof, an atheist', of the prefatory 'Advertisement'. (p. 76)

The extract which Cameron quotes from Shelley's letter of 12 January 1811 was printed by Hogg as 'and you [Hogg] disbelieve not the existence of an eternal, omnipresent Spirit'; whereas it should read 'yet you disbelieve the existence of an eternal omnipresent spirit'. Understandably a commentator could gain the impression that Hogg was here trying to cover his atheistic tracks. But there is a good deal more to be said, and a reader must be wary, since even as careful a scholar as Cameron can plant atheistic steps for Hogg. 'On January 6 [writes Cameron], came a further refutation from Hogg — an "argument against the existence of a Deity" ' (p. 74). But what Shelley actually wrote to Hogg was 'I consider your argument against the non-existence of a Deity.'[17] Clearly the 'non-' is of the utmost importance. Hogg must have been arguing against, and not for, atheism in his previous letter. But this hardly accords with the interpretation of him as an atheist trying to proselytise his friend. Apparently Hogg was trying to persuade Shelly to *abandon* his atheism, or, on my interpretation, Shelley's sympathetic speculation on the possibility of atheism.

We must also question whether, as Cameron maintains, during this period Hogg denied 'Christian doctrine'; for in his letter to Hogg of 12 January Shelley speaks of Hogg's 'argument of the necessity of Xtianity'. The argument, it would appear, embodied a form of the orthodox position. Hogg must have been defending Christian belief on the basis of its utility. I can see no other way of interpreting Shelley's remarks in this letter, or in his letter of 1 January. Hogg's allegiance to the orthodox position is even more evident from Shelley's letters of 24 April and 28 April 1811. In the latter Shelley quotes Hogg as follows: 'You say "I have no idea how society wd be if freed from false ideas on almost any subject." ' For Hogg, Christianity would seem to be necessary even if it were false. But did Hogg believe that Christianity was false? Shelley's letter of 26 April certainly suggests that Hogg was trying to paint a rosy picture of Christianity, for Shelley tells him: 'You omit to mention the weeds' of Christianity. This letter also suggests that Hogg was a believer, as Shelley speaks of 'your religion'.

It is difficult to accept that as a supporter of the orthodox position

Hogg could also be an atheist. It is also hard to believe, from the evidence of Shelley's letters, that Hogg was an enemy to Christianity. One piece of evidence which some Shelley scholars have adduced for Hogg's atheism is particularly extraordinary, for it seems to prove the very opposite. In his letter of 17 January 1810 Shelley writes to Hogg: 'Your systematic cudgel for Xtianity is excellent, I tried it again with my Father who told me that 30 years ago he had read Locke but this made no impression.' Cameron and Frederick Jones have suggested that this is a reference to Hogg's share of the *Necessity*. Their main reason for holding this are (1) that the *Necessity* was systematic and (2) that it is supposed to be based on Locke's empiricism. Yet there is nothing in the *Necessity* which directly relates to Christianity; and Locke wrote a great deal in favour of Christianity.[18] But most astounding in their hypothesis is that it overlooks the preposition 'for': Hogg's systematic cudgel was *for*, not *against*, Christianity. And that this was no slip on Shelley's part is confirmed by his next letter to Hogg, in which he informs Hogg that he is now welcome at Field Place. Shelley's father had formed a positive view of Hogg: 'Your principles are *now* as divine as before they were diabolical.' Surely this change was brought about by Shelley's having tried Hogg's cudgel for Christianity on his father. Hearing Hogg's Lockean arguments must have convinced Timothy that Hogg favoured Christianity. Moreover, it is hardly likely that Shelley would have told his father about Hogg's anti-religious arguments, even if Hogg had had any, for Shelley was anxious that his friend should receive an invitation to visit Field Place.

It is difficult to know what the beliefs of the prudent Hogg were during this period. The available evidence suggests that they were not very settled. His theological thoughts may have been, as he later said, idle speculations. He may have been merely entering into the spirit of his more earnest friend. I suspect that Hogg was, at the very most, a midwife to Shelley's atheism, and not its begetter. Perhaps the only piece of solid evidence that Hogg was at one time an atheist is the remark quoted by Cameron from the letter of 12 January. Admittedly, this letter does pose problems for my interpretation. For in it Shelley also undertakes to prove the existence of God. But it should be noticed firstly that Shelley ends his letter by asking Hogg to 'excuse my mad arguments, they are none at all, for I am rather confused'; Shelley also speaks of being in a 'fever'. Secondly, after saying that Hogg does not believe 'the existence of an eternal omnipresent spirit' he writes: 'Am I not mad? alas I am, but I pour my ravings in the ear of a friend who will pardon them.' Does this mean that

Shelley was not prepared to stand by his previous assertions? Thirdly, it must be noted that Shelley does not say that Hogg does not believe in God. The question is: Did Shelley think that Hogg's apparent disbelief in the 'existence of an eternal omnipresent spirit' amounted to a disbelief in God? This cannot be taken for granted; for Shelley's mental categories were in a highly fluid state at the time. Thus in his letter of eight days previous Shelley had said that the word 'God' does 'not imply "the Soul of the Universe the intelligent & *necessarily* beneficient actuating principle".' 'This,' he affirms, '*I* believe in.' The implication here is that he does not believe in the conception normally connoted by the world 'God'. Clearly, the situation is very complicated. Thus in denying the 'existence of an eternal omnipresent spirit' Hogg may not have been denying, in Shelley's view, the existence of God. Hogg's denial may have been made from the perspective of a Christian fideist. Like Eusebes in the *Refutation* he may have been denying a pantheistic/deistic God in the interest of Christianity. This hypothesis would explain Hogg's 'argument of necessity of Christianity' and 'systematic cudgel for Christianity'. It would also fit in with Hogg's High Church family background.[19] A High Church fideist might well have much in common with a deist who was moving towards atheism. Whether Hogg was or was not the prototype for Eusebes, the bulk of evidence supports Shelley's assertion that Hogg was not the 'original corruptor of my principles'. Shelley's atheism, I conclude, is not to be explained by Hogg. It had deeper roots.

Notes

1. See Priestley, *Letters to a philosophical unbeliever*, 2 edn (1787), Preface, pp. vi–viii.

2. See *Necessity*, p. 37 and note in *Queen Mab*, p. 97 (in *Shelley's prose*, edited by Clark, see Chapter 6, note 4). All quotations from Shelley's letters are from Jones's edition (see Chapter 6, note 9).

3. See *Shelley's prose*, p. 38, note 3, and Vaughan's *Early Shelley pamphlets*, p. 19.

4. See Barnard's *Shelley's religion*, p. 23 note.

5. See Hume's *Enquiry concerning human understanding*, Section V, Part 2. Belief, according to Hume is 'not in our power' and 'depends not on the will'; it 'is excited by nature'. In Chapter IX, vol. 1 of the *System*, d'Holbach states that man's 'thoughts, his reflections, his manner of viewing things, of feeling, of judging ... is neither voluntary nor free.'

6. See Collins's *Philosophical inquiry concerning human liberty* (London, 1717), pp. 33–4; 'what is judging of propositions, but judging that propositions do

appear as they do appear; which I cannot avoid doing, without lying to myself, which is impossible' (p. 33). In his *Nascent mind of Shelley* (Oxford, 1947), A.M. Hughes suggests that Shelley's principle 'may have come from Rousseau's Savoyard vicar: "I believe in God as I believe in any other truth because to believe or not to believe are the things in the world that are least under my control" ' (p. 67 note). After Shelley, the principle was taken up by the reformer Robert Owen, for whom 'convictions of the mind ... are impressions produced upon us independent of our will ... therefore ... it is irrational to attribute merit or demerit for belief'. ('The creed of Owen', printed in Carlile's *Prompter* [1831], p. 234.)

7. Shelley's sensitivity is apparent in a letter of 16 May 1811 to Janetta Philipps: 'In justice to myself [he writes] I must also declare that a proof of *His* [God's] existence, or even the divine mission of Christ would in no manner alter one idea on the subject of morality' (*Letters*, vol. 1, p. 88).

8. See his *Philosophical commentaries*, no. 279, in George Thomas's edition (Alliance, 1976), p. 32.

9. See 'Proceedings of the trial of Eaton for blasphemous libel', in *A complete collection of State trials*, vol. 31 (London, 1823), compiled by T.J. Howell, p. 930-1.

10. During his atheistic years, 1823 and 1824, Carlile's commitment to rationalism seems to have been closer to the extreme position of Hammon rather than to the more moderate one held by Shelley. In his letter to Fitton, Carlile declares: 'Whatever is not founded on truth cannot be moral.' *Republican*, vii, p. 408.

11. On the connection between Shelley and Blake, see Cameron's *Shelley, the golden years* (1974), p. 134.

12. See *Letters*, vol. 1, p. 77.

13. See below, Chapter 9, Section III, and the *Republican* vii, p. 397. The cause of atheism was also unintentionally helped by the imprisonment of William Hodgson, M.D., for sedition in 1793; for it was while in prison in Newgate that Hodgson produced the first English translation of d'Holbach's *System*, printed in 1795-6.

14. See Hogg's *Life of ... Shelley* (London, 1906), with an introduction by E. Dowden, pp. 211-14.

15. See *New Shelley letters*, p. 36. The letter from which this extract is taken is attributed to Shelley by the editor, W.S. Scott; but see *Letters*, vol. i, p. 114 note, where Jones convincingly argues that it is by Hogg.

16. For arguments in favour of Hogg's co-authorship of the *Necessity*, see Cameron's *The young Shelley*, pp. 328-31, and Jones's 'Hogg and the *Necessity of atheism*', *Publications of the Modern Language Association*, li (1937), pp. 423-6.

17. I should note that Cameron has the correct reading in his *Shelley and his circle*, vol ii (New York, 1961), p. 690; but he still thinks that this 'must be incorrect' (p. 693).

18. See Vaughan's *Early Shelley pamphlets* for a different account of Shelley's empiricist sources.

19. See his *Life of Shelley*, p. 190.

9

The Atheists: 1822–1842

I. The *Analysis*

The *Analysis of the influence of natural religion on the temporal happiness of mankind* (London, 1822) was, according to J.M. Robertson, 'the most stringent attack made on theism between d'Holbach and Feuerbach.'[1] The *Analysis* also exerted a profound influence on J.S. Mill, who says in his *Autobiography* (London, 1873) that it 'contributed materially to my development [and] was one of the books which by the searching character of its analysis produced the greatest effect on me' (pp. 69–70). Yet despite such tributes, the *Analysis* has received little scholarly attention and has been out of print for more than a hundred years. Nor is there even general agreement about its authorship. It was originally published with the pseudonym 'Philip Beauchamp'. According to Croom Robertson, it was almost entirely the work of George Grote, although 'founded upon a mass of written material committed to him by [Jeremy] Bentham.'[2] Yet M.L. Clarke, Grote's most recent biographer, states: 'It may be assumed that Grote conscientiously reproduced Bentham's arguments, and that there is nothing of his own in the substance of the Book.'[3] J.S. Mill, who saw the *Analysis* in manuscript, says that it was 'understood to have been partly compiled from manuscripts of Mr Bentham.'[4] There are various compelling reasons for accepting Mill's *via media* between Croom Robertson and Clarke. Firstly, Mill was friendly with both Bentham and Grote, and hence was in a position to know the extent of Grote's authorship. Secondly, there is now no way of knowing to what extent Grote drew on Bentham's manuscripts, because we cannot be sure whether the manuscripts deposited in the British Library by Grote's wife, Harriet, were all or even most of those Bentham originally gave Grote for the *Analysis*.[5] Furthermore, not all the papers in the so-called Bentham Papers (British Library Add. MSS 29,806–9) are in Bentham's hand; some items were almost certainly, written by Grote.[6] Thirdly, my impression, after examining the four *extant* manuscript volumes, is that the *Analysis* is largely the work of Grote, although inspired by Bentham's point of view. Fourthly, the extant correspondence between Bentham and Grote suggests that there was considerable and flexible collaboration between the two men; thus in a letter of 9 November 1821, Bentham tells Grote that as the work proceeds he (Bentham) will look it 'over and see whether I could do anything more towards rendering the work more methodical, correct, clear, concise and comprehensive'. Yet, he adds, 'Should it be found necessary, grudge not the trouble of recomposing ... think of the matchless importance of the subject.'[7] My conclusion, for positive and negative reasons, is that the *Analysis* should be regarded as the joint work of both men, with Grote as the major and Bentham the minor partner.

This conclusion has a bearing on our interpretation of the *Analysis* as a work of atheism. Some of Bentham's contemporaries as well as modern scholars have confidently stated that Bentham was an atheist. Yet it also seems to be accepted that Bentham nowhere explicitly denies the existence of God, or describes himself as an atheist. Thus in a recent article, 'Bentham on religion: atheism and the secular society',[8] J.E. Crimmins speaks of 'Bentham's unmitigated atheism' (p. 96) and his 'outright denial ... of the existence of God'; yet concedes (somewhat inconsistently) that 'Bentham never in so many words publicly avowed his atheism' (p. 98). That there should be no such avowal in Bentham's voluminous *private* papers and letters is most noteworthy, and should make us reluctant to endorse Crimmins's confident judgements that 'Bentham was an atheist' (p. 95), indeed 'an active, not to say a zealous, atheist' (p. 99).

What, then, of Bentham's collaborator George Grote? Until recently, a similar judgement would have to be passed on him. It has always been clear that Grote was an opponent of religion, but it has never been possible to determine precisely the extent of his unbelief. There has been a wide range of opinion. In his *Life and writings of George Grote* (1884), W. MacIllwraith writes that Grote's mother, the daughter of a clergyman, forced religion on her son, and that this 'misdirected sincerity ... tended to repel rather than convince, and the result was that to the end of his days Grote was not religious in the general acceptation of the term' (p. 6). Alexander Bain, the editor of Grote's works, also hints at Grote's irreligion.[9] But nothing that

Grote published in his own name reveals the extent of his irreligious position. Grote was a prudent man.

It is therefore of great interest that a collection of his private letters on religious topics has recently come to light, particularly as they were written close to the publication of the *Analysis*. The letters give a unique view of a crypto-atheist. For not only does Grote argue against the existence of God, he also discusses strategies of concealment. The letters, transcripts of which are in the Watson Library, University College, London, were written between 10 May 1822 and 20 December 1826 to Frances Lewin, the younger sister of Harriet, Grote's wife. They are largely concerned with Frances's intellectual development, especially her growing disbelief in religion. 'I do truly hope [writes Grote on 10 October 1822] that it may be my lot to see you emancipated from this & all other [religious] inconsistencies of mind, which disguise ... the true path conducting to happiness.'[10] He is pleased to note, on 28 January 1824, that 'It is scarcely more than a year since you fully shook off the Jug [i.e. Juggernaut, the code-name Bentham and his followers gave to religion] ... at your age, I was ... beset with all the miserable phantoms of Jug.'

Grote's main atheistic argument is based on the existence of pain and evil: 'where there is a *grain* of misery existing — *a single grain* — this must be because the Maker of it (granting the hypothesis) either wants the will or wants the power to prevent it. The evil that exists is a plain proof that there is no being existent ... *an aching finger* proves that there *can* be none such' (letter of Tuesday, circa 1824; A2.14.2). Confident (as befits a utilitarian) that pain is evil, Grote confidently rejects God's existence or His goodness. (A perfect God would surely have created the world for the greatest good for the greatest number — yet plainly He has not.) Grote's atheism comes out most clearly and defiantly in the following passage from his letter of 23 February 1823:

> there cannot be a benevolent God who suffers evil and pain to exist. And if there be a God of any other character, who does not design the happiness of mankind, then all I can say is, that I shall prefer serving & benefitting my fellow-men & take the risk of his displeasure. But all these superstitions are really altogether on a fictitious basis: There is exactly as much reason to believe that there are ghosts, as that there is a God; indeed there is not so much evidence for the latter, inasmuch as his reputed attributes are thoroughly incompatible & contradictory.

Clearly, at least *one* of the authors of the *Analysis* was a strong-minded covert atheist. Once this is appreciated it becomes easier and more cogent to see the *Analysis* as an atheistic work. Although the book is largely concerned to show the many-sided miseries caused by religious belief, and hence the falsity of the orthodox position on theoretical and practical atheism, it also attacks theoretical theism itself. Its complete attack on 'Jug', or religion, has three prongs: religious belief is shown to be (1) irrational (2) naturalistically explicable and (3) pernicious.

Let us first consider (1). Religious beliefs are irrational because they are 'extra-experimental' (p. 87), by which Grote and Bentham mean something similar to Karl Popper's notion of non-falsifiability.[11] An extra-experimental belief is one which 'precludes you from applying the process of refutation, and thus from detecting any falsehood whatever' (p. 90). As belief in 'God cannot be founded on experience' (p. 87), no empirical evidence can either prove or disprove His existence. Similarly, belief in divine design (p. 87), a life after death (p. 88), miracles (p. 89), the justice of trial by ordeal (p. 93), and the existence of witches (p. 91), are all extra-experimental. There is no way of falsifying them. It is in *this* sense that there is no point in considering whether extra-experimental beliefs are true or false (p. 5). Yet to detach experience from belief is to unhinge the mind, producing a 'thorough depravation of the intellect' (p. 91) or 'phrenzy' (p. 106). No possible belief can be rationally rejected if extra-experimental belief is accepted. 'To him who believes in the intervention of incomprehensible and unlimited Beings, no story can appear incredible' (p. 92).

This reduction to extra-experimental belief is damning, but Bentham and Grote do not rest their case here. They try to show how religionists acquire their crazy extra-experimental beliefs. In this second prong of their attack on 'Jug' they argue that we endow God with moral and intellectual perfections, such as goodness and wisdom, because we are intimidated by His power. (In the *Analysis*, Grote and Bentham grant, at least initially, that there is a most powerful and incomprehensible Being.) This genealogy is based on an analysis of praise and blame, according to which 'the employment of praise or blame bears an exact ratio to the comparative weakness or strength of the critic ... The greater the disparity of power, the more severe is the blame heaped upon [an] inferior, [and] the more excessive the blame lavished upon [a] superior ... the employment of praise and blame is [also] in inverse proportion to each other. [So] he who praises the most, blames the least ... [Finally] the vehemence of our praise is ... not measured by the extent of the kindness bestowed, but by the superiority of the donor to the receiver' (pp. 28-9). Because we fear God's *overwhelming* power, we flatter Him as we would a powerful human tyrant (pp. 29-31). We convince ourselves that He is benevolent just as a Roman sycophant might persuade himself that Caligula was a god. And, of course, we puny mortals stand in an even more humble relationship to omnipotence than a Roman sycophant would to Caligula. To argue that the Deity is *really* good, and that evils in His creation arise because the material He has to work with resists His good intentions, would imply not only that He is comprehensible but that 'His power only extends to the production of the already existing amount of good. [But if] He can produce no more good ... it is vain to trouble ourselves about Him' (p. 24n). In fact, this attempt to save God's goodness — which Grote and Bentham associate with Plato — is really extra-experimental. To show this, they ingeniously employ the device of

constructing a similar phantom on [their] side in order to ex-pose the absurdity of the first hypothesis by its resemblance to the second. Conformably to this rule, I affirm that the Deity is perfectly and systematically malevolent, and that he was only prevented from realizing these designs by the inherent goodness and incorruptible excellence of matter. I admit that there is not the smallest evidence for this, but it is just as well supported, and just as probable as the [alternative] ... theory of Plato.

It is likely that this device was largely Grote's idea, for he uses a similar technique in a letter to his sister-in-law:

no benevolent being can possibly have been the cause of what exists in this world. A single aching finger is enough to prove that ... it matters not whether the good or evil preponderates ...If you say that the good part of Nature comes from this benevolent being; & the bad part by itself & without his agency; then I ask you, why, if one part of Nature can exist without this cause, the other part could not exist also? If the bad part of Nature could exist uncaused, so could the good. Besides, you would have just as good reason to say, that the good part of Nature came by itself, and that the bad part was superadded by some malevolent being — as you would have to say, that the bad part came by itself, and the good from some benevolent being. Take the doctrine as you will, the supposition of such a cause is both useless and contradictory.[12]

So the *Analysis* shows that our belief in God's endearing moral and intellectual attributes actually arises from our desire to flatter a capricious and powerful despot. And this explains a curious conflict in the believer's account of God — i.e. how God is always said to be most perfect, and yet His behaviour is often depicted as capricious and cruel.[13] I should point out that Grote and Bentham recognise that this whitewashing of a black tyrant may occur at an unconscious level. For

> Suppose than any tyrant could establish so complete a system of espionage, as to be informed of every word which any of his subjects might utter. It is obvious that all criticisms upon him would be laudatory in the extreme, for they would be all pronounced as it were in the presence of the tyrant, and *there* no one dares to express [any] dissent. The unlimited agency and omniscience of the Deity is equivalent to this universal espionage. He is conceived as the unseen witness of everything which passes our lips — *indeed even our thoughts*. It would be madness, therefore, to hazard an unfavourable judgment of his proceedings, while thus constantly under his supervision. (My italics, p. 30.)

Their next step is to subject to genetic analysis the essential attribute of omnipotence, which has hitherto been assumed. Some men appear to perform astonishing deeds, and 'We ascribe to the man who astonishes us by an incomprehensible feat, the ability of astonishing us still more by a great many others. Nay, the power, which we are led to conceive as exerted, seems too vast to be ascribed to him alone. We therefore introduce an omnipotent accomplice into the scene.'

> Such is the prompt and forcible transit whereby *the extra-experimental* believer is hurried on to swell the power which he beholds into a greater, and that still farther into the greatest — until at last an act of legerdemain is magnified into an exhibition of omnipotence. (pp. 106–7)

So our belief in God's goodness stems from our fear of His power, which in turn is rooted in our amazement at wonder workers, for whom Grote and Bentham also offer a naturalisatic account. That is, firstly there are more wonder workers in primitive societies where little is known of the laws of nature (104–5); secondly, it gives wonder workers (i.e. priests) profit (p. 107). Thirdly, since no one prays for the removal of a disease by supernatural aid when he once knows an appropriate surgical remedy (p. 108), the priest has an interest in maximising extra-experimental belief. In effect, Bentham and Grote are telling the believer: 'You do not really believe in God because of some mysterious faith, your fideism is explicable as the natural outcome of certain psychological — that is, pathological — tendencies.'

Finally, there is a third prong of their assault. Faith in 'Jug' is not simply irrational and naturalistically explicable: it is also pernicious. It produces the greatest unhappiness for the greatest number. Hence even if God did exist, it would be better for our happiness *in this life* if we did not believe in Him. This is the book's central argument. Religious belief is 'impotent for the purpose of resisting any temptation, and efficient only in the production of needless and unprofitable misery' (p. 62). Thus devotion to God is measured by 'the amount of intensity of pain which you … gratuitously inflict upon yourself' (p. 64). Bentham and Grote list: fasting; celibacy; abstinence from repose, cleanliness, personal decoration, and mirth; gratuitous surrender of property, time, labour, and honours (p. 65).

Predictably, they dwell on 'the universal prevalence of religious hatred' (p. 76f); more characteristic is their reply to the common objection that only 'posthumous apprehensions' are able to prevent the 'secret crime': 'To say that earthly laws do not actually perform this, is merely to affirm, that governments are defective and ought to be reformed' (p. 61). Thus Jug's all-seeing God can be replaced by Bentham's architectural plan for universal inspection — the Panopticon.[14] An apparent supernatural necessity points to a real need for social reform or scientific insight.

II. Grote's atheism

Whereas Shelley was an atheist who became an immaterialistic follower of Berkeley around 1819, Grote seems to have been a Berkeleian immaterialist who became an atheist around 1818. The evidence suggests that Berkeley's immaterialism encouraged Grote's atheism; indeed, Grote might well be called a Berkeleian atheist. Not that this comes out in any work Grote published under his own name. For his contemporaries Grote was the honoured historian of Greece, the distinguished associate of Bentham, of James and J.S. Mill, the MP and reformer, a founder of University College, London, of which he was to become President and Vice-Chancellor, a FRS, with honorary doctorates from Oxford and Cambridge. Publicly, there was little in Grote's life that suggested his radical atheistic position. Even the pious Gladstone offered him a peerage — which, however, he declined. Yet, as his friend Croom Robertson wrote: behind 'the calm exterior there lay ... fires of passion which it took all his strength of reason and will to control'.[15]

With the help of Grote's early correspondence with Frances Lewin, we can appreciate some of these secret fires. The correspondence should also help to banish the idea that theological insincerity and secrecy are inconsistent with high moral character. Thus after his protégé, Frances, had become an unbeliever, Grote commends her duplicity:

> I highly approve your having taken the Sacrament: It was equally judicious & resolute on your part, & I give you great credit for the step. With regard to ordinances, I sh—ᵈ always conform to those with whom I was passing my time, & particularly when in a subject state to some extent, as you now are. (25 February, 1823)

With regard to conversation, however, Grote advises Frances that

> The only method is to maintain an obstinate silence & to say that as you interfere with no one else's opinions, you will tolerate no interference with your own. [For] Interference with other people's opinions, even on the subject of Jug, is hardly approved of in England. (20 December, 1826)

Grote, himself, seems to have followed this prudent advice. On the whole, he confined his philosophical enthusiasms to his notebooks, some of which have fortunately been preserved. From these it is possible to chart his radical development. Sometime before 1818, when he was 24, he was sympathetic to the views of Thomas Reid and Dugald Stewart. At this time, he accepted the existence of both God and matter. Thus in an early undated manuscript (Add. MS 29, 528, fos. 98—9) he tries to show that Helvetius (i.e. d'Holbach) was wrong to suppose an infinite regress of causes, rather than a First Cause: 'I choose ... to suppose that matter had a creator,' he writes;

and in a notebook in the Goldsmith Library, labelled 1817, he criticises Berkeley. At this Reid/Stewart phase he holds that touch, unlike vision, 'conveys to us sensations which are necessarily attended with the perception of certain qualities in an external object. We learn by means of touch the existence of external objects' (p. 24). However, after reading Berkeley's works in 1817 — his annotated copy is now in the University of London Library — he writes: 'Berkeley's observations are vastly acute and ingenious, yet I cannot yet exactly comprehend the true extent of his theory ... I hope, however, to study him more and understand him better.' (*Posthumous Papers* of Grote [London, 1874], pp. 18–19). Five years later, as Alexander Bain put it, Grote was 'a Berkeleian and something more' (*Minor works*, p. 333). What more, the discrete Bain does not say. But it seems reasonably clear that he, like Croom Robertson, is hinting at Grote's atheism, as anonymously presented in the *Analysis* and privately in his notebooks.

Grote's most extensive Berkeleian essay was written in 1822, according to Bain, the same year he was working on the *Analysis*. Bain prints an extract in *The minor works of Grote*, but the whole manuscript is in the British Library (Add. MS 29, 528). In much of the essay Grote astutely defends Berkeley's rejection of matter against Reid and Stewart. He also argues that Berkeley's destructive analysis of matter must be applied to spirit. Because Berkeley 'believed Religion to be involved in the question ..., his reasonings against material substance are as piercing & irresistible, as his endeavors to protect spirit from annihilation by the same arguments, are weak & futile' (fol. 108). It is 'a matter of melancholy certainty that neither the Bishop [Berkeley] himself, nor any one else at the time (indeed I might say since) comprehended the full extent & cogency of [Berkeley's] reasonings' (fol. 111). Grote's criticism of Berkeley's defence of spirit show a close reading of Berkeley's *Principles*. Thus Grote takes Section 23 to be an 'admission' that spirits for Berkeley are not independent substances but merely objects of thought. 'For what else is implied by "framing the idea of books, and omitting to frame the *idea of some one perceiving them*" ' (fol. 111). This shows that for Berkeley (other) minds can and must be perceived; hence they are not independent of perceptions, as Berkeley officially holds. For Grote, Berkeley must either accept both matter and spirit, or reject both: 'the question was, which side of the Bishop's doctrine should destroy the other' (fol. 111). For Grote, both matter and spirit should be rejected. Hence his world seems to consist of 'states of mind' (fol. 105), with no substances and, of course, no God. Unfortunately,

Grote does not work out this extreme empiricist position in any of the extant manuscripts. He seems to take it that as 'other minds' are for me ideas, or states of my mind; and as I am for them also ideas, it follows that everything is an idea, or state of mind, with no real independent mind or minds (fol. 110).

Grote's radical empiricist position is reflected in the *Analysis's* critique of 'extra-experimental belief', i.e. 'belief altogether unconformable to experience' (p. 87), which, as we have seen, was one of the work's atheistic prongs. The Berkeleian nature of Grote's atheism can be more specifically seen in an early manuscript in the Sterling Library, University of London (MS 429). In a section entitled 'Anti-Teleology Aug. 14. 1823' (pp. 496–9), Grote argues that we cannot legitimately infer anything about a God from the state or states of the physical world. He then, in a section entitled 'Creation' (pp. 500–1), argues even more radically against divine creation itself; and he does so with the help of a 'remarkable passage out of Berkeley's *Principles*', i.e. Section 103, which he quotes at length. Whereas Berkeley had criticised the doctrine of attraction as used by physicists, Grote directly applies Berkeley's criticism to creation as used by theologians. When we are told that the world was created, does this, Grote asks,

distinguish the process by which the beginning of the world came to pass, from the process by which the beginning of anything came to pass? If it does, by what circumstances does it distinguish the former process from the latter? If it does not, we may ask with Berkeley, how are we enlightened by being told, that this is done by Creation. All exertions of the human will presuppose the existence of the other laws & properties of nature … We have experience of volition only in ourselves, & must therefore lay down its limits as we find them to exist by experience. But if we are allowed gratuitously to enlarge the power of volition — if we may multiply to infinity the results which volition may be affirmed constantly to precede or will account for — such an unwarrantable licence of overlapping all experimental limit would enable us to solve the difficulty by means of any supposition whatever. If we are allowed to suppose the powers of fire & water aggrandized to infinity & capable of producing unlimited results, we may account for the origin of the world exactly as well by the hypothesis of fire & water, as by that of an omnipotent willing spirit.

I have quoted this passage at length not only because it shows Grote exploiting Berkeley for atheistic ends, but also because it implicitly shows Grote using the rigorous Berkeley against the theological Berkeley. For Berkeley was, of course, a believer in divine creation — indeed, in a constant divine creation — which is known by analogy with human volition, particularly our mental creation of imaginative ideas. Like Shelley (Chapter 6, Section IV), Grote attacks Berkeley at this vital point. Our volitions, Grote seems to be saying, are restricted by laws of nature; whereas the alleged creation of the world by a divine volition would have to be a volition totally different from human volition, because such a divine volition must precede and produce the laws of a nature. Human volition is, for example, subject to the law of association of ideas. Hence we cannot make sense of the concept of divine volition by reference to our experience of willing. It would involve 'an unwarrantable licence of overlapping all experimental limit'; it would, in short, be extra-experimental. On the other hand, if we are 'allowed gratuitously to enlarge the powers of volition', then this extra-experimental technique will enable us to prove that anything — fire and water, for example — may have created the world. For really we are only saying that *something*, which differs from its nature as we experience it, created the world.

III. Richard Carlile

British atheism, from Hammon and Turner to Bentham and Grote, is extremely heterogeneous. There is little evidence that any of the atheistic writers of the period from 1782 to 1822, which would include Francis, Scepticus, and Shelley, were even aware of each other. This situation was to be changed by the next figure in British atheism. With the indomitable Richard Carlile there is the beginning of a cohesive, more or less continuous atheistic movement. Before Carlile, Erasmus Perkins had provided a limited forum for atheism in his periodical the *Theological inquirer* (London, 1815). Perkins reprinted Shelley's *Refutation of deism* (pp. 6–24 and pp. 121–31); he also published a few essays and letters sympathetic to atheism, see especially pp. 96–102, 200–1, 249–52. But the *Theological inquirer* seems to have had little circulation or impact, and Perkins lacked Carlile's dynamism and publicising genius; nor did Perkins himself either avow or defend atheism.

Carlile had firm links with at least four of the previous atheistic works: he reprinted the *Answer, Watson refuted*, and in 1822 he published both *Queen Mab* and the *Analysis*, thereby drawing together an indigenous atheistic tradition. It is as publicist and publisher of atheism that Carlile is most important. In the early 1820s Carlile moved from a deism to atheism. Before 1821, writes G.D.H. Cole, Carlile 'had described himself as a Deist; but the fruit of his prison reflections [for printing Paine's *The age of reason*] was a conversion to thoroughgoing atheism.'[16] According to G. J. Holyoake, his first biographer, Carlile 'reached the climax of his atheism on the title page to his tenth volume of the *Republican*, where he declared "There is no such a God in existence as any man has preached; nor any kind of God." '[17]

Not all scholars agree, however, that Carlile was a 'thoroughgoing atheist', or an atheist at all. Robertson holds that 'Carlile had always been a deist, and, now near his end [he lapsed] into a kind of theistic mysticism.'[18] He also asserts that Carlile (among others) regarded atheism as 'something outrageous, dangerous, offensive to the moral instincts, and therefore to be carefully repudiated by free-thinkers as such'[19] Robertson, however, is definitely wrong in ascribing deism to Carlile throughout the 1820s, that is, after his straightforward deistic period and before his final phase of mystical theism. At the very least, Carlile's pronouncements of this period are those of an agnostic. He frequently speaks of the deity as an 'unknown' and 'incomprehensible' power (*Lion*, vol. 1, no. 1, 4 January 1828, p. 9). Eight years previously, in the *Republican* (vol. 4, no. 18, 29 December 1820), he had written: 'I feel that there is a power in nature superior to my comprehension, and that I am content to call this power god, or by any other respectful and appropriate epithet' (p. 621). But while Carlile wished to be respectful to this unknown power, he became less and less willing to endow it with any anthropomorphic feature, such as intelligence. And by 1823 he was certainly more than a deist or an agnostic. In various essays and letters in the 1823 volume (vii) of the *Republican* he avows atheism and defends it at some length. In one notable letter he flatly asserts: 'I am an atheist' (p. 402) and 'there is no God' (p. 406), and he concludes the letter in the manner of Shelley, signing himself: 'Your atheistical friend, Richard Carlile' (p. 402). His strong-minded atheism lasted at least until 1824. I would also argue that most of Carlile's agnostic pronouncements of the 1820s amount to atheism. But, with the exception of 1823/4, it is probably going too far to describe his position (as do Cole and Holyoake) as 'thoroughgoing' and persistent atheism. In the *Republican* 1822 he was still prepared to assert that 'I call ... myself a Deist' and 'I adhere to that God of Nature of which

Mr. Paine writes' (p. 197). But at the same time, he says, 'I do not reject the Appellation of atheist, if any man thinks proper to bestow it upon me' (p. 197).

Carlile's vacillations in the 1820s between avowals and denials of atheism probably reflected the fluctuations in his conscious beliefs. He was, as Joel Wiener has recently shown, a volatile personality.[20] And the instability of his beliefs is probably to be explained by such factors as, firstly, the relative newness of avowed atheism, secondly, the varying pressures and hostility from opponents, and, thirdly, the negative emotive meaning of the word 'atheism'. At times he seems indifferent as to what name, or label, he was given. In the Preface to his edition of *The true meaning of the System of nature* (London circa 1825), Carlile writes that 'he is quite proud of being called a Deist, Materialist, or Atheist, just as the idolaters may please, so [long] as he is distinguished from them' (pp. v–vi); and in the *Republican* of 1822 he says 'the words *Deism* and *Atheism*, upon my view of them, differ more in sound than in meaning' (vol. vi, p. 197).

But a further year in Dorchester Gaol for blasphemy seems to have hardened Carlile. In a public letter to William Fitton of 8 March 1823 he declared himself an atheist. It is interesting that he also stresses his unoriginality: 'As I shall have to traverse a beaten track, I do not expect to offer any thing new to the public generally ... in defence of what you call *Atheism*' (vol. vii, pp. 396–7). He seems anxious to give the impression that atheism was already a well-established position, with a considerable history behind it — probably a comfortable reflection for an early, incarcerated, atheist. Similarly Humphrey Boyle, an atheistic associate of Carlile, asserted in the same volume of the *Republican*: 'In almost all ages and countries there have been men who scouted the popular doctrine of the existence of a supreme, intelligent, immaterial being' (p. 286). Boyle was probably aware, however, that this was historical invention rather than historical description, as he immediately adds the qualification: 'but they were men of genius and learning, and their opinions were seldom known farther than amongst their own friends' (p. 286). In his letter to Fitton, Carlile described Boyle's essay as 'a masterpiece, as a compendium in defence of atheism' (p., 397). This again gives the impression that the creative work had already been done; all that remained was to summarise the previous atheistic arguments.

In fact, there *is* little that is original in either Boyle's or Carlile's apologies for atheism. Most of their arguments are to be found in the works of Hammon, Turner, Scepticus, Shelley or Grote. At the basis of their atheism is the assumption that materialism is unquestionably true: 'matter does exist [writes Carlile, and] we know of no other existence, nor of the possibility of any other existence, ... and being to all our senses indestructible and infinite, we have no other sense or perception, that it must be the cause of all things, itself without a cause' (p. 403; see also pp. 287, 399). Here Carlile dismisses an 'incomprehensible power' behind this world. Yet he had agnostically posited such a power before in 1823, and would return to it in 1827. Since everything which we can properly know is material, it follows that if we know God, then He must be material. Most theologians, according to Carlile and Boyle, regard God as essentially immaterial; but if this is so, it follows that we cannot know anything about God: we cannot know that He is intelligent or even has a mind, for only material beings have such features. Like their atheistic forerunners, Carlile and Boyle regard the material world as eternal and self-explicable. They put the onus on the theist to prove that the material world is an effect, standing in need of a divine cause. As Carlile forcibly puts it: 'It is not fair to call upon me to prove a negative, to prove a creation for instance [of matter out of nothing], when it is quite impossible for any one to conceive the world as not existing: the proof rests with you' (pp. 400–1). Whereas Grote had used Berkeley's immaterialism for atheistic purposes, Carlile saw the Bishop as a formidable opponent of atheism:

> We know nothing distinct from those states and qualities which we consent to call matter [writes Carlile in his *Every Man's book: or what God is* (1826)]. Bishop Berkeley saw the force of this conclusion and to get rid of it, he denied the existence of matter ... his book on the subject is well worth the reading of every student, as a deep exercize for the mind.

Carlile's mode of refuting Berkeley is similar to that later used by Marxists, such as Lenin: 'I surmount the difficulty which Berkeley raised by perceiving, that, though our knowledge of matter is ideal, there could have been no idea without the previous existence of matter to form it' (p. 25).

Some of Boyle's criticisms of theism recall those of Scepticus. Boyle asks:

> Why ... should we conclude, that because a material being can make a piece of machinery out of *something*, that an *immateriality* could produce a universe out of *nothing*? (p. 287)

[According to the deists] God is infinite, eternal and immutable ... [But the] deists themselves say that he is incomprehensible; how, then, do they know anything of that which
is incomprehensible? (p. 288).

A distinguishing feature of Carlile's atheism is the firm link he
establishes between the denial of God and social change (pp.
399–400). In this respect, too, he looks ahead to Marxist atheism,
and he departs from (what some Marxists call) bourgeois atheism:
atheism that stops at bare denial of God, with no concern for the
economic, legal and cultural implications of that denial. Carlile's
contribution to the development of atheism was less as a theorist than
a propagandist. With him the popular periodical became a chief
vehicle and focal point of atheism; and it remained so for most of
the nineteenth century. He carried on the Painite tradition, but instead of deism he advocated atheism — at least in the mid-1820s —
among the lower orders. He was the first public champion of atheists.

How extensive was Carlile's atheistic following? According to
Humphrey Boyle, 'it is now not uncommon to see individuals among
the lower orders avowing themselves atheists' (p. 287). Yet there is not
much concrete evidence of this in the late 1820s. In Carlile's
periodical, the *Lion* (1828), there is a short letter by someone who
signs himself 'An Atheist' (p. 26). Of more interest is a letter of 30
March 1828 by one Octavius Hall, who avows atheism, endorses
Carlile's views on God, and also mentions the influence Carlile's edition of *Queen Mab* had on him. Hall's account of his own intellectual
development is interesting and probably not atypical. From being an
evangelical Christian he moved to Unitarianism, which in turn
yielded — under the influence of William Godwin's *Political justice* —
to Necessarian deism.

For some time, [writes Hall] I stopped at this point; because,
according to the doctrine of Necessity, we can owe no duties
to an Deity, and, consequently, the enquiry into the existence
or non-existence of such an equivocal Being, becomes a mere
matter of curiosity. But about twelve months ago, wanting
matter for speculation, I read Paley's Natural theology, more
attentively than ever I had done before, and finding no argument on that side of the question more valid, I became an
Atheist. (p. 443)

With Carlile atheism and free-thought become closely identified with the lower orders. Bentham, Grote and Shelley — who defended Carlile in an unpublished letter of 1819 to the *Examiner* — are lingering representatives of the long line of upper-class free-thinkers, which included Lords Rochester, Shaftesbury, Molesworth, Hervey and Bolingbroke. The all too plain connection of free-thinking and egalitarianism, forged especially by Paine and the French Revolution, was no doubt largely responsible for discouraging free-thinking among the upper classes and encouraging it among the lower.

Carlile is the first atheistic leader who exerts a wide influence by means of the periodical, mass meetings and the courtroom. After Carlile we can trace a fairly clear line of succession: Charles Southwell, George Jacob Holyoake, Robert Cooper, Charles Bradlaugh, G.W. Foote, Chapman Cohen. Only in the early twentieth-century is there a revival of more upper-class atheism, with John Ellis McTaggart, G.E. Moore and Bertrand Russell, all Fellows of Trinity College, Cambridge. In some respects, McTaggart and Russell merge with the more popularist tradition; e.g. in belonging to, and publishing pamphlets with, the Rational Press Association. Yet they also represent a new development in British atheism, in that all three men are respected academic philosophers.

IV. Southwell and Holyoake

As editor of *The Oracle of Reason; or Philosophy Vindicated* (London, 1842), Charles Southwell took over the championship of atheism from Carlile, who had moved away from atheism in the 1830s to a confused form of mystical theism. According to Southwell — who was the youngest child of a family of 33 — *The Oracle of Reason* was 'the only exclusively *atheistical* print that has appeared in any age or country' (Preface, p. ii). *The Oracle* was certainly the most vociferous and militant atheistic periodical, and Southwell, like Carlile, paid for militancy with incarceration. A prison sentence for blasphemy became an almost necessary attainment for leadership. While Southwell was in prison, the editorship of *The Oracle* passed to Holyoake, who was himself imprisoned in 1843. Southwell resembles Carlile in volatility. Both men also came to repudiate their former atheism. Their atheistic statements have in common a derivative and *ad hoc* character. Thus Southwell published two works in which he 'atheised' previous theistic pamphlets. In *The existence of God disproved by believers of God* (Edinburgh, 1844) he assembles quotations from prominent theists such as Lord Brougham and William Gillespie who, in the course of defending theism, undermine each other's arguments. Thus Brougham casts scorn and criticism on the *a priori* argument for God's existence and Gillespie on the sentimental argument, i.e. on the appeal to feelings. In the end all the possible arguments — which are five in number, according to Southwell — are exploded by one or another champion of theism.

A similar technique is used in Southwell's *Literary legerdemain: the argument,* a priori, *for the being and attributes of God, by William Gillespie, atheised ... by the substitution of a score or two proper words for as many improper ones* (London, 1851). By substituting 'matter' for 'God', 'movable' for 'unmovable' — all substitutions are printed in italics — Southwell is able to turn Gillespie's theistic demonstration into an atheistic one. There is something theatrical about Southwell's atheism, as perhaps befits a former Shakespearian actor.

When Southwell was sentenced to a year's imprisonment, the editorship of *The Oracle* passed to Holyoake, who was not, at that time, an atheist.[21] However, persecution led him — as it had led Shelley and Carlile, and was to lead Bradlaugh — to atheism: 'I had not become [an atheist] till after the imprisonment of Mr. Southwell, which led me to inquire into the grounds of religious opinion more closely than I had before done, and it ended in my entire disbelief'.[22] At a lecture in Cheltenham in May 1842 he was goaded into making some irreligious statements for which he was arrested in June and indicted at the Gloucester Assizes on 15 August 1842. Part of the indictment was that Holyoake,

> being a wicked ... person, and disregarding the laws and religion of the realm, and wickedly and profanely devising and intending to bring Almighty God, the Holy Scriptures, and the Christian religion into disbelief and contempt among the people of this kingdom, on the twenty-fourth day of May, ... maliciously, unlawfully, and wickedly did compose, speak, utter, pronounce, and publish with a loud voice, of and concerning Almighty God, the Holy Scriptures, and the Christian religion, these words ... 'I do not believe there is such a thing as God; I would ... place Almighty God on half pay.' (*History*, p. 22)

Holyoake wrote a book on this episode, called *The history of the last trial by jury for atheism in England*. In her *Penalties upon opinion* (2nd edn, London, 1913), Hypatia Bradlaugh Bonner notes that 'the title of this pamphlet is somewhat of a misnomer ... [because] Holyoake was not tried for atheism, but for blasphemy, as the indictment [quoted above] clearly shows' (p. 64n). Yet her criticism seems mistaken, for part of the indictment, as we can see, specified Holyoake's 'intending to bring God Almighty ... into disbelief' and quoted his assertion of disbelief in 'such a thing as God'. The misnomer in Holyoake's title is not, I would suggest, in the word *'atheism'*, but in the word *'last'*. For Holyoake may well have been the *first* person tried for — in part at least — atheism. The evidence indicates that before Holyoake all such offenders were indicted exclusively for crimes against revealed, rather than natural, religion. Carlile was tried for printing Paine's *The age of reason*; Southwell for offensive comments on the Bible — that 'odius Jew production', as he called it.

What is not quite so clear is whether Holyoake was *imprisoned* (in part) for atheism. In his summing up, Mr Justice Erskine told the jurors that if they were convinced that Holyoake's words 'were uttered with levity, for the purpose of treating with contempt the majesty of Almighty God,' then the defendant was guilty. And in sentencing Holyoake 'to be imprisoned in the Common Gaol for six months', he said:

> You have been convicted ... of having uttered these words with improper levity. The arm of the law is not stretched out to protect the character of the Almighty; we do not presume to be the protectors of our God, but to protect the people from such indecent language. And if these words had been written for deliberate circulation, I should have passed on you a severer sentence. You uttered them in consequence of a question [and] ... in the heat of the moment. (*History*, p. 64)

It would seem from this that Holyoake's atheistic remarks were offensive less for their matter than for the mode of their delivery, i.e. for their 'indecent language'. Yet this is not altogether clear. Holyoake and some of his religious opponents, at any rate, thought that his offence was atheism. For in defending himself at his trial Holyoake addressed the jury:

> Learned divines, and sage writers on atheism, agree that it is too absurd to need refutation — too barren to satisfy, too monstrous to attract, too fearful to allure, too dumb to speak, and too deathly not to appal its own votaries. It is styled too grave to entertain youth, and too devoid of consolation for the trembling wants of age — too abstract for the comprehension

of the ignorant, and too unreasonable to gain the admiration of the intelligent, ... Gentlemen, will you disturb the harmony of these conclusions by a verdict against me, and attack that which never existed, and place upon the grave records of this court a slaying of the self-slain? Will you thus draw attention to a subject you perhaps think had better be forgotten? (*History*, pp. 59–60)

With these words Holyoake brought out in the open both the repression and suppression of atheism and showed their power. While in prison Holyoake was able to observe their continuing power. He recounts an extraordinary conversation he had with the prison chaplain on religion, part of which runs as follows:

Are you really an atheist, Mr. Holyoake?
Really I am.
You deny that there is a God?
No; I deny that there is sufficient reason to believe that there is one.
But if the atheist has so much on his side, why does he not make it known?
Is it generous in you to taunt him with lack of evidence, when you are so prepared to punish its production?
The reason is that your principles are so horrible; as Robert Hall said, 'Atheism is a bloody and ferocious system.'
And, my dear sir, has it never occurred to you that the language of the Christian is shocking to atheistical feeling?
Atheists have a right to their opinions, I allow, but not to publish them.
I shall think you speak reasonably when you permit the same rule to be applied to the Christian.
But you really cannot be an atheist?
And you say this who have been a party to imprisoning me here for being one! If you believe yourself, go and demand my liberation. (*History*, pp. 80–81.)

The last interchange is especially noteworthy, first because it indicates that Holyoake thought he was imprisoned for atheism, secondly because of the revealing clash in the chaplain's opinions. He wants atheists to publish their atheistic opinions. He is trying to convert Holyoake from his ferocious atheism; yet he does not believe that Holyoake can be an atheist. It is almost as though we are seeing here the naive religious unconsciousness, striking out childishly in all (inconsistent) ways against 'bloody' atheism. It shows again the repressive nature of the denial of atheism.

Notes

1. Robertson, *Short history of freethought* (1906), p. 376 n. Robertson altered his assessment in the *History of freethought in the nineteenth century* (1929), pp. 86–8.

2. 'Grote', in *Dictionary of national biography* (Oxford, 1959–60), vol. VIII, pp. 728–9.

3. *George Grote* (London, 1962), pp. 30–1.

4. *Three essays on religion*, p. 76.

5. On 20 June 1875 Mrs Grote wrote to J.W. Jones, of the British Museum: 'I have arranged the various items connected with the Bentham Papers, and propose sending, or bringing, the box to Br. Museum tomorrow, or Tuesday.' (See Acquistion Material, fol. 405). She does not say that she is giving all the papers to the Museum. It should also be noted that Bentham had asked Grote to note the number of manuscript pages sent to him. On the first page of Add. MS 29, 808 someone has written: '332 pages', yet the manuscript volume has 236 folios.

6. See, for example, Add. MS 29, 807, fos. 196 and 197.

7. Add. MS 29, 807, fol. 12.

8. *Journal of the History of Ideas* (1986) vol. XLVII, no. 1.

9. *The minor works of George Grote* (London, 1873), Introduction, p. 170.

10. See Add. MS 266, A2.6.5 The typescripts of the original letters were transcribed by Dr Eva Grunwald. The letters are arranged in chronological order.

11. I shall be quoting from, and referring to, Edward Truelove's (London, 1875) edition of the *Analysis*.

12. See A2.5.2–3; the letter is dated 22 June (1822).

13. See *Analysis*, pp. 30, 112–13.

14. See *Panopticon: or, the inspection house* (1791). That Bentham did consider the Panopticon as a substitute for the omniscient God of Christianity is fairly evident from Letter Four of *Panopticon*, where he daringly writes: 'I flatter myself there can now be little doubt of the plan's possessing the fundamental advantages I have been attributing to it: I mean, the *apparent omnipresence* of the inspector (if divines will allow me the expression) combined with the extreme facility of his real presence.' Like God, the inspector (who lives in the centre of the building) sees 'without being seen' (Bowring [ed.]. *Bentham's Works* (1843), vol. iv, p. 45).

15. See *Dictionary of national biography*, vol. viii, pp. 728–9.

16. *Richard Carlile, 1790–1843* (London, 1943), p. 16. Also see Guy Aldred, *Richard Carlile, agitator, his life and times*, 3rd edn (Glasgow, 1941).

17. *Life and character of Richard Carlile* (Circa, 1845), p. 24.

18. *History of freethought in the nineteenth century* (1929), p. 75. This is also the opinion of Joseph McCabe, who states that 'Like Paine, [Carlile] was a

Deist'; *Rationalist encyclopedia* (London, 1948), p. 82.

19. Ibid., p. 70. In his *Life and letters of G.J. Holyoake* (London, 1908), McCabe makes the remarkable claim that 'Carlile hated atheism' (p. 73).

20. Joel H. Wiener, *Radicalism and freethought in nineteenth-century Britain: the life of Richard Carlile* (Westport, Conn., 1983).

21. Holyoake, *History of the last trial by jury for atheism* (London, 1851), pp. 11–12. I shall refer to this work as *History*.

22. *History*, p. 12.

10

Militant and Academic Atheism

I. Holyoake and Bradlaugh

Although Charles Southwell and G.H. Holyoake were avowed atheists, neither considered himself a dogmatic atheist. They claimed only to disbelieve in God, because there was no sufficient reason for belief. They did not, as they put it, directly deny there is a God.[1] Like Southwell, Holyoake exploited theistic texts to refute theism. This is most evident in his *Paley refuted in his own words* (1843), composed while he was in prison, which contains his distinctive rebuttal of the argument from design. If the design argument entitles us to believe that there is an intelligent and personal cause of the apparent order and purpose in nature, then, Holyoake insists, we are also obliged to believe that the super-intelligent person is, like human beings, organised. Hence God must have a brain, senses and nerves. But if so, then God (as an organised body) must Himself have had a maker.

Although Holyoake was important as a theoretician, he was even more influential as a publicist and organiser.[2] He was largely responsible for uniting the various secular societies scattered over Britain. Holyoake also brought to the cause of atheism a certain sobriety, steadiness, moderation and respectability largely lacking in Carlile and Southwell. Like Carlile, Southwell was to muddy the waters of his (former) atheism. In 1852 he published a pamphlet entitled *The impossibility of atheism*, which Holyoake criticised in the *Reasoner* for that year.[3] Southwell, Holyoake concluded, was probably still an atheist, but not so frank as previously (p. 129).

Holyoake, in his turn, was chastised by Charles Bradlaugh for backsliding from atheism. Having popularised the title 'secularist' — a term he derived from Comte — Holyoake preferred it to 'atheist'. He also suggested that a secularist need not be an atheist. In 1870 the two British champions of unbelief — Bradlaugh and Holyoake — clashed in a debate on *Secularism, scepticism and atheism*, at which Holyoake argued for a more practical, less doctrinaire line: 'the world will never have time to stand still to listen to secular propositions [he urged], if you have to settle the Atheistic first'.[4] The secularist therefore neither affirms nor denies God or atheism; he ignores them (p. 6). Recognising that the term 'atheism' carries with it the inherited suggestion of immorality, Holyoake rejected the term: because that is 'the public use of the term ... I repudiate the word atheism in that sense' (p. 21). Bradlaugh saw this as prevarication and betrayal of atheism: 'Holyoake objects to [atheism] because of [its] opprobrium ... I maintain the opprobrium cast on the word atheism is a lie' (p. 34). With Bradlaugh we return to the 'fisticuffs style' of Southwell. Indeed, Bradlaugh described himself as a 'rough English skirmisher' in the army of free-thought.

Holyoake was always a somewhat reluctant atheist. Even in his critique of the backsliding Southwell in 1852, he admits that he is not overfond of atheism as a satisfactory description of his position.[5] Holyoake eventually came to adopt Huxley's label 'agnostic', because, as his biographer put it, he

> resented the term Atheist, because most of those who apply it to him understood it to invoke a more or less dogmatic denial of the existence of a Supreme Being ... [whereas Holyoake] was without such belief, not that he considered it could be disproved.[6]

In his *Victorian infidels*, Edward Royle argues that this is what largely distinguished Holyoake from his younger rival, Bradlaugh. Whereas Bradlaugh 'stated a philosophical position which denied the existence of God *a priori*' (p. 119), Holyoake, as we have seen, made it quite clear — e.g. in his dialogue with the prison chaplain (Chapter 9, Section IV) — that he did not sanction such a denial. For evidence of Bradlaugh's more extreme and positive atheism, Royle quotes from his 1861 debate with the Reverend Woodville Woodman, *The existence of a God*, in which Bradlaugh asserted:

> Mr Holyoake and I do not hold the same opinions. I am an Atheist, and say I can demonstrate one existence. Mr Holyoake does not hold this opinion; Mr Holyoake simply says to the Theist, you cannot prove your Theism. (p. 31)[7]

Clearly, Bradlaugh does think that he goes further than Holyoake; but it is not clear from this that he *denies* the existence of God. Robertson, Bradlaugh's associate and interpreter, maintained that Bradlaugh 'said a hundred times, to "deny the existence of God" is meaningless' (*Charles Bradlaugh*, London, 1920, p. 29). Bradlaugh's considered view is that

> The atheist does not say 'there is no God', but he says: 'I know not what you mean by God; I am without idea of God ... I do not deny God, because I cannot deny that of which I have no conception.'[8]

This is in line with Holyoake's position. Both men agree, too, that no specific assertion of the existence of God has been rationally sustained. Their criticisms of previous theistic conceptions and arguments are also similar. Where Holyoake and Bradlaugh seem to part company is in their confidence that no form of theism will ever be proven. Holyoake is not prepared to say this, whereas Bradlaugh is. Yet his degree of confidence varies. In his formal essays, he tends to keep his confidence closely under control, in keeping with his recognition that it is absurd to deny something that has not been defined and asserted and which may take conceptual forms not yet devised. In his debates, however, he tends to be less restrained; thus is his 1881 three nights' discussion with McCann on *Secularism: unphilosophical, immoral*, he boldly states:

> By 'Atheism' I mean Monism, that is the affirmation of one existence, of which existence I only know mode, each mode being distinguished in thought by its qualities. This affirmation is a positive, not a negative, affirmation, and is properly describable as Atheism, because it does not include in it any possibility of Theos. (p. 75)

On the other hand, in his *Two nights' public discussion* with Thomas Cooper some 16 years earlier he had taken a different line, which, apart from its passion, might well have come from Holyoake:

> I wish, before concluding, to point out to you that in the position I have taken up I do not stand here to prove that there is no God. If I should undertake to prove such a proposition, I should deserve the ill words of the oft-quoted psalmist applied to those who say there is no God. I do not say there is no God,

214

but I am an Atheist without God. To me the word God conveys no idea, and it is because the word God, to me, never expressed a clear and definite conception — it is because I know not what it means — it is because I never had sufficient evidence to compel my acceptance of it. (p. 9)

There is, then, a certain tension or vacillation in Bradlaugh's atheism, perhaps explicable partly by the immediate polemical intent, and partly by his wanting to be, or appear, a complete atheist, as distinguished from the more reticent, qualified positions of his rivals, particularly Holyoake. Bradlaugh's motto was 'Thorough'. Yet rarely is he carried away into absolute atheism, i.e. into a flat denial of the existence of God. In one of Bradlaugh's last essays, one of the *Doubts in dialogue* (London, 1891), originally published in the *National Reformer* less than a year before he died, he asks himself the question: 'But in any case you deny "God"?', to which he replies 'Not unless you define the word' (p. 50). It is interesting, too, that Holyoake did not seem to regard Bradlaugh as an absolute atheist. For in his autobiography, *Sixty years of an agitator's life* (6th impression, London 1906), published after Bradlaugh's death, Holyoake describes W. Chilton as 'the *only* absolute atheist I have known' (p. 142, my emphasis).

I am not claiming that Bradlaugh's tendency, or temptation, to absolute atheism was entirely temperamental. It had, I shall argue, a more solid basis in his monistic metaphysics, which is probably the most striking, indeed oddest, feature of his atheism. It is odd because, firstly, it derives its inspiration from Spinoza's seventeenth-century metaphysical system, and, secondly, it is extremely abstruse and must have been perplexing to Bradlaugh's working-class followers.

There is clear evidence of Bradlaugh's debt to Spinoza. Writing in 1890, he said:

In 1855/6 I was much influenced by the glimpse of the Ethics of Spinoza first presented by Lewes, and a good deal of my advocacy [of atheism] shows traces of this influence. For thirty years my position has been atheistic ... My position has always been that the word 'God' is either undefined, or that the attempted definitions are self-contradictory or meaningless:[9]

Bradlaugh's Spinozistic monism helped him in particular to the latter conclusion, that the attempted theistic definitions are either self-contradictory or meaningless:

'Nature' is with me the same as 'universe', the same as 'existence'; *i.e.*, I mean by it: The totality of all phaenomena, and
of all that has been, is, or may be necessary for the happening
of each and every phaenomenon. It is from the very terms of
the definition, self-existent, eternal, infinite. I cannot think of
nature commencement, discontinuity, or creation. I am unable
to think backward to the possibility of existence ceasing to be.
I have no meaning for the word 'create' except to denote change
of condition.

In this typical statement, from Bradlaugh's essay 'Is there a God?'
(p. 3), monism rules out creation and a creator as meaningless. It
also precludes any meaningful assertion of an existence that
transcends nature or the one existence. By this means, Bradlaugh
was striking a blow not only against theism, I suggest, but also
against agnosticism. 'The "God" of the Theist, the "unknowable"
of the Agnostic, are equally opposed to the Atheistic Affirmation'
(p. 7). The atheist recognises that 'there is much that is unknown'
(p. 6), but such unknown elements are for him modes of nature or
existence; there is nothing which transcends nature. In this sense,
Bradlaugh goes further than Holyoake, who, as we have seen, was
sympathetic to agnosticism, and was not prepared to exclude the
possibility that something existed which transcended what we know of
nature.

Yet since Holyoake and Bradlaugh both agree in attacking the
known conceptions of God and showing the invalidity of the
arguments brought in their defence, it might be felt that the
difference between them is insignificant — a distinction without a
difference. The question is a complicated one. For some, like J.M.
Robertson and Chapman Cohen, there is no real difference because,
I think, they tend to collapse agnosticism into atheism. For others,
the difference is denied by collapsing atheism into agnosticism, and
showing thereby that there are no atheists. Yet there is a difference
at least in the sense that an agnostic, like Herbert Spencer or
Winwood Reade but unlike Holyoake, may be a reverent towards the
Unknowable. It was the reverent agnostics, I suggest, that would have
attracted Bradlaugh's criticisms. For there is a dangerous similarity
between reverent agnosticism and certain forms of fideistic negative
theism (as we saw in Chapters 2 and 3). I can bring out the
similarity by quoting Winwood Reade, whose 1872 *Martrydom of man*
became one of the nineteenth-century classics of rationalism. In the
Martrydom Reade openly rejected any belief in a 'personal God', or

'a God of the anthropoid variety'.[10]

In one place Reade shows his allegiance to Feuerbachian atheism: 'those who desire to worship their Creator must worship him through mankind'; yet on the same page (p. 441) he seems better cast as a religious disciple of Spencer: 'God is so great that he cannot be defined.'

Plainly Bradlaugh would not have accepted the latter claim. If something cannot be defined, then there is no sense in assenting to it. That is Bradlaugh's most persistent opening gambit against theism. Even more objectionable, from Bradlaugh's point of view, is Reade's affirmation that

the Supreme Power is not a Mind, but something higher than a Mind; not a Force, but something higher than a Force; not a Being, but something higher than a Being; something for which we have no words, something for which we have no ideas. (p. xxxix)

It is this agnostic sort of theism, the assertion of 'something higher than a Being', which Bradlaugh's abstruse Spinozistic monism can attack. For, according to Bradlaugh, it is nonsense to talk about 'two existences', or a kind of existence which is different from the one existence which constitutes phenomena (see *A plea for atheism,* pp. 22–3). It is nonsense not only because as utterly undefined it is 'mere jingle' (*Doubts in dialogue*, p. 60), but also because there can be only one being, nature, or existence.

Thus Bradlaugh's metaphysical monism (derived from Spinozistic pantheism) undercuts both agnosticism and theism: there can be no transcendent being, whether knowable or unknowable. But although Bradlaugh's atheism is distinctively and primarily metaphysical, it also contains an empirical component. Having used pantheism against agnosticism, he now uses empiricism against pantheism in order to purge its religious content. For whereas the pantheist would like to say that substance, or existence, is itself eternal, infinite and intelligent, and hence that substance is God, Bradlaugh denies that these familiar theistic attributes can be applied to existence itself. Rather, insists Bradlaugh, we are only entitled to say that existence is illimitable and of indefinable duration. More important, intelligence can only be predicated of (finite) modes, i.e. organisms. In arguing for these negative theses Bradlaugh uses the more common British epistemological and empirical approach. 'I can only think beginning, progress, and cessation of duration' (*Doubts in dialogue*,

p. 49), not positive eternity and infinity — as Spinoza held. Again, intelligence is something which concerns conditioned beings, capable of comparing, reflecting, and judging in ways 'sometimes clear, distinct' sometimes 'vague and blurred' (p. 50). Intelligence, in short, 'is limited by the organism'. It is not something that could be attributed to existence as such; for, since existence includes everything, there would be no difference between perceiver and perceived, thinker and that which is thought on; but that is utterly different from what we understand by intelligence or intellectual activity.

II. The thorough atheist

There is, then, something *thorough* about Bradlaugh's atheism. It does go further than that of Holyoake. Bradlaugh tries to take the war into the enemies' camp. Whereas Holyoake was content to show flaws in the traditional arguments for God's existence, Bradlaugh is also anxious to point out internal conflicts in the putative divine attributes. For example:

> The word 'unchangeable' contradicts the word 'creator'. Any theory of creation must imply some period when the being was not yet the creator, that is, when yet the creation was not performed, and the act of creation must in such case, at any rate, involve temporary or permanent change in the mode of existence of the being creating...
>
> To speak of an infinite personal being seems to me pure contradiction of terms. All attempts to think 'person' involve thoughts of the limited, finite, conditioned. To describe this infinite personal being as distinct from something which is postulated as 'what he has created' is only to emphasise the contradiction, rendered perhaps still more marked when the infinite personal being is described as 'intelligent'. (*Is there a God?*, p. 5)

There is another less theoretical sense in which Bradlaugh was a more thorough atheist than Holyoake or his atheistic predecessors. Most of them, as we have seen, repudiated their former strong assertions of atheism. Yet unlike Carlile, Southwell, Holyoake and Annie Besant, Charles Bradlaugh never wavered or recanted. He does, more than any other prominent atheist, explode the long-standing denials of atheists, even in the extreme form expressed by Bishop

Fotherby, for example, according to whom: 'we deny that there be any *Atheists*, as be properly so called, namely, which generally and constantly believe *there is no God*, and hold so onto the end: (of which sort there can be none)' (see Chapter 1, Section IX). Bradlaugh made it abundantly clear, time and time again, that he *did* 'generally and constantly believe *there is no God*'. He and his family were anxious that there should be no doubts that his disbelief lasted 'onto the end'.

G.W. Foote, Bradlaugh's successor as President of the National Secular Society, was also interested in the persistence of Bradlaugh's disbelief, and the likely clerical denial of it. For Foote had previously tried to expose bogus infidel conversions in his *Infidel death-beds* (London, 1886). In *The Freethinker*, he writes:

Directly after Charles Bradlaugh's death we expressed a belief that the Christians would concoct stories about him as soon as it was safe to do so. It took some time to concoct and circulate the pious narratives of the deathbeds of Voltaire ... Already, however, the more superstitious and fanatical Christians are shaking their heads and muttering that 'Bradlaugh must have said something when he was dying, only they wouldn't allow believers in his sick room to hear it.' ... We are well aware that his daughter took every precaution. She has the signed testimony of the nurses, that her father never spoke on the subject of religion during his last illness. But this may not avail, for similar precautions are admitted to have been taken in the cases of Voltaire and Paine.[11]

It did not avail, as Foote was to point out in an article in *The Freethinker* of 19 November 1893. Thus the Revd Allen Rees had suggested that Bradlaugh 'materially modified his views before his death'.[12] This was pounced upon by Bradlaugh's daughter, Hypatia, who managed to extract a qualification from Rees that amounted to a virtual retraction.

But the most interesting and amusing attempt to call Bradlaugh's unwavering atheism into question was examined by Foote in a delightful essay entitled 'Bradlaugh's Ghost'. If it could not be plausibly suggested that Bradlaugh recanted *before* death, then it could be maintained that it occurred *after* death. And this is precisely what happened. The *Medium and Daybreak*, a spiritualist newspaper, carried a detailed report of a message sent from the next world by Bradlaugh through a Birmingham medium. In this message the 'ghost' of Bradlaugh affirmed that there is 'a life beyond the grave that I did not wish for nor believe' and, even more noteworthy, that 'there is a God! There is a Divine principle.'[13] This attempt by the spiritualists to show that Bradlaugh did in the 'end' recant, whether it was conscious fraud or unconscious self-deception, shows, once again, the power of the suppression (if conscious) or repression (if unconscious) of atheism.

Bradlaugh had a number of able atheistic followers or associates, most notably Annie Besant, whose *My path to atheism* was published in 1877 but who was to abandon atheism for Madame Blavatsky's Theosophy in 1889. J.M. Robertson and Foote were also atheistic followers; yet although they avowed atheism, neither of them was as concerned as Bradlaugh to develop and defend atheism theoretically. Robertson's distinctive contribution is as a historian, Foote's as a militant journalist and publicist.[14] A similar judgement can also be passed on Foote's successor, Chapman Cohen — probably the last popular and popularist champion of atheism in Britain. Even though he wrote widely and intelligently on atheism, he made little or no original contribution. As he himself observed in the preface to his *Theism or atheism: the great alternative* (London, 1921): 'one cannot hope to say anything that is strikingly new on so well worn a subject as the existence of God' (p. vii).

Yet Cohen does have some interesting, critical things to say about Bradlaugh's atheism. In his *Bradlaugh and Ingersoll* (London, 1933) Cohen criticised the Spinozistic and metaphysical component of Bradlaugh's atheism, the thesis that existence or substance can be 'conceived in itself', with 'no relation to any other thing'. This Cohen calls 'metaphysical moonshine' and 'unthinkable'. 'If existence is the sum of phenomena [as Bradlaugh holds], then whether we use the one term or the other [i.e. substance or the sum of phenomena] we are saying the same thing.' Yet neither term is acceptable to Cohen, because both are metaphysical abstractions. Cohen might also have pointed out, with more justice, that Bradlaugh's affirmation of one substance (or existence) in itself is gratuitous. How, in other words, could Bradlaugh defend this monistic assertion? In fact, he seems to take it as intuitively self-evident — a defence which would hardly impress his theological opponents.

Cohen's next criticism might have wounded Bradlaugh even more: 'The truth is, I think, that Bradlaugh ... did not realize that this 'one existence' with infinite [?] phenomenal 'modes' was really the ghost of a God that had been permitted to intrude into philosophy' (op. cit., pp. 42–3). If Cohen is right here, then even the most *thorough* British atheist was not entirely atheistic! Yet it is not clear that

Cohen's alternative is more completely atheistic. For according to him, the correct way of developing Spinoza is to 'treat his two known attributes, thought and extension, as mere categories of experience, and [in that way] we have a complete Atheistic philosophy' (p. 44). But if thought and extension are ways of experiencing, then what is the stuff or substance that they are categorising or structuring? If we can only experience the world, or existence, through extension and thought, then we can know nothing of existence or the world itself. But that opens the way to the reverent agnosticism of Winwood Reade, in which existence in itself might be 'higher' than existence as we experience it.

III. G.E. Moore

G.E. Moore, John Ellis McTaggart and Bertrand Russell are the first three academic atheists of note. They were also friends, and prominent members of the Apostles, a Cambridge Society with a distinctively irreverent attitude towards God and religion.[15] Although Moore is not generally thought of as an atheist, he did publish one atheistic essay in the *International Journal of Ethics* (vol. xii, 1902) with the title 'The value of religion', an essay previously delivered to the London School of Ethics and Social Philosophy. Moore also helped McTaggart with *Some dogmas of religion* (London, 1906). McTaggart's acknowledgement in the preface goes well beyond mere courtesy: 'to Mr. Moore, in particular, I owe the deepest gratitude for criticisms which revealed — and, I trust, enabled me to correct — many lurking errors.'

Moore also exerted a considerable influence on Russell, although there seems to be no evidence of his direct influence in the area of religion. Of the three Trinity College philosophers Moore published the least on the subject. Unlike McTaggart and Russell, Moore never issued any popular pamphlet for the Rationalist Press Association. His attitude to religion and atheism was also, if we can judge by his 1902 paper, more detached. The essay is urbane, self deprecatory and at times flippant and sardonic (see especially pp. 81 and 87). Yet for all that, it is a forceful work which deserves to be better known.

Typically, Moore's essay is argued with almost microscopic precision, as when he characterises his irreligious position:

> I am an infidel, and do not believe that God exists; and I think
> the evidence will justify my disbelief. But just as I think there

is no evidence for his existence, I think there is also no
evidence that he does not exist. I am not an atheist in one
sense: I do not deny that God exists. My arguments will only
urge that there is no reason for thinking that he does: they will
not urge that there is reason for thinking he does not. I do *not*
believe that he does exist, but also I do *not* believe that he does
not exist. (p.88)

Moore qualifies his atheistic position in two ways: he does not 'deny
that God exists', nor does he believe that God 'does not exist'. For
as he states earlier in the essay, 'there is not one atom of evidence,
establishing the smallest probability either that God exists or yet that
he does not exist' (p. 86). Although I shall question Moore's
qualification, I think it is clear that his position — as stated — is
atheism. After all, even Bradlaugh often claimed that he did not
'deny that God exists'. Also, whereas the later Holyoake felt that the
new label 'agnosticism' more exactly suited his atheological position,
Moore does not describe himself as an agnostic, although the term
was then available and very much in vogue. Instead, he calls himself
an 'infidel', and says that he is an atheist in all but one sense. [15a]

Yet I think Moore should have more carefully qualified his
qualification of atheism. For one thing, although he critically
examines (and rejects) arguments *for* God's existence (pp. 88-95), he
does not examine arguments against. That is, he tries to show —
very briefly, of course — that there is no valid argument for the
existence of a personal God, who has intelligence and wisdom to a
great degree. But there had been atheistic arguments, developed,
e.g. by Bradlaugh (whom Moore mentions, p. 81) against such a
theistic conception. Moore's friend McTaggart had also argued that
God could not be a person, if, as some Hegelians thought, He
includes or embraces other (finite) persons. My point is that certain
conceptions of a personal, intelligent and good God may be either
impossible or improbable. Indeed, at the end of his essay Moore
himself argues that the belief in a God who can 'interfere in the
course of natural events' is 'demonstrably untrue' (p. 97). However,
Moore might have responded that there are certain theistic conceptions which cannot be reached by atheistic attack; and that is enough
for his purposes. In any case, Moore is concerned, as I hope to show,
to undermine theism, not atheism. He is particularly concerned to
rule out empirical support for theism by showing that there is a
logical flaw in the design argument.

Moore develops the following fork: the cause of putative good and intelligent natural events — like the orderly motion of the solar system, the structure of animals — is either natural or non-natural. If it is natural, then that cannot be God (for then that cause would need a cause and would not, in any case, satisfy the theist). If it is non-natural, then there is no reason to believe that such a being exists; for the design argument depends on the analogy between God's causing or creating things and human beings' causing intelligent effects, like works of art. But as human beings are natural causes, the analogy will break down if we suppose that God is a non-natural cause:

> Either then God is a cause in some sense utterly different from that in which man is a cause: and then we cannot infer either to his existence or his nature; or else he is a cause in the sense in which man is a cause, and then we can infer his existence but not his nature: we can infer that the events in question had a cause, but not that their cause was God. (p. 91)

This fork disposes of arguments for God; yet Moore has another fork which advances atheism one step further. There has been an important confusion, he argues, in statements on the value of religion. When a theist tells us that we ought to believe in God and religion, he can mean two things: (1) that, for example, morality requires a God, or (2) believing in God has desirable consequences. Now (2) is a factual statement, which has nothing to do with the truth of theism: (1), on the other hand, is usually developed as an argument for the truth of theism; i.e. because there are moral facts or laws, there must be a divine moral-law-giver. Moore attributes this sort of argument to Matthew Arnold and Lord Balfour (p. 86). The other argument, (2), that we have 'a right and duty to indulge in positive belief, where the evidence alone would give us no right', he does not attribute to anyone, but he may well have had pragmatists like William James in mind. Moore takes (2) to be an interesting argument, but one which loses its force once it is clearly distinguished from (1):

> It does not usually occur to them that they are bestowing their enthusiastic praises on a belief, which, failing other arguments to prove its truth, *may* be a mere delusion. A mere delusion may, no doubt, have very good effects: but I think I am right in saying that earnest men are very loth to think so. If, then, it be brought home to them that religious belief is possibly

223

mere error, they will then be apt either to cool in their praises of its excellent effects, or else to argue that its effects themselves are evidences of the truth. (p. 87)

Against the position — (1) — held by Matthew Arnold, Moore argues: 'In order to verify the fact that righteous conduct is rewarded, we must already know what righteous conduct is: and to know that it is righteous is to know we ought to do it' (p. 96).

For Moore, moral judgements 'are independent of beliefs about the world' (p. 95). To try to derive an ought from an is, as he later argued, is to commit the naturalistic fallacy. We intuitively perceive that such and such is good. Moral truths cannot be inferred from the fact that God exists. Moore is a fideist concerning moral truths, and he holds that the intelligent theist must be a fideist concerning God's existence. 'An appeal to faith, then — to intuition — is the sole ground for asserting the truth of religion ... And so far it would seem that religious belief stands in the same position as our moral beliefs' (p. 95). But he is not prepared to allow that the moral fideist (or intuitionalist) is on no better footing than the religious fideist.

the religious believer may be tempted to say, 'I have as much right to my belief that God exists, as you have to any of your moral beliefs.' But this claim, it should be pointed out, refutes itself. For his assertion that he has 'as much right' to believe in God is itself a moral judgment. It can only rest upon the moral principle that necessity will justify beliefs: and this principle must have a prior validity to that of any particular instances which may be brought under it. The believer is therefore admitting that there is one moral principle to which he has more right than to his belief in God. ...In fact he cannot attempt to *defend* his belief in God except by a moral judgment; and by so doing he gives up the supposed parity between moral and religious beliefs in general, although it may still be true that such parity exists between religious belief and *most* moral judgments. (p. 96)

There is another sense in which moral beliefs are more fundamental than religious ones. Although Moore is prepared to admit that some believers are pure fideists, i.e. they 'really cannot help believing in God', he doubts whether this is often the case:

Their religious belief gains much of its strength from the fact that they think they ought to have it. They have a direct moral feeling that it is wicked to doubt of God's existence; and without this belief, which is a strong one, their direct religious certainty would offer but a weak resistance to scepticism. For such persons the final question arises: Are they right in thinking that infidelity is wicked? (p. 96)

If the theist's belief is immediate and intuitive, then nothing, according to Moore, can be said against him. Yet if, consciously or unconsciously, his belief is motivated by a moral feeling, as Moore suggests it is, then it may be possible to undermine the religious belief by criticising the moral feeling. It is here that Moore's second fork comes ingeniously into play. For the feeling that infidelity is wicked can no longer derive its force from the falsity of infidelity — since that side of the fork has been exploded — it must be accepted because believing it produces desirable effects. But once we clearly recognise that our feeling that atheism is wicked can have nothing to do with the falsity of atheism, then, Moore suggests, the feeling may lose its power.

In short, Moore is proposing a genetic and therapeutic strategy. The feeling that one ought to believe in God may arise from a conflation of two sorts of belief in the value of religion. The fideist may also be confusing the moral compulsion to believe with the religious or fideistic one. If so, the question becomes: how can it be wicked to believe the truth?

IV. McTaggart

John McTaggart Ellis McTaggart is, arguably, the most outstanding British atheist. Whereas Moore published his atheism in one article, McTaggart avowed and developed his atheism at length in *Some dogmas of religion* (London, 1906), and also in *Studies in Hegelian cosmology* (London, 1918) and his philosophical masterpiece, *The nature of existence* (London, 1921 and 1927). McTaggart's atheism is also more distinctive, assertive and unqualified than either Moore's or (as we shall see) Russell's. *Some dogmas* develops atheism in a semi-popular way in two senses: firstly, it is written in a direct, relatively simple prose — for the intelligent general reader rather than only professional philosophers. Secondly, the book's atheism is relatively independent of McTaggart's distinctive and difficult metaphysics. Yet despite McTaggart's forthright expression of atheism, both in print and person, his atheistic philosophy is scarcely known outside academic circles. It has made little impact on the general public, or even on the free-thought community. His name does not appear even once in the voluminous index of David Tribe's *100 years of freethought* (London, 1967). Yet McTaggart was (and still is by some) considered one of the leading philosophers of the first quarter of this century. He is also the first major philosopher whose distinctive philosophy is openly, even aggressively, atheistic. How then has it (and he) had so little impact? Part of the answer lies in the curious and (apparently) contradictory elements of McTaggart's personality and philosophy. Although a strong atheist, McTaggart was also a firm believer in immortality and the non-existence of matter — a position which must have appeared incredible to those who thought, as Royle puts it, that 'the [Chapman] Cohen era saw the development of materialism as the philosophy of atheism'. According to Royle, 'philosophical materialism [in this period, *circa* 1920] became the principal ground of debate'.[16] Also, though a member of the Rationalist Press Association, McTaggart was at the same time a strong supporter of the Church of England. He had the gift of combining — with apparent rationality — views that most people regarded as utterly incompatible. Though a rationalist, he was a mystic; though famous for his disbelief in the reality of time, he could ridicule the Irish for lacking a sense of precise time.[17]

And yet, having said this, it should also be clear that some elements in McTaggart's atheism are not really so unusual. Thus we have found immaterialism in Shelley and Grote.[18] Nor is it quite true to say — as his friend and biographer Lowes Dickinson does — that 'in one point, so far as I know, he is unique. He believed in immorality but did not believe in God' (pp. 86–7), for Shelley and Turner did too, although not so clearly or interestingly as McTaggart.[19] According to Dickinson, McTaggart's atheism went back to his schoolboy days, when he was 'a materialist and an atheist' (p. 11). McTaggart's opposition to theism and Christianity was by no means a superficial or incidental part of his life. Thus in a letter of December 1898, he says: 'it can't be nice to believe in God I should think. It would be horrible to think that there was anyone who was closer to one than one's friends' (Ibid., p. 87).

Belief in God affronted McTaggart's strong theoretical and personal committment to the ultimate value of love. In a letter to Bertrand Russell of 17 May 1902, he writes: 'I don't see how the ideas of a personal God and real love can co-exist with any vigour'[20] At times McTaggart's condemnation of Christianity is almost Bradlaughian, although tempered by a certain wry Oxbridge humour:

> Besides, if one was a Christian one would have to worship Christ and I don't like him much. If you take what he said in the first three gospels (for St John's has no historical value I believe) it is a horribly one-sided and imperfect ideal. Would you like a man or a girl who really imitated Christ? I think most of the people I know are living far finer lives than anything you could get out of the gospels. The best thing about him was his pluck at the Crucifixion, and other people have shown as much.[21]

McTaggart's atheism is set very much in the Hegelian context, a point of view that dominated British philosophy when McTaggart was writing. McTaggart's neo-Hegelian idealism is another likely reason for his general neglect, since that standpoint was never likely to appeal to a wide audience, and it lost favour — even with philosophers — as a result of attacks from McTaggart's friends, Moore and Russell, who had earlier shared McTaggart's Hegelian sympathies. With the vanquishing of Hegelianism in the 1930s and 40s, McTaggart's atheistic development of Hegel seemed to lose its point.

Yet McTaggart's atheism was perceived as a formidable threat by his fellow Hegelians; thus in a review of *Some dogmas* in 1908, H. Rashdall wrote: 'I regard the present work as the most formidable challenge that has for a long time been presented to the theistic Philosopher.'[22] Perhaps the most notable word in this judgement is 'Philosopher', for McTaggart's *Some dogmas* is probably the first book by a British philosopher of any standing that goes carefully and destructively through the possible conceptions of God, the divine attributes, the probability for this or that conception of God. The book is a first rate work of analysis and argumentation, carried through with apparent fairness and with little or no rancour. Its tone is reminiscent of Moore's work; Russell's irreligious essays by comparison are slighter and far more polemical.

McTaggart's atheism is difficult to summarise because it is so interconnected and closely argued. It might be considered under two headings: (1) atheistic arguments derived from a general philosophical standpoint and (2) atheistic arguments drawn from McTaggart's distinctive philosophy. Of course, this is hardly a clear-cut or satisfactory division, since most of McTaggart's arguments bear the mark of his singular intellect, and the division suggests that (1) is true or acceptable and (2) idiosyncratic and untrue. On the other hand, McTaggart himself seems to have made this sort of distinction in *Some dogmas*, where he defers bringing in some of his more distinctive and challenging philosophical ideas.

There are at least four atheistical lines of argument in McTaggart's writings. (1) McTaggart argues, particularly in Chapters VI and VII of *Some dogmas*, that there are internal conflicts and difficulties in the usual theistic arguments and conceptions of God; here McTaggart's conclusions are derived, for the most part, from a generally accepted philosophical basis. (2) His most distinctive argument is based on the unreality of time: i.e. if time is unreal, then God could not have created a world subordinate to himself. This has been seen, by P.T. Geach for example, as McTaggart's most powerful argument against traditional theism.[23] (3) McTaggart also argues that our conception of God includes personality or selfhood; but because one self cannot include another self, the pantheistic and Hegelian idea of God — or the ultimate or total reality — is mistaken. Here McTaggart's argument is partly distinctive and partly general, although his conclusion would be applicable specifically to his fellow Hegelians. (4) McTaggart also develops a rather different sort of argument in the first and second chapters and conclusion of *Some dogmas*. As I shall be saying more about this ethics-of-belief argument in the Epilogue, I need only quote McTaggart's summary here. We are not entitled to believe in a religious dogma on authority, he holds, because there is no consensus, i.e. there is

> no dogma of religion ... which is not also denied by able students. It follows that a man is not entitled to believe a dogma except in so far as he has investigated it for himself. And since the investigation of dogma is a metaphysical process, and religion must be based on dogma, it follows further that no man is justified in a religious attitude except as a result of metaphysical study. The result is sufficiently serious. For most people, as the world stands at present, have not the disposition, the education, and the leisure necessary for the study of metaphysics. And thus we are driven to the conclusion that, whether any religion is true or not, most people have no right to accept any religion as true. (pp. 292–3)

In Chapter V of *Some dogmas* McTaggart criticises the two most popular arguments for God's existence — the cosmological and design arguments. For example, if in causing something God changes, then He, too, must have been caused; hence He is not the first cause. If He does not change, then it is hard to conceive how He could be a cause (Section 158). Against the design argument, McTaggart suggests that when the theist points to facts in the universe which are useful to the divine purpose, he is showing that God is not omnipotent. For if God is omnipotent He need not work indirectly through means (Section 164).

McTaggart offers a number of arguments against the reality of time, and hence the impossibility of divine creation. For example, while I write this sentence, my writing *is* in the present, *was* in the future and *will be* in the past. But then we are ascribing to the event — my writing — incompatible characteristics; for something cannot be past, present and future, but only past at one moment and future at another moment, because these moments are themselves events in time to which we must ascribe the contradictory qualities of past, present and future.

'If there is no time, there can be no creation', says McTaggart in the *Nature of existence*, (Section 492). But that still leaves as possible a God who is coeternal with His creation; and it is here that McTaggart's argument against the Hegelian and neo-Hegelian conceptions of God comes into play. If God is not a self or person, then He does not satisfy the accepted idea of a God. But if He is a self then either He (1) includes other selves, (2) is coeternal with and different from other selves, or (3) is the only self. McTaggart argues at some length against (1); e.g. it would mean that two minds had the same mental states, and so when one mind felt a pain, God would also feel that pain. However, McTaggart is prepared to allow the possibility of a God who was one self among others. In that case, He would not be a supreme being, but only a God of limited but great power. But there is not reason to believe that such a being exists (see *Some dogmas*, Section 215).

McTaggart's conclusion is that 'there can be no being who is God, or who is anything so resembling a God that the name would not be very deceptive' (*The nature of existence*, Section 500). I have been able to give only the faintest idea of McTaggart's intricate and elaborate argumentation, but it should be evident that it rests on a foundation that few would accept, despite McTaggart's philosophical virtuosity and prestige in the philosophical community. The uncommonsensical denial of time came under fire from McTaggart's Cambridge colleague, Moore, who attacked it as simply incredible.

V. Russell

For many people Bertrand Russell is the most formidable British atheist, if not *the* atheist. James Thrower is probably expressing this popular view when he asserts that 'Russell's atheism is classic not to say monumental'.[24] Yet even a cursory examination of Russell's anti-religious works should reveal that they are neither very formidable, nor are they straightforwardly atheistic. Russell's criticisms of theism are to be found primarily in his *Why I am not a Christian* (1927) and his debate with Father Copleston. Even the forms of these works should suggest their peripheral character. *Why I am not a Christian* was originally a lecture delivered at Battersea Town Hall, on 6 March 1927, under the auspices of the South London Branch of the National Secular Society; the debate with Copleston was originally broadcast in 1948 on the Third Programme of the BBC. Neither offered Russell an appropriate format for a considered and adequate critique of theism. They are closer in spirit to the writings of Carlile and Bradlaugh than to the work of Moore and McTaggart. Nor are they, despite their reputation, straightforwardly atheistic. Thus in the debate, when asked by Copleston whether his 'position is that of agnosticism or atheism', Russell replied: 'agnostic'.[25]

Yet if Russell did not consider himself an atheist, then why, it might be asked, is he being considered in this history? Because, I should answer, Russell is, at the least, an *exoteric* atheist. Russell's clearest statement on this point is in a little-known essay 'Am I an atheist or an agnostic?', published in Kansas by Haldeman-Julius in 1949. 'I never quite know', writes Russell, 'whether I should say "Agnostic" or whether I should say "Atheist".' He calls this 'a very difficult question' and one 'which has often troubled me'. His answer is as follows:

> As a philosopher, if I were speaking to a purely philosophic audience I should say that I ought to describe myself as an Agnostic, because I do not think that there is any conclusive argument by which one can prove that there is not a God. On the other hand, if I am to convey the right impression to the ordinary man in the street I think I ought to say that I am an Atheist, because when I say that I.cannot prove that there is not a God, I ought to add equally that I cannot prove that there are not the Homeric Gods. (p. 4)

This does not quite accord with Russell's description of himself in the BBC radio debate a year previously, where he was hardly addressing 'a purely philosophical audience'. Yet he was answering a question posed by a philosopher. In any case, even if Russell is an esoteric agnostic, he is an exoteric atheist. In this he curiously reverses what we have found in the seventeenth century, since Hobbes (as I have suggested in Chapter 2, Section VII) was an esoteric atheist and an exoteric Christian. Yet it may be questioned whether Russell is any less an atheist than Bradlaugh or McTaggart, neither of whom thought he could conclusively prove that there is not a God. However, unlike Bradlaugh and McTaggart, Russell is content to attack arguments for God's existence rather than producing pro-atheistic arguments. In *Why I am not a Christian* Russell briefly considers at least four arguments — 'the first cause argument', 'the natural law argument', 'the argument from design' and 'the moral argument' — and points out weaknesses in all of them. He makes no pretension to being comprehensive:

> To come to this question of the existence of God, it is a large and serious question, and if I were to attempt to deal with it in any adequate manner I should have to keep you here until Kingdom Come, so that you will have to excuse me if I deal with it in a somewhat summary fashion. ... There are, of course, a number of them [i.e. arguments for God's existence], but I shall take only a few. (p. 3)

His critique of theism is developed from his usual empirical point of view, with his usual lucidity. But one feels that Russell is happier to pass on to a criticism of the practical disadvantages of religion.

After being published as a pamphlet in April 1927 *Why I am not a Christian* went through at least nine impressions in a dozen years. It was republished (with changes) in a book of that title in 1957, which has often been reprinted. The lecture has also been translated into no fewer than eighteen languages. Yet despite its popularity, it can hardly be considered a satisfactory statement of atheism. Indeed, what I take to be Russell's most interesting atheistic statement (which I shall consider in the Epilogue) is missing from it.

It has been suggested by Ronald Clark that Russell's militantly irreligious phase, which began somewhat abruptly in 1925, was partly the result of his (second) wife Dora's influence.[26] It is also possible that McTaggart was an underlying influence. As a student at Cambridge Russell very much admired McTaggart's philosophical ability.[27] The two philosophers became friendly, although their friendship ended during the First World War, as a result of McTaggart's hostility to Russell's pacifism. My suggestion is that Russell may, unconsciously, have set himself to follow in McTaggart's atheistic footsteps; for McTaggart died in 1925, the year Russell published his *What I believe* (London, 1925) which, as Ronald Jager has wittily said, 'is mostly a record of what he does not believe'.[28] It is this work which initiates Russell's militant phase, which Jager describes as 'quite sudden and unexplained' (p. 485). Another curious coincidence is that Russell's *Why I am not a Christian* was delivered in the same year as McTaggart's posthumous second volume of *The nature of existence*, whose forty-second chapter, 'God and immortality', contains McTaggart's most succinct and powerful statement of atheism.

Why I am not a Christian is interesting less for its intrinsic merits than as the work of Russell, a great philosopher and human being. It is of interest, too, for the reaction it drew from the general public and from a former student and friend of Russell's — T.S. Eliot. In a review, published in *The Monthly Criterion* of 1927, Eliot seems to be both obsessed with what he supposes to be Russell's atheism and also unwilling to think that Russell is a genuine atheist:

> Mr. Russell supposes that he is not a Christian, because he is an Atheist. ... As we become used to Atheism, we recognize that Atheism is often merely a variety of Christianity. In fact, several varieties. There is the High Church Atheism of Matthew Arnold, there is the Auld Licht Atheism of our friend Mr. J.M. Robertson, there is the Tin Chapel Atheism of Mr. D.H. Lawrence. And there is the decidedly Low Church Atheism of Mr. Russell. For one only ceases to be a Christian by being something else definite — a Buddhist, a Mohammedan, a Brahmin. Mr. Russell is essentially a Low Churchman, and only by caprice can call himself an Atheist. ... we cannot take Mr. Russell's Atheism [seriously]. Just as Mr. Russell's Radicalism in politics is merely a variety of Whiggery, so his Non-Christianity is merely a variety of Low Church sentiment. That is why his pamphlet is a curious, and a pathetic, document. (p. 179)

Eliot seems to be ruling out not only Russell's atheism but the possibility of any feasible atheism: 'For one only ceases to be a Christian by being something else definite — a Buddhist, a Mohammedan, a Brahmin.' Russell, therefore, is *really* a Low

Church Christian, despite himself. While it is hard to understand exactly what Eliot is trying to say here, it is not difficult to see what he is getting at. Atheism and Russell's atheism need not be taken seriously, for real atheism is impossible. We have encountered this sort of repressive (or suppressive) denial throughout this study and it is fitting to find it in the year 1927, probably the high-water mark of British atheism.[29]

Notes

1. See Royle, *Victorian infidels: the origins of the British secular movement 1791–1866* (Manchester, 1974), p. 115, and Holyoake, *History of the last trial*, pp. 33 and 41–2.

2. Royle, *Victorian infidels*, pp. 91–6, and Robertson, *History of freethought in nineteenth century* (London, 1929), pp. 73–5.

3. Holyoake, *Reasoner* (London, 1852), vol. 13 (nos. 323 and 324), pp. 113–16, 129–30.

4. *Secularism, scepticism and atheism verbatim report of ... debate between Holyoake and Bradlaugh* (London, 1870), p. 7.

5. Thus he calls 'atheist' a 'worn-out name' (*Reasoner* [1852], p. 130) and a term 'we have disused ... a long time' (p. 115).

6. See J. McCabe, *Life and letters of George Jacob Holyoake* (London, 1903), vol. 2, p. 266.

7. *Victorian infidels*, p. 118.

8. *A plea for atheism* (London, twenty-fifth thousand, 1883), p. 4; also see *Is there a God?* (London, 1883), p. 1.

9. This is quoted in C. Cohen, *Bradlaugh and Ingersoll* (London, 1933), p. 57.

10. *Martrydom of man* (London, 1925), with an Introduction by F. Legge, pp. 441 and 446.

11. The essay is reprinted in Foote's *Flowers of freethought* (London, second series, [1894]), pp. 28–9.

12. *Flowers*, p. 238.

13. *Flowers*, p. 30.

14. See my 'J.M. Robertson: Freethinker and historian of freethought', *New Humanist* (Summer, 1984) pp. 12-16.

15. See Paul Levy, *Moore: G.E. Moore and the Cambridge Apostles* (London, 1979). Thus in February 1895 Moore read a paper to the Apostles with the title 'Can God be serious?' (p. 148); also see p. 214.

15a. Moore is less explicitly atheistic in his *Ethics* (London, 1912), Chapter 4.

16. Royle, *Radicals, secularists and republicans* (London, 1980), pp. 172–3.

17. G. Lowes Dickinson, *J. McT.E. McTaggart* (Cambridge, 1931), p. 113.

18. See above Chapter 6, Section IV and Chapter IX, Section II. Bradlaugh himself was attracted to Berkeley's views on matter; see his 1861 *Discussion with Woodman*, pp. 31 and 34.

19. See above Chapter 5, note 25 and Shelley, *Essays, letters from abroad* (London, new edn, 1845), pp. vii–viii.

20. *The autobiography of Bertrand Russell 1872–1914* (London, 1967), vol. 1, p. 70.

21. Dickinson, *McTaggart*, p. 88.

22. *Mind* (1908), p. 535.

23. Geach, *Truth, love and immortality: an introduction to McTaggart's philosophy* (London, 1979), pp. 162–3.

24. Thrower, *A short history of western atheism* (London, 1971), p. 132.

25. *Why I am not a Christian and other essays on religion and related matters*, edited by Paul Edwards (London, 1957), p. 144.

26. *The life of Bertrand Russell* (London, 1975), p. 413.

27. *Autobiography*, vol. 1, p. 63.

28. *The development of Bertrand Russell's philosophy* (London, 1972), p. 485.

29. This is the opinion of Joseph McCabe, who mentions a poll carried out by the London *Daily News* in 1925; *A rationalist encyclopedia* (London, 1950), pp. 36–7, 265. McCabe's opinion seems plausible, if only because McTaggart, Moore and Russell were then probably the most respected philosophers in Britain, and each of them was — albeit in a different way — a professed atheist.

Epilogue:
The Ethics of Unbelief

In Tom Stoppard's play *Jumpers* (London, 1972) there is a striking, if fanciful, reflection on the history of atheism: 'Well, the tide is running his [the atheist's] way, and it is a tide which has turned only once in human history ... there is presumably a calendar date — a *moment* — when the onus of proof passed from the atheist to the believer, when quite suddenly, secretly, the noes had it' (p. 25). In nineteenth-century Britain two historical moments suggest themselves: T.H. Huxley's encounter with Wilberforce in 1860 and J.S. Mill's impassioned declaration (against Mansel) in 1865. What made these moments momentous was not the presentation of any new atheistic argument — indeed, neither Huxley nor Mill ever defended atheism — but the moral superiority they evinced. As righteousness was perceived to pass from the champions of belief (Bishop Wilberforce and Dean Mansel) to the critics, Huxley and Mill, so, I shall argue, the onus of proof passed from unbelievers to the believers.

Mill's moral victory is, more than Huxley's, directly relevant to the history of British atheism; hence I shall try to chronicle it. Mill's blow occurs in his otherwise rather turgid *Examination of Sir William Hamilton's philosophy* (London, 1865), in a section directed against Dean Mansel's *Limits of religious thought* (London, 5th edn. 1867). Mansel, a follower of Hamilton, had argued that we have no direct or literal knowledge of God, and that any philosophical attempt to conceive God leads to contradiction. Thus, writes Mansel,

> we are landed in an inextricable dilemma. The Absolute cannot be conceived as conscious, neither can it be conceived as unconscious: it cannot be conceived as complex, neither can it be conceived as simple: it cannot be conceived by difference, neither can it be conceived by the absence of difference: it cannot be identified with the universe, neither can it be distinguished from it.[1]

The dilemma is present, too, in the case of God's moral attributes; for we must recognise, according to Mansel, that some effects of God's 'natural providence' are not explicable by 'the highest human morality':

The infliction of physical suffering, the permission of moral evil, the adversity of good, the prosperity of the wicked, the crimes of the guilty involving the misery of the innocent ... these are facts which no doubt are reconcilable, we know not how, with the Infinite Goodness of God, but which certainly are not to be explained on the supposition that its sole and sufficient type is to be found in the finite goodness of man. (p. 101)

About Mansel's position, Mill says that 'it is simply the most morally pernicious doctrine now current'.[2] Mill's resounding condemnation must be quoted at some length. It opens on a Luther-like note:

Here, then, I take my stand on the acknowledged principle of logic and of morality, that when we mean different things we have no right to call them by the same name, and to apply to them the same predicates, moral and intellectual. If in ascribing goodness to God I do not mean what I mean by goodness; if I do not mean the goodness of which I have some knowledge, but an incomprehensible attribute of an incomprehensible substance, which for aught I know may be totally different quality from that which I love and venerate — and even must, if Mr. Mansel is to be believed, be in some important particulars opposed to this — what do I mean by calling it goodness? and what reason have I for venerating it? To say that God's goodness may be different in kind from man's goodness, what is it but saying, with a slight change of phraseology, that God may possibily not be good? ... I am informed that the world is ruled by a being whose attributes are infinite, but what they are we cannot learn, nor what are the principles of his government, except that [as Mansel says] 'the highest human morality which we are capable of conceiving' does not sanction them; convince me of it, and I will bear my fate as I may. But when I am told that I must believe this, and at the same time call this being by the names which express and affirm the highest human morality, I say in plain terms that I will not. Whatever power such a being may have over me, there is one thing which he shall not do: he shall not compel me to worship him. I will call no being good, who is not what I mean when I apply that epithet to my fellow-creatures; and if such a being can sentence me to hell for not so calling him, to hell I will go. (pp. 102–3)

A reader familiar with the Berkeley/King/Browne debate, partly examined above (Chapters 3 and 4), can scarcely fail to feel a certain *déjà vu*. For Mansel's doctrine is very close to that of King and Browne, with whose writings he was familiar. And Mill has become Berkeley — a philosopher he greatly admired. Compare, for example, Berkeley's description of King's God as an 'unknown subject of attributes absolutely unknown' (*Alciphron* IV.17) with Mill's characterisation of divine goodness (for Mansel) as 'an incomprehensible attribute of an incomprehensible subject'. It is not clear whether Mill was drawing on Berkeley's *Alciphron*. That he was probably not familiar with the earlier debate is suggested by his statement that 'the novelty [of Mansel's position] is in presenting this [negative theological] conclusion as a corollary from the most advanced doctrines of modern philosophy' (p. 90). For the same could be said with equal validity of King and Browne, whose negative theology was based on the advanced epistemology of Locke.[3]

Although Mill hardly presents a substantial criticism which is not already in Berkeley, he does give the case a different — moral — turn. He may be said to inaugurate the ethics of belief — a merging of logic and morality. Because of his political and social standing, Mill brought an element of drama to the discussion. He did what Hobbes said no one had the courage to do. In a discussion of atheism (see above Chapter 2, Section V) Hobbes had asked: 'Upon what confidence dares any man, deliberately I say, oppose the omnipotent?' Mill had the confidence to do this 'on the acknowledged principle of logic and of morality', and he did so openly and boldly and with devastating effect.

In the celebrated passage, Mill is showing himself to be something more and something less than a speculative atheist: he is, in effect, a theoretical blasphemer. He will not call the omnipotent being God if its goodness is unlike human goodness. He is defying an omnipotent being (who may be able to to send him to Hell) thereby taking up Hobbes's challenge (probably without knowing it). More important, he broke a spell and, I shall argue, opened up a new irreligious era. This may seem an extravagant claim. It is certainly a difficult one to substantiate. Yet it is supported by a number of authorities, and also by the profound effect it had on men such as Grote, McTaggart, Bradlaugh, and less directly, W.K. Clifford and Russell.

In some ways, Grote's reaction is the most interesting. It appeared in an anonymous review of Mill's *Examination*, first published in *The Westminster Review* of 1 January 1866 and then separately reprinted. After quoting the whole of Mill's long defiant passage, Grote testifies to its extraordinary impact:

This concluding declaration is memorable in many ways ... We are not surprised that a declaration so unusual and so impressive should have been often cited in critical notices of this volume; that during the month preceding the last Westminster election, it was studiously brought forward by some opponents of Mr Mill, and more or less regretted by his friends, as likely to offend many electors, and damage his chance of success.[4]

Yet for all his admiration of Mill's declaration, Grote suggests that Mill had gone too far: 'For ourselves, we cordially sympathize with his resolution. But Mr Mill must be aware that this is a point on which society is equally resolved that no individual shall determine for himself, if they can help it.'

Socrates's judicial death for irreligion shows, Grote urges, that all societies are determined to dictate in religious matters; hence overt deviants must 'count upon such treatment as will go far to spoil the value of the present life to him, even before he passes to those ulterior [otherworldly] liabilities which Mr Mill indicates in the distance.' Grote then contrasts Mill's position with the

more cautious proceeding of men like Herodotus. That historian, alike pious and prudent, is quite aware that all the Gods are envious and mischief-making, and expressly declares them to be so. Yet, far from refusing to worship them on that account, he is assiduous in prayer and sacrifice.

I take it that Grote is here signalling to Mill and others about the social and legal dangers of being overtly irreligious, of coming out openly against God. It is, perhaps, ironic that he himself gave vent to a Mill-like outburst, albeit in a private letter to his sister-in-law:

...There cannot be a benevolent God who suffers evil & pain to exist. And if there be a God of any other character, who does not design the happiness of mankind, then all I can say is, that I shall prefer serving & benefiting my fellow-men & take the risk of his displeasure.[5]

Perhaps one reason why Grote was recommending 'more cautious proceedings' to Mill was that he felt responsible for Mill's stand. I suggest that behind Mill's memorable declaration is the *Analysis's* discussion of how and why we attribute goodness to the capricious and omnipotent God (see above Chapter 9, Section I), where our worship of God is shown to be a fearful, sycophantic flattery of a tyrant. Yet anyone, writes Grote, who was not cowed by such a great power 'would justly be extolled as a man of heroic firmness' (p. 22). Mill (who was greatly influenced by the *Analysis*) did heroically refuse to flatter such a being by calling Him good.

Grote himself, like Cicero, was 'content with that "semi-liberty under silence and concealment" ', although, as Croom Robertson said, under 'the calm exterior there lay ... enthusiasms and fires of passion which it took all his strength of reason and will to control' (see above, Chapter 9, Section II). Grote's control and strategic 'concealment' is impressively displayed when he moves from 'Mill's declaration of subjective sentiment' to the logical issue between Mill and Mansel. The following passage comprises Grote's last and, perhaps, most fascinating esoterical statement of atheism:

> The problem was [he writes] how to reconcile the actual evil and suffering in the universe (which is recited as a fact by Mr Mansel, though in terms conveying a most inadequate idea of its real magnitude) with the goodness of God. Mr Mill repudiates the explanatory hypothesis tendered by Mr Mansel, as a solution, but without suggesting any better hypothesis of his own. For ourselves, we are far from endorsing Mr Mansel's solution as satisfactory; yet we can hardly be surprised if he considers it less unsatisfactory than no solution at all. And when we reflect how frequently and familiarly predicates applicable to man are applied to the Supreme Being, when they cannot possibly be understood about Him in the same sense — we see no ground for treating the proceeding as disingenuous, which Mr Mill is disposed to do. Indeed, it cannot easily be avoided: and Mr Mill himself furnished us with some examples in the present volume. At page 491, he says:–

> > 'It would be difficult to find a stronger argument in favour of Theism, than that the eye must have been made by one who sees, and the ear by one who hears.'

> In the words here employed, *seeing* and *hearing* are predicated of God. (p. 303)

Grote then goes on to argue against such univocal predication empirically, using Mill against himself:

Now when we predicate of men, that they *see* or *hear*, we affirm facts of extreme complexity, especially in the case of *seeing*; facts partly physical, partly mental, involving multifarious movements and agencies of nerves, muscles, and other parts of the organ... All the real objects in nature known to us by observation are finite, and possess only in a finite measure their respective attributes. Upon this is founded the process of Science, so comprehensibly laid out by Mr Mill in his 'System of Logic'

It is easy, amidst Grote's smooth sentences, to miss his point. He first notes that Mansel rightly tried to overcome theism's great difficulty — the problem of evil — although even Mansel is not aware of its magnitude. Mansel's solution — negative theology — Grote then gently although firmly dismisses. He then tries to show that Mill's anthropomorphic alternative is even less acceptable, because it is not tenable to predicate univocally the same properties of men and God. So the great problem remains. Mansel's solution is illogical and immoral; Mill's is facile. The only sensible conclusion the intelligent reader can draw is (silent) atheism.

With this contribution of Grote, we have the final character in the repetition of intellectual history: with Mansel playing King and Browne, Mill playing Berkeley, and now Grote playing Anthony Collins, (see above). For like Collins and Lysicles, Grote is esoterically exploiting both Mansel and Mill for atheistic ends: he is suggesting — as he did more openly in his 1820s letters — that the problem of evil is an overwhelming problem; that Mansel's desperate solution is understandable but untenable; that Mill is right to reject Mansel's solution, but wrong to think that his theistic alternative is any less untenable.

Mill was very much aware of Grote's review, which he calls an 'admirable article'; he appreciated particularly its tribute to his father. In a letter to Robert Pharazyn he discusses the review and says that Grote (whom he does not name)

is quite right in saying that I have thrown no light on the difficulty of reconciling the belief in a perfectly good God with the actual constitution of nature. It was not my business to do so, but if I had given any opinion on the point it would have been that there is no mode of reconciling them except the hypothesis that the Creator is a being of limited power. The appearances ... of contrivance in the universe ... seem to point

... to a benevolent design limited by obstacles than to a malevolent ... character in the designer.[6]

Mill was to develop this position in his posthumously published *Three essays on religion* (London, 1874), in the third essay, 'Theism'. As this essay was written between 1868 and 1870 it is just possible that some of Mill's comments (particularly on pages 191–2) were written with Grote in mind. Thus Mill tries to show that there is a 'preponderance of evidence' that the non-omnipotent Creator 'desired the pleasure of his creatures.' for 'pleasure of one description or another is afforded by almost anything' and 'Even in cases where pain results, like pleasure, from the machinery itself, the appearances do not indicate that contrivance was brought into play purposely to produce pain' (pp. 191–2). As far as I know, there is no extant correspondence between Grote and Mill on this crucial topic. (In a letter to Grote of 25 December 1866, Mill mentions a writer who attacks Mansel and is on 'our' side in the controversy.[7]) However, it is possible to reconstruct Grote's likely objection to Mill's notion from the *Analysis*, especially where Grote attacks the theory that 'the Deity is perfectly ... well intentioned, but that he was prevented from realising these designs, by the inherent badness and intractable qualities of matter' (see Chapter 9, Section II). Such a theory is 'insulting' to God's power, according to Grote; it is also no more credible than the theory that the 'Deity is perfectly ... malevolent, and that he was only prevented from realizing these designs by the inherent goodness and incorruptible excellence of matter.' It is a pity that we do not have Mill's explicit comments on this argument, or on Grote's esoteric statement of atheism in the review. Mill may implicitly have accepted some of Grote's argument, however, for in 'Theism' he concedes that God is not solely or perfectly well-intentioned to man. Yet still, Mill says in an assertion that may be a retort to Grote's 'similar phantom', there is 'much appearance that pleasure is agreeable to the Creator, while there is little if any appearance that pain is so.'[8]

There is something almost symbolical about Grote's funeral in 1871. According to Alexander Bain, 'Mill disliked [Grote's] being buried in [Westminster] Abbey, but of course attended the funeral. He resisted the proposal that he should be one of the pall-bearers, and gave way only under pressure.'[9] It is hard to know which to admire more: the atheistic Grote ironically allowing himself to be religiously buried in the Abbey, or the honest Mill's uneasy repugnance at this farce.

McTaggart's judgement on Mill's 'famous outburst' — as one scholar has recently called it[10] — is that it forms 'one of the great turning-points in the religious development of the world' (*Some dogmas*, p. 214). After paying such a solemn tribute, McTaggart goes on to ask, with characteristic perversity, whether Mill really would have been well advised to defy the omnipotent. McTaggart's reservations are prudential, but not — as in the case of Grote — entirely this-worldly. Admittedly, he says,

> To call such a being good, and to worship him, is to lie and to be degraded. But it is not certain that nothing could be a greater evil than to lie and to be degraded. ... Unless it is said that moral degradation is absolutely incommensurable with suffering — and I doubt if this can be maintained — the case does not seem impossible. We may doubt, then, whether we should be bound, or justified, in refusing to misapply the predicate good to such an omnipotent being, if the use of the word would diminish our chances of unending torture.

There is, McTaggart suggests, something most imprudent (particularly, one would imagine, for a Utilitarian) in risking so much excruciating pain. McTaggart may well be right. And yet that only makes Mill's stand more courageous, indeed heroic. It is understandable that Gladstone called Mill 'the Saint of Rationalism'.[11]

McTaggart's own aproach to the question is somewhat flippant. He considers whether it would in fact be more prudent to worship God, and suggests that God (if He exists) might actually be angered by such servile worship, particularly if it is not whole-hearted.

> Many men, bad as well as good, are not appeased by such flattery, but rather irritated by it, especially if they know it to be insincere, or to have been insincere when it began. God may resemble these men rather than the others. Indeed, the probability seems to be that he would do so, since pleasure in such flattery is generally a mark of a weak intellect, and even if God's goodness is like our wickedness, it can scarcely be suggested that his wisdom is like our folly...
>
> When everything is so doubtful there does not seem to be the least prudence in flattery. Nor can we rest our action on any statement made by God as to the conduct which he will pursue. For, if goodness in God is different from goodness in us, we should have no reason to believe a statement to be true

rather than false, even if it were certain that it came from God. Divine goodness may not exclude the desire to destroy our happiness by false statements. (pp. 215–6)

Mill might have repudiated the irreverent spirit of this passage, but it has a clear family resemblance with his own. It is probably mediated by W.K. Clifford, who is usually regarded as the proponent, *par excellence*, of the ethics of belief.

Clifford's debt to Mill's stand is most evident in his 1877 essay, 'The ethics of religion'. His approach is less direct than Mill's. He take as an example the Greek story that Zeus kicked Hephaestos out of heaven for trying to help his mother. There are, Clifford thinks, two issues here. First, is the story true? This is something which must be determined by the evidence; nor should the possible immorality, or immoral consequences, of the story deter us from believing it. Yet, secondly, there is the question: if Zeus behaved as he is said to have behaved, ought he to be worshipped? Clifford firmly answers no. Clifford's next move is clearly modelled on Mill's stand against Mansel. It will not do, he argues,

to say that the divine attributes are far above human comprehension; that the ways of Zeus are not our ways, neither are his thoughts our thoughts. If he is to be worshipped, he must do something vaster and nobler and greater than good men do, but it must be like what they do in its goodness. His actions must not be merely a magnified copy of what bad men do. So soon as they are thus represented, morality has something to say. ... If there really is good evidence that Zeus kicked Haephaistos out of heaven, say so by all means; but say also that it is wrong to salute his priests or to make offerings in his temple.[12]

This twofold probing in terms of truth and morality, which is also characteristic of the passage I quoted from McTaggart, must have been painful to believers. Clifford then observes, coyly but acutely, that

When men do their duty in this respect [refusing to worship an immoral God], morality has a very curious indirect effect on the religious doctrine itself. As soon as the offerings become less frequent, the evidence for the doctrine begins to fade away; the process of theological interpretation gradually brings out the true inner meaning of it, that Zeus did not kick Haephaistos out of heaven. (p. 105).

Clifford then becomes more direct, moving from Greece to his real target in the Holy Land:

> Now to condemn all mankind for the sin of Adam and Eve; to let the innocent suffer for the guilty; to keep anyone alive in torture for ever and ever; these actions are simply magnified copies of what bad men do. No juggling with 'divine justice and mercy' can make them anything else. This must be said to all kinds and conditions of men: that if God holds all mankind guilty for the sin of Adam, if he has visited upon the innocent the punishment of the guilty, if he is to torture any single soul for ever, then it is wrong to worship him. (p. 106)

This is the true and formidable spirit of Mill against Mansel: by its means irreligion or (negative) atheism has conquered. In short, Mill and his followers made it immoral, or at least unfashionable, to frighten people into worship or religious belief. This is not to say that the pragmatic argument had gone out of fashion. It was used by William James, who brilliantly attacks Clifford in his 'The Will to believe'.[13] But James, although in the direct line of Pascal and Mansel, introduces an important change. He appeals almost exclusively to hope, not fear, to heaven, rather than hell. He appeals to man's better nature and to the desire for perfection (p. 120). Yet on occasion we can see the shade of Mansel and smell the brimstone, as when James says that 'if we take the wrong road we are dashed to pieces' (p. 121).

James sees the agnostic approach as essentially atheistic; for to suspend judgement concerning the truth of religion is practically tantamount to saying that it is not true. As Mansel was attacked by Mill, so James was vigorously attacked by McTaggart, who speaks of his 'degraded position'.[14] Russell, too, criticised James in 'Pragmatism' (1909), pointing out that James 'tacitly assumes that there is no evidence for or against religion'.[15] The battle, at least for James, has moved from truth to morality or value.

Bradlaugh's atheism is also informed by Mill's stand, which is quoted at great length in Bradlaugh's *Freethinker's text-book* (London, circa 1875), pp. 108–11. In *Is there a God?* Bradlaugh aligns himself with Mill on the question of divine analogy:

Here I maintain the position taken by John Stuart Mill in his examiniation of Sir W. Hamilton (p. 122). Righteousness and benevolence are two of the words of description included in the definition of this creator and governor of nations. But is it righteous and benevolent to create men and govern nations so that the men act criminally and the nations seek to destroy one in war? (p. 4)

And this argument runs through Bradlaugh's essays, taking various shapes, as the following from *A plea for atheism*:

Every Theist must admit that if a God exists, he could have so convinced all men of the fact of his existence ... If he could not do this, he would not be omnipotent ... Every Theist must also agree that if a God exists, he would wish all men to have such a clear consciousness of his existence and attributes ... But as many men have doubts, disagreements, and disbeliefs as to God's existence and attributes, it must follow that God does not exist, or that he is not all-powerful, or that he is not all-good. (p. 19)

Mill's approach also seems to be behind the apocryphal 'watch' stories, in which Bradlaugh usually figures as the leading character. According to the earliest (1867) version, Bradlaugh offered

as a proof of his assertion that 'there is no God,' the fact that if, on taking out his watch from his pocket, he held it in his hand for some minutes and was not struck dead, it would be conclusive evidence of the truth of his opinions. He was not struck dead because of God's long-suffering mercy.[16]

One can appreciate, from the previous quotation, why Bradlaugh would be brought into the story. The former represents a theoretical, the latter a practical and dramatic challenge to God. Both are in the tradition of Mill, as is this telling story about Mill's godson, Bertrand Russell:

when asked after a lecture what he would say if he was confronted with the deity after his death Russell replied, 'God' I should say 'God why have you made the evidence for your existence so insufficient?'[17]

Epilogue

In this, as in the preceding examples, God is being defied because it is unethical to believe in Him. A God who wants us to believe in Him in clear opposition to the available evidence is simply immoral and incredible. Mill's stand was a good deal more than 'an extraordinary outburst of rhetoric' — as Mansel optimistically claimed.[18] Rather, it cleared the air of the hell-fire and the God who prospered on fear. More than any other event, I maintain, it shifted 'the onus of proof ... from the atheist to the believer'. 'Probably no English writer' said Viscount Morley, 'has done so much as Mr Mill to cut at the root of the theological spirit.'[19]

Notes

1. Mansel, *The limits religious thought examined in eight* [Bampton] *lectures ... in the year 1857* 5th edn (London, 1867), p. 97.

2. *An Examination*, ed. J.M. Robson, Introduction by Alan Ryan, in *Collected works of John Stuart Mill*, vol. IX (Toronto, 1979), p. 90.

3. See my Introduction to *Archbishop King's sermon on predestination* (Dublin, 1976), pp. 9–20.

4. *The minor works of George Grote*, ed. Alexander Bain (London, 1873), p. 301.

5. University College, London, MS Add.; letter of 23 February 1823; see above Chapter 9, Section I.

6. *The later letters of John Stuart Mill 1849 to 1873*, ed. F.E. Mineka and D.N. Lindley, in *Collected works of Mill*, vol. 16 (Toronto, 1972), pp. 1195–6; the letter is dated 21 August 1866.

7. Ibid. vol. 16, p. 1223.

8. *Three essays on religion*, p. 192.

9. Bain, *John Stuart Mill. A criticism: with personal recollections* (London, 1882), p. 113.

10. That is, Alan Ryan in his Introduction to the *Examination*, in *Collected works*, vol. IX, p. xxxvi.

11. Quoted in J.M. Robertson, *Modern humanists* (London, 1891), p. 109.

12. Clifford, *The ethics of belief and other essays*, ed. L. Stephen and F. Pollock (London, 1947), p. 105. 'The ethics of religion' originally appeared in the *Fortnightly Review*, July 1877.

13. 'The will to believe' was originally published in the *New World* in 1896; it is reprinted in James's *Selected papers on philosophy* (London, 1929), see especially pp. 105–10.

14. *Some dogmas*, p. 66.

15. See *Philosophical essays* (London, revised 1966), p. 82.

16. See Hypatia Bradlaugh Bonner and J.M. Robertson, *Charles Bradlaugh: his life and work* 2nd edn (London, 1895), see vol. 2, Chapter 8, 'The "watch" story'.

17. The story is told by Russell's friend and fellow philosopher Sir Alfred Ayer; in a letter to me of 3 December 1984, Ayer comments: 'I can give you

no source for this story, except that I have a, possibly delusive, recollection of hearing it from Russell himself.'

18. See *Collected works of Mill*, vol. IX, p. XXXVII.
19. *Critical Miscellanies* (London, 1886), vol. 3, p. 43.

Index

Adam 124, 129, 244
Adam, J.Q. 151n1
afterlife
 see immortality
agnosticism 94, 136-9, 142, 202, 213, 216, 221, 222, 230
anthropomorphism 73, 87-8, 141, 148, 217, 240
Arnold, M. 223-4, 232
atheism
 demonstration 72, 74, 78, 82, 87, 90n21
 exoteric 230-1
 exploders 17
 high-church 46n39, 164, 189, 232
 Hobbesian 48, 50, 57, 61-2, 70, 96
 malicious 57-61
 mixt 13-15, 17-18, 20-1
 odious name 93-4, 100-1, 105, 164, 213
 practical 2, 8-9, 11-12, 15-18, 33, 96, 153-72
 repression 5-6, 9, 21-2, 37, 44n9, 48, 105, 112, 122, 141, 176, 210, 233
 Restoration 51, 56
 secret viii, 59, 64, 66-7, 79, 110, 143, 193, 198, 240, *see also* esoteric
 speculative viii, 2-5, 8-10, 12, 14-15, 17, 19, 20, 21, 27-30, 37-8, 57, 59, 71, 74-5, 78, 93-7, 102, 143, 147, 153-5
  absolute 11-13, 18, 33, 215
 suppression 5, 48, 104, 106, 233
 unthinking 2-4, 7, 11-12, 15, 17, 29, 33, 38, 156
atheology 89n13
Atterbury, F. 157, 172n30
Aubrey, J. 61, 64

Axtell, J. 62
Ayer, A.J. 246n17

Bacon, F. 47n51, 141
Badcock, S. 47n57
Bain, A. 192, 199, 241
Baker, C. 136, 139, 141
Baldaeus, P. 38-9, 47n47
Balfour, Lord 223
Balguy, J. 6, 10, 13, 23, 29, 35-6
Barnard, E. 142
Bayle, P. 21, 83, 88, 159, 160-1, 182
belief
 extra-experimental 194-7, 200-1
 passive 135, 138, 142, 179-83, 189n5, 190n6
Benn, A. 134
Bentham, J. 116, 151n1, 191-7
Bentley, R. 16-17, 19-20, 21, 34, 39, 41, 54, 64, 71, 104, 158
Berkeley, G. 42, 72, 75, 77, 79, 82, 87, 88n3, 90n15, 90n21, 95, 100, 137-40, 147, 155-7, 161-2, 169, 199-200, 237
 see also immaterialism
Bernard, Prof. 49, 64
Besant, A. 218, 220
Bible 121, 127-9, 133n36, 207
Billopp, T.S. 123
Bion 96
Birkenhead, J. 61
Blake, W. 185
Blackmore, R. 16, 21, 81, 95, 98-9, 131n2, 171n8
Blackstone, W. 159
blasphemy 35, 48-9, 51, 59, 76, 116, 154, 159, 203, 206-7, 237
 Act of 1697 35-6, 39, 48-9
 Theoretical 237, 245-6
Blount, C. 63, 68n13, 95-6, 108n8

Bolingbroke, Lord 76, 206
Boswell, J. 102, 165, 173
Boyle, H. 203-5
Bradlaugh, C. x, 38, 206, 212-13,
    214-17, 220, 222, 231, 244-5
    'thorough' 215, 218
    ghost 219
Bradlaugh, H. 207, 219
Bramhall, J. 57, 61, 158
Brooks, J. 119
Brougham, Lord 206-7
Broughton, T. 1-2
Brown, J. 157
Browne, P. 90n15, 100, 237
Browne, T. 42
Buckley, G.T. 46n37
Burke, E. 40-1, 93
Burnet, G. 52-6, 81
Butler, J. 107, 146

Cambridge 57, 59, 206, 229
    Apostles 221, 233n15
Cameron, K. 142, 151n10, 180,
    186-8
Campodonico, A. 64
Carlile, R. 38, 63, 114-15, 119,
    123, 185, 201, 202-5, 212
causes 117, 119, 125, 147, 198
    see also matter
chance 3, 7, 27, 29, 37, 44n11,
    46n33, 53, 55, 126
chemistry 113, 115
Cherbury, Lord Herbert of x,
    16-17, 30-4, 38-9, 40, 93
Chilton, W. 215
Chinese 97-8
    Literati 80
Chubb, T. 163, 173
Cicero 66, 179, 239
Clark, D.L. 139-41
Clark, R. 231
Clarke, M.L. 191
Clarke, S. 2, 4, 79, 86, 89n13,
    91n24, 92n30, 118, 163
Clifford, W.K. 237, 243-4
clubs 74, 77, 90n15
Cohen, C. 216, 220-1, 226
Cole, G.D.H. 202
Collins, A. 36, 42, 50, 70, 93,
    104, 106-7, 116, 118, 124, 130,

135, 146, 164-5
Comte, A. 212
confessions 24-6, 46n29, 51-2, 57
consensus 8, 31, 135, 148, 228
Cooper, T. 113-15, 214
Copleston, F. 230
Corry 91n24
Crimmins, J.E. 192
Cudworth, R. 17-21, 29, 33, 41,
    62, 78, 89n13
Curteis, T, 7-10, 12-13, 21, 23,
    26, 29-30, 34, 40, 54, 90n14

Darwin, C. 38
Darwin, E. 134
David, King 58, 160
Davison, M. 132n13
death 8, 11, 26, 52, 76, 96, 117,
    123-4, 219, 245
deism 55, 70-2, 76, 90n14, 93-4,
    95, 120-2, 126-30, 136, 146-7,
    162, 170, 179, 202, 205
Demaizeaux, P. 79
Descartes, R. 139
determinism 81, 82, 180
devil
    see Satan
d'Holbach, Baron viii, 37, 42,
    44n6, 47n56, 50, 63, 68n22,
    101-2, 119, 124, 126, 135, 147,
    169, 180, 182, 190n13, 198
Diagoras 11-14, 32, 47n47, 72-4,
    93
Dickinson, L. 226
Diderot, D. 50, 101
divine attributes 53, 55, 72-3,
    82-8, 98, 100, 125, 127, 196,
    218, 227, 235, 239-40
    see also negative theology
Dod, Doctor 74, 89n7
Doddridge, P. 163
Dodwell, H. 82
Drummond, W. 132n28
Dryden, J. 63, 107
duck/rabbit 59, 61, 63
Dudgeon, W. 124

Eaton, D. 183-4
Edwards, J. 2, 158
Eliot, T.S. x, 232-3

Ellis, J. 131
empiricist 118, 135, 150, 160-1, 167, 188, 200, 217, 231
Epicurus 11, 13, 28, 46n33, 81, 93, 99, 131n2, 141, 160
Erskine, Mr Justice 208
esoteric 61, 65, 67, 75, 78-9, 86-7, 89n9, 95, 102, 105-6, 107, 238-9
eternity 78, 91n23, 97-8, 104, 117, 146
 see also matter
ether 116, 132n13
Evans, J. 42
Evelyn, J. 171n6
evil 83, 118, 168, 193, 239-40

Fanshaw, W. 68n15
Feuerbach, L. ix, 191, 217
fideism 34, 83, 104, 130, 189, 197, 216, 224
 see also negative theology
Fitton, W. 203
Flint, R. 42
Foote, G.W. 219, 220
Fotherby, M. 16, 17, 32-4, 40, 93, 219
Fox, C. 134
Francis, S. 120-3, 130, 146, 178
Freud, S. ix, 4, 12, 21, 23-4, 35-7, 44n9

Gastrell, Bishop 79
Gawlick, G. 69n30
Geach, P.T. 228
Gibson, E. 79, 90n21, 107
Gildon, C. 51, 95, 97, 99, 100, 103, 106, 108n4
Gillespie, W. 206-7
Gladstone, W. 198, 242
Glover, W.B. 65
Godwin, W. 180, 205
Gordon, T. 104-5
Grabo, C. 136, 141
Grote, G. 116, 191-201, 237-41
Grove, H. 180-1, 191, 193, 210n5
Grunwald, E. 210n10

Hale, Lord Justice 159
Hall, O. 205

Hall, R. 209
Hammon, W. 42-3, 44n6, 110, 112-15, 125, 127, 135, 173, 175-8, 183-4
Hegelian 222, 227, 228
Hell 236-7, 242, 244
Hepburn, R. 67
Hephaestos 243-4
Herodotus 238
Hervey, Lord 104, 206
Hickes, G. 49, 89n14
Hitchener, E. 141-3, 150, 151n15
Hobbes, T. 34, 36, 48, 49, 51, 55, 57-61, 64-6, 67n10, 68n14, 68n34, 93, 95, 111, 131n2, 158, 231
Hodgson, W. 151n3, 190n13
Hogg, T.J. 134, 181-9
Holmes, R. 144
Holyoake, G.J. x, 38, 202, 207-10, 213-18, 222
honour 43, 173, 176
Hughes, A.M. 190n6
Hume, D. x, 42, 64, 101-3, 105-6, 109, 112, 116, 119, 135, 141, 147, 150, 165-8, 175, 180, 182
Hutcheson, F. 164
Hutchinson, A. 74
Huxley, T.H. 70, 213, 235

immaterialism 124, 147, 197, 199, 204, 226
 see also Berkeley
immortality 70, 82, 126, 132n25, 157, 194, 226
immutability 86, 125, 218
imprisonment 202-3, 206-9
 see also blasphemy
innate 7-8, 16, 33, 38-40, 96, 137, 140, 150
insinuation 67, 73, 78, 99
 see also esoteric
Ireland 166-7, 226
Italy 165

Jackson, J. 124
Jager, R. 232
James, W. 223, 244
Jessop, T.E. 109n14

Johnson, S. 74, 76, 82
Jones, F. 188
'Jug' 193-4, 197, 198
  see also Bentham

Kaimes, Lord 151, 152n17
Kant, I. 27-8, 38, 119, 132n25,
  137, 168, 169, 178
King, P. 75, 89n9
King, W. 73, 82, 88, 100, 236-7
Kippis, A. 77-8
Kors, A.C. 109n13

Laird, J. 57
Lange, F.A. ix, 68n14
Lawrence, D.H. 232
Leland, J. 63, 171n8
Leslie, C. 95
Lewin, F. 193, 198, 238
Liverpool 113-15
Lloyd, C. 149
Locke, D. 151n2
Locke, J. 17, 38-9, 46n35, 108n5,
  130, 137, 140-4, 145, 150,
  153-7, 161, 169, 180, 188
London Magazine Essayist, 1-13,
  23, 29, 36
London University 198-200
love 226-7

McCabe, J. 211n19, 234n29
McTaggart, J. 148, 221-2, 225-9,
  231-2, 237, 242-3
MacIllwraith, W. 192
Mackie, C. 78
madmen 30, 93, 120-1, 132n28
Manichean problems 83-5, 88,
  92n29
Mansel, H. 235-7, 239-40, 244,
  246
Marischal, Lord 102
Martin, B. 47n55
Marx, K. ix, 169, 204-5
massacre 167-8
materialism 27, 111, 119, 124,
  203-4, 226
matter 68n13, 78, 86, 199,
  233n18
  creation *ex nihilo* 79-80, 84, 88,
  91n23, 130, 200-1, 204

Meteyard, E. 115
Mill, J. 198, 240
Mill, J.S. 191, 198, 235-46
Milton, J. 157
Mintz, S. 67n10
miracle 145-6
Mitchell, J. 78
Molyneux, W. 90n23
monism 214-17
monster 8, 10, 105, 135
Moore, G.E. 221-5, 227, 229
morality 78, 118, 121, 155,
  163, 168, 170, 174, 175, 182,
  185, 223-5, 235-6, 243, 246
More, H. 14, 15, 21, 30
Morgan, T. 90n15
Morley, Viscount ix, 246
Mosaic God 126-7
Mossner, E. 101

National Secular Society 219,
  230
naturalistic fallacy 224
negation 22-3
negative theology 66, 69n38,
  73, 86-7, 92n30, 180, 237,
  243
  see also fideism
Nietzsche, F. ix, 185

oaths 43, 60, 76, 154-5, 158-9,
  165
  see also morality
O'Higgins, J. 70-1, 75-6, 92n30
Oxford 135, 179, 186
Owen, R. 190n6

pain 118, 120-3, 193, 197, 238,
  241-2
  see also evil
Paine, T. 38, 93, 128-30, 135,
  153, 169, 173, 183, 202, 206
Paley, W. 205, 211
panopticon 197, 210n14
pantheism 68n14, 89n8, 91n24,
  111, 119, 124, 167, 217
pantheistic materialism 80, 94-5,
  130
  see also materialism
Parsons, R. 52-3

Pascal, B. 172n35, 244
Penelhum, T. 109n14
Percival, J. 74, 77
Perkins, E. 201
persuasive definition 103, 164
Pharazyn, R. 240
Philipps, J. 190n7
physicians 113, 115, 120
Place, F. 151
Plato ix, 122, 195
Pope, A. 77
Popper, K. 194
power 68n13, 194-6, 240
    see also divine attributes
Priestley, J. 64, 112-16, 119,
    132n25
prophecies 84-5, 106
providence 54, 75, 97-9, 235
    see also divine attributes
Puritans 58, 60-1

Quinton, A. 64, 65

Radcliff, Doctor 56
Radicati, A. 55, 64, 93-5,
    99-101, 106, 108n3, 124
Rashdall, H. 227
rationalism 161, 167, 177-9, 184,
    190n10, 226
    see also truth
Rationalist Press Association 206,
    221, 226
Reade, W. 216-17, 221
reason 117, 185, 236
Redwood, J. 46n37
Rees, A. 219
Reid, T. 198-9
Robertson, G.C. 191, 198-9, 239
Robertson, J.M. 45n23, 50-1,
    71-2, 120, 122-3, 134, 191, 202,
    214, 216, 220, 232
Rochester, Lord x, 52-7, 61,
    67n10, 68n22
Rogers, N. 139-44
Royle, E. 213, 226
Russell, B. x, 221, 225, 227,
    230-3, 237, 244, 247n17
Russell, D. 231
Ryan, A. 242, 246n10

Saint-John, J. 38-40, 47n47
Satan 99, 160, 167, 171n14
Sault, R. 51
Scargill, D. 57, 59-62
scepticism 94, 181, 225
Scepticus Britannicus 123-31,
    135, 178, 184
Schopenhauer, A. ix, 16, 27-8,
    41, 126
Scot, R. 62
Scott, W. 63
secularist 212-13
Seddon, J. 115
sexuality 21-4, 35, 46n39
Shaftesbury, Lord 63, 159, 161-2
Shelley, P.B. 38, 116, 125-6, 131,
    134-52, 179-90, 201-2
Shelley, T. 184, 188
Smith, N.K. 109n12, n14
Socrates 30, 93, 179, 238
Southey, R. 141, 149
Southwell, C. 38, 206-8, 212
Spencer, H. 216-17
Spinoza, B. 28, 34, 55, 60,
    68n18, 78, 81, 87, 91n24, 93-5,
    99, 111, 124-6, 129-30, 154,
    160, 182, 215-18, 221
    see also pantheism
Stephen, J. 132n11
Stephen, L. 142
Stevenson, C. 103
Stewart, D. 198-9
Stoppard, T. 235
Strato 80
superstition 40, 65-6, 166, 170
Surenhusius, W. 82, 84
Swift, J. 76, 89n13
Synge, E. 47n55, 107

Tenison, T. 62, 68n13
Theodorus 11, 13-14, 47n47, 96
Thrower, J. 230
Tillotson, J. 73, 85, 108n4, 153
time 226, 228-9
Tindal, M. 79, 121, 158
Toland, J. 46n32, 75-6, 89n8,
    91n24, 106
toleration 138, 155, 160-1, 182,
    184
    see also morality

Trapp, J. 89n12, 108n9
travel literature 38-9, 96, 102,
    108n5
    see also consensus
Trelawny, E. 143, 152n13
Tribe, D. 226
Trinity 35, 116
truth 75, 124, 142, 176, 178, 184,
    190n10, 223, 224-5, 243
    see also rationalism
Turner, M. 44n6, 112-19, 122,
    125, 135, 174-8, 183-4

Vaughan, P. 131n5
vice 45n23
Voltaire 169-70, 173, 219

Wake, W. 171n1
Waller, E. 68n18
Warburton, W. 63, 91n23

Ward, S. 62
Warrington Academy 115, 131n10
watch stories 245
    see also blasphemy
Waterland, D. 171n8, 172n35
Watson, Bishop 120-2, 130-1
Webb, J. 37-8, 93
Wedgwood, J. 115
Weiner, J. 203
Whiston, W. 75, 82, 84, 89n9
Wilberforce, W. 45n23
Willms, B. 64
Wise, T. 11-15, 19, 21, 26, 29-30,
    33-5, 91n23
Wollheim, R. 109n14
Woodman, W. 213
Woolston, T. 76, 78, 132n19

Zeus 243-4